Genesis

Literal

Iapetus Ducq

2014
ISBN 978-0-9839522-5-1
Publishing rights reserved
by *Iapetus Ducq*
sufferingduckman@gmail.com

Genesis

A New Literal Translation

from

**The Text
The Roots
The Grammar
The Style**
and
The Context

having

The Meaning of the Words, Names, and Text Plainly Presented

showing

The Original Form
of
the Sacred Text

Table of Contents

Introduction..........1

Chapter	Page	Chapter	Page
1	11	26	95
2	14	27	98
3	19	28	102
4	23	29	104
5	27	30	107
6	30	31	111
7	33	32	116
8	36	33	119
9	41	34	121
10	45	35	124
11	50	36	127
12	54	37	132
13	56	38	136
14	58	39	139
15	61	40	141
16	64	41	142
17	65	42	147
18	67	43	151
19	70	44	153
20	74	45	156
21	76	46	158
22	79	47	164
23	82	48	168
24	85	49	171
25	91	50	174

Index to the Appendices.......................178

The Twelve Text Sections

	Section	Chapter	Page
I	In the Beginning	1:1	11
II	Generations of the Heavens and the Earth	2:4	15
III	Scroll of Genealogies of Adam	5:1	27
IV	Genealogies of Noah	6:9	32
V	Genealogies of the Sons of Noah	10:1	45
VI	Genealogies of Shem	11:10	52
VII	Genealogies of Terah	11:27	54
VIII	Genealogies of Ishmael	25:12	93
IX	Genealogies of Isaac	25:19	94
X	Esau		
	1. Genealogies of Esau	36:1	127
	2. Genealogies of Esau, Father of Edom	36:9	128
	3. Sons of Seir	36:20	129
XI	Genealogies of Jacob	37:2	133
XII	Names of Jacob's Sons	46:8	159

Index to the Appendices

Appendix I *What Genesis One Does Not Say*..........................180
Before we approach the text with all our answers, it is useful to consider the questions.

Appendix II *The Changes to Adam: Original Sin that Isn't*...190
An ordinary look at Adam and Eve's bodies demystifies religious dogma; did we fall from a state of goodness, or rise to a state that we couldn't handle?

Appendix III *The Two Trees: Morality vs. Mortality*..............199
A look at what being mortal means, and what God is and has always been doing about it.

Appendix IV *Jehovah vs. Elohim*..206
Ancient warring factions or common sense that a child could understand?

Appendix V *The Woman and the Seed*..................................212
  A look at the ramifications of being a woman ...to Jesus.

Appendix VI *The Stories in the Genealogical Histories*.........220
  It's far more than a list of names.

Appendix VII *Time*..228
  Time is not *longer* than we think, it's *broader*.

Appendix VIII *The Days of the Deluge, Peleg, and Eber*......234
  How the initial power centers that are still around were set up.

Appendix IX *Sarai, Mother of Faith*........................247
  How Sarah picks up where Eve left off.

Appendix X *Mother of All Living*............................251
  Eve, Rebecca, and the dialogue between sister, mother, and wife.

Appendix XI *Seventy Souls to Egypt*........................259
  is set that way.

Appendix XII *Year/years: Hidden Cycles in the Text*............262
  How the grammar and the numerics work together.

Appendix XIII *Themes Within Themes: the Ephesian Pattern*..270
  How the overarching saga of Genesis is summarized in Ephesians as a model of reality.

Appendix XIV *Where Was the Field?*........................274
  An investigation into this strange word that begins the second account of creation suggests a world that we are missing.

Appendix XV *Translator's Comment*..........................284

Introduction

Making a literal translation is not that difficult—in Greek. It has been attempted in Hebrew, with some little success. Merely looking up the meaning of a word leads to severe myopia; Hebrew is a *contextual* language; the same word means "raven" in one verse and "evening" in another. Thus the faithful using of the same word every time that it appears, while almost a necessity in the Greek, produces language that is flat, uninspiring, and completely lacking the rich imagery of Hebrew. A Hebrew word means whatever it happens to want to mean in the context in which it appears—provided that one is faithful to both the roots from which it is derived and the context in which it appears. Thus the word *chalel* (to bore, to wound, to dissolve, to break, to begin; Strongs 2490) is often translated in Genesis 4:26 as, *then began men to call upon the name of Jehovah*. Yet *chalel* is a primitive root sharing a connection with *chalah* (to be rubbed or worn, sick, afflicted, to grieve; Strong's 2470) and neither word implies the sense of 'starting' to call on the name of Jehovah, unless one imagines that one is wearing out Jehovah and grieving him by calling on his Name. *Chalel*'s sense of *to bore* is from the idea of wedging a crack into something, thus its association with *chalah*'s to be rubbed or worn. It is the enduring effort of getting something that is closed to expose its treasures. Thus in this text it is translated, *he is wedging open hope, causing to call on—in name of—Jehovah*; the sense of which must also appeal to the context of the previous verse in which Abel has been "reduced" and Seth is somewhat of a replacement rather than the reinstitution of that hope. Enosh, already named after the weakness of mortality, needed to establish himself as a viable beacon of steadfastness—as a weak mortal—to his progeny. A strictly literal—and less Hebrew—approach would be to translate it *he was wounded to herald the name of Jehovah*, which while viable, misses the richness of the story being told.

The point here is that Hebrew is like the Dreaming; all associations, including puns, paronomasia, and parallel passages, must be taken into account. While there are puns in the New Testament, they characteristically have reference to the Hebrew.

In the Greek, one can with a measure of confidence say, "This is what it says." In the Hebrew, the best one can hope for is "This is something of what it is saying but we need to read the entire passage."

Having said all that, this translation is still likely the closest you will find in English to word-for-word.

The Hebrew Old Testament has been said to be one long sentence connected with 'and'. And it is. To leave out that little word 'and', who begins the vast majority of the verses, is to completely miss one of the most valuable aspect of the accounts—the flow. There are striking examples where the scribe breaks from the flow, such as "He lied to him" in First Kings 13:19. The passage sticks out like a sore thumb, and for good reason: it is exactly what is needed to bring special attention to that verse. This is lost when "modernizing" the Bible. That word is in quotes because most of the attempts to modernize the scriptures are far more interpretive than translative. And this is a crying shame, for today we have in the English language far more tools for expression than in previous centuries. It is analogous to the material plastic; we developed an amazing material which can be put into any shape, any color, at any strength ...and we use it to make trinkets with which to crowd our landfills. The increase of ability and knowledge leads the more often to laziness than creativity.

Yet while the Hebrew text is one long sentence connected by *and*, the individual sentences are distinct and orderly. There is a subject—present or missing, a verb or verbs, and direct objects as well as prepositional phrases which act as direct objects. The structure is so well set out that no confusion need exist as to where one sentence stops and another begins, including (or especially) in long lists of names. Within this structure are figures of speech and grammatical devices that are so rich and varied that virtually no passage lacks them. And the fact that the subject acts as an *interruption* to the flow of verbs rather than having a set place in the sentence leads to the subject of the flow.

Two vital points need to be made regarding the flow: the placement of the subject of the sentence, and the series of verbs it supports. "Vital" is not used lightly here. The clue as to how to read a sentence is found in the placement of the subject. All of the following renditions are possible:
- And he is appearing to him in Oaks of Mamre—Jehovah—
- And he is appearing to him—Jehovah—in Oaks of Mamre
- And he—Jehovah—is appearing to him in Oaks of Mamre
- And—Jehovah—he is appearing to him in Oaks of Mamre

...and the text uses the second one. In that list, the last one would be extremely emphatic, and is used so rarely that it hits the reader like a symphonic climax. English translations generally do not carry forward this Hebrew sense of emphasis and thus miss what the poetic art of the text is communicating. There are two elements at play here: firstly, the closer the subject to the beginning of the sentence, the more emphatic it is meant to be. Secondly, the more verb phrases that are attached to a subject, especially if the subject is placed at the end, the greater the diminishing of its contextual importance. A good example of this phenomena is found in 25:34 where *five* verb phrases are attached to the single subject of Esau thusly:

"...and Jacob, he gives to Esau bread and stew of lentils, and he is eating, and he is drinking, and he is rising, and he is going, and he is despising—Esau—the **birthright**."

The verbs are underlined for emphasis here. Note that the text attaches the direct object (birthright) to the last verb, which by the sentence's construction, carries all the weight of the four previous verbs, each of which wanted a direct object but did not get one. Furthermore, the text adds insult to injury by emphasizing **birthright** after all this deliberate diminishing of Esau. This is a poetic device, in which in a single statement, more is said about the relationship between Jacob and Esau than could be said in a long paragraph (such as this one) in English. The next time five verb phrases are used (preceded by two conjoined ones) will be with Tamar in 38:18-19 to emphasize determination rather than insignificance, as the subject is entirely left out; that is, there is nothing to diminish about *her*, but there certainly is *something* going on which needs humbled, in this case Judah's inaction.

In the rare occasions that multiple subjects are used in a sentence, the reader's attention is opened to the extremity or complexity of the situation, as in 47:20,
"And he is buying—Joseph—**all of** ground of Egypt to Pharaoh, that they sold—Egyptians—♂man his field, that he grips over them—the famine—and she is becoming—the land—to Pharaoh." Here we have Joseph, Egyptians, the famine, and the land all serving as subjects for the same sentence. We could attempt to break it into smaller sentences, but that is not the sense; all of the players contribute equally the central idea, and all are needed.

A note on the prepositions; in Hebrew they are exact and strong. One might say that one comes *from* Pennsylvania; in Hebrew one would say that one comes *of* Pennsylvania, for to use the word *from* is too strong; it would mean that one has utterly left Pennsylvania. So when the text says that the waters were gathered *from* the face of the earth, it is clearly stating that there is no more water left there whatsoever. Likewise with *on*, *over*, and *to*. To have the Spirit hovering *over* the waters connotes that he has complete mastery of the waters. To have the Spirit hovering *on* the waters means that he is associated with them and that they are his place of abode. And the Hebrew prepositions can be rich and deep; see the note in 20:7 for a beautiful example.

When a double or triple preposition is used—which occurs frequently—layers of meaning are insinuated, many of which must be wrestled to the ground in order to discern the writer's intent, of which there are always more than one. In English we have few resources to handle an expression such as "*And they become for luminaries in atmosphere of the heavens to to light of on the earth*," yet this must be deconstructed one layer at a time with great sensitivity rather than, as most translations, merely discarding the extra prepositions and giving a weak equivalent. We are used to leaning heavily on our verbs in order to emphasize meaning, but verbs cannot provide *direction, position,* or *sequence,* from which we get relations of causality …in the manner that Hebrew does so richly. For an example of the hierarchies of meaning in the Hebrew, see the note in 20:6 of the text.

The verbs are also affected by the prepositions in a unique manner; there is both a causative and passive use of verbs. Causative involves purpose and action, passive simply involves action. For example, in Exodus 7:3 and elsewhere in the account, Jehovah says, *"And I—I harden Pharaoh's heart..."* which like most verb usage is passive. The sense is that he would allow Pharaoh's heart to take it's natural course, not magically make it hard. But when the causative sense is used, as in 9:16, *"...And nevertheless, on this account I cause you to be raised up, in order to your showing my power..."* it means that purpose and action are both utilized, which is why it is chosen—from the multitude of references to the hardening of Pharaoh's heart in the text—by Paul in Romans 9:17. The distinction can make quite a difference in a passage, so this translation uses phrases such as *"to cause to"* to show active verbs with purpose in the text. Once again, it is our powerful friend the preposition who points this out to us.

As to conventions in the text:
"Man", "men", or "Adam" will be used for *adam*, meaning universal man.
"•Man" or "•men" will be used for *enosh* or *enoshim*, meaning weak or mortal man. The use of this word begins with 4:26, the naming of Seth's son Enosh. In its normative sense in the text it simply means undistinguished men. In its full meaning it connotes tranquil power and gentle movement in the context of the patient endurance of mortality.
"♂Man" or "♂men" will be used for *Ish* meaning intelligent or individual man as a male, and as often, husband. "Male" or "males" will be used when applied to animals.
"›Man" or "›men" will be used for *Gibbor* or *gibborim* meaning mighty man, hero.
"Male" or "males" will be used for *zakar* meaning the male (of any species). It's root means to mark as special, thus also to remember, recount, record.

A word on punctuation; The Hebrew has oodles of punctuation, but uses letters, prefixes, and suffixes, and grammar to express it. English, depends; heavily, on: punctuation, as the first half of this sentence demonstrates. Thus to satisfy both languages, the conventions are freely broken where more useful to the meaning; usually placing the punctuation where it actually occurs in the Hebrew. For example, in English, we would write:

"I wondered who was following me, when a thug shouted from behind me, 'Stop for a sec, matey!"
And in Hebrew it would be more:

"And I am wondering ? who, he is following me, that *then* **thug**, he shouts from on opposite behind, 'Stop you ! for piece *of* duration—you! matey."

The latter is richer and less constrained by English conventions, and after a few sentences settles easily into the mind of the reader just as the flow of a song's lyrics does once the flow is familiarized.

A note on gender; in Hebrew there is masculine and feminine only; when you see the word "it" in the text, as *And it becomes* (*And it comes to pass* in other translations), know that the original reads *And he becomes*. The feminine is preserved in the text; so unless otherwise noted, English neuter is Hebrew masculine. Generally in Hebrew, the fifth letter Heh, the sign of life, is added to a word to denote the feminine. The modern custom of appending Yod for the the masculine and Yod-Tav for the feminine does not belong to the original Hebrew.

As to the roots; if English were a lost language, and one were translating the phrase, "He swung the bat mightily towards the ball," one might go to an English dictionary and find out that a 'bat' is a furry flying animal, and a 'ball' is a lavish party for dancing. The resultant image would turn out quite amusing, but would likely fail to convey the original meaning. Thus when one looks up the meanings of the names in the Text, one finds that "Ajah" means variously a "falcon", a "kite" or a "screamer", from which one can see that translators simply flipped over to Leviticus 11:14, Deuteronomy 14:13, and Job 28:7 to find a similar word, though with different accent points. Why they didn't turn to

Genesis 18:9 or Jeremiah 37:19 to find the same word meaning "where?" is probably because "where" is hardly a suitable name for a prince of Seir. It turns out to mean "the place of desire, the manifestation of the will" in context.

The point is easily seen here. While looking up similar words can be somewhat helpful with the context once one has gotten the root meaning, it is not only useless but distracting without an initial understanding of the roots themselves. In the case of "Ajah" (Aleph-Yod-He) from 36:24, the roots are all vowels, so must be considered in light of the first two (the center of activity), the last two (the showing of life), and the first and the last (the ability to will) as three distinct and possible roots. Fortunately, and as with all languages, all three combinations contribute nicely toward one idea, that of the place (the "where") of the desires or will, which in a restricted sense is an animal who is focused on one spot where his prey is, as does a falcon. In Ajah's case he was the brother of Anah who found the fountains in the wilderness, gaining prominence; thus his less fortunate brother would be eying that success as a vulture eyes a carcass. The imagery is all there, yet wants ordering for us to understand the impact of the text and the motivation of the writer to put things as he did.

The fact that Hebrew always references the human body and its actions is very helpful, and makes the meanings that much more down to earth, unlike Greek in which the concept is primary. Like many indigenous cultures, the stories are all told with verbs; the actual subject and the far less frequent direct object come into the sentences almost as 'surprises' that interrupt the flow. Thus the long dash is used to demonstrate the interruptive character of the subject in most cases, as pointed out earlier with the importance of the placement of the subject in the sentence. It is a rare case when the meaning cannot be derived from examining the roots and the context, and these cases can be attributed to a lack of familiarity with the language rather than some fault on the part of the text. It was written to be understood.

Etymology and syntax (word meaning and grammar) are beautifully interwoven in Hebrew by a dynamic ongoing dialogue. The fact that it was written without spaces between the words is perhaps the best example. It is of no little amusement to me when people discard this as a 'primitive' practice; you mean to tell me that for over two millennia not a single person thought that it might be easier to read with spaces? The reason that Hebrew can say something in one sentence that takes me two paragraphs to say is because it allows for interrelationships that an analytic language does not. One can argue the meaning of a particular word ad infinitum, but one cannot argue its place among its neighboring words, nor its place in the sentence, which often tell more about its meaning than the word itself.

Scripture has another peculiarity about it that goes beyond even the Hebrew. In virtually every passage there is a contradiction, a hiccup, a turning from what is expected; in short, a mystery. These mysteries are beyond the scope of a work like this although a few have been indicated; thus the effort here is somewhat different from merely translating. In translation there necessarily comes in a great deal of *explaining*. The difficulty produced is that as soon as the meaning of a passage is *explained*, the mystery is gone; further, access to the mystery is subsequently blocked in the reader's mind by acceptance of the initial explained meaning. It is difficult to relearn how to drive. This process of replacement of that which is not understood with something that is far more easily understood is addressed throughout scripture in the subject of idolatry. Here the effort has been to have left the door to the mysteries ajar; in most cases this means using phrases which stumble the reader: sentences without verbs, fragment of phrases with no apparent reference, etc. When the text uses a subject without a verb or a dangling phrase it is not because the language was undeveloped or because the text is just too old for us to understand. These are all, without exception, *powerful literary devices* that indicate additional layers of meaning. It is helpful if the text is read as English *poetry* in which the strict rules of grammar are relaxed. However, in Hebrew when structural conventions are broken, it is not relaxing the rules, but artfully using them to compose far more depth—with fewer words. If the reader is aware that the Bible is neither a dictionary nor an encyclopedia, but the *manifestation of an incomprehensible Truth*, his apprehension will be that much more rewarded, albeit his comprehension may suffer some lessons in humility. We cannot wrap our arms around it, but we can dive in and swim around.

Another point comes into relief when we begin to look at the actual wording of the text, which can be called the the *"Well, what it really meant was..."* syndrome. There is no such thing. Various aspects of our ignorance, when faced with jarring or obscure passages, quickly jump in with excuses based on this ignorance; such as *it was a primitive language and they didn't know how to express themselves properly*, or *the text must be corrupted*, or any of a thousand like ideas which assume that we are smarter than the text. Thus whatever simplistic idea we *think* it might mean is what it actually means. Let it be stated here unequivocally that what the text says is precisely what it means, down to the last letter. When the text leaves out a subject or verb or direct object where one belongs, it is a literary device of a depth and complexity that we are simply unfamiliar with, having learned a language (English) which attempts to define things by ascription rather than inference, and by indication rather than relation. What the text leaves out is often far more important than what it iterates. The reader can rest assured that this translation is often deliberately strange *because the text is deliberately strange*. A fine Walnut table is not made from Spruce 2 x 4's. The account you have before you does not insert "the" where there is none in the Hebrew, nor does it supply "the" just because it sounds better to the English ear. In both Hebrew and Greek (and most ancient languages) there are very good reasons for leaving out or inserting an article. When we find a mystery, or what appears for all the world like a oddly phrased idea, we think about it. That is what the Hebrew text was designed to make us do. It is a valuable exercise.

Genesis

In the beginning, he creates[1]—God—the **heavens**[2] and the **earth**. ² And the earth, she becomes chaos and vacancy[3], and darkness over the face of Abyss[4], and Spirit of God ready-hovering over face of the waters.

³ And he is saying—God—'he becomes light;' and he is becoming light.

⁴ And he is seeing—God—the **light**, that *as* good; and he is separating—God—between the light and between the darkness.

⁵ And he is calling—God—to[5] the light 'Day,' and to the darkness he calls 'Night;' and it[6] is becoming evening[7], and it is becoming morning[8] . . . day One.

⁶ And he is saying—God—'he becomes space in the middle of the waters, and he becomes separating between waters toward waters.' ⁷ And he is making—God—the **space**, and he is separating between the waters which, from-under to the space,

---

[1] *Creates*—The word has always the sense of a new head of God`s purposes from which all subsequent purposes will take their form. It is less *making from nothing* and more *establishing a center*—yet this center in contradistinction from God as center—as an element which one must necessarily address in the process of approaching their Creator.

[2] Bold words are emphatic in the Hebrew.

[3] *Chaos* Isaiah 45:18, c*haos and vacancy* Jeremiah 4:23.

[4] *Face of Abyss* Job 38:30, Proverbs 8:27. Note that *Abyss* and *Waters* are as different from each other as *Heavens* and *Earth*, the former in the earth, and the latter on the earth. When the light appears *out of the darkness* as II Corinthians 6:4 informs us, it is evident that it is proceeding from inside the earth itself, the face of the Abyss; not from the sun, who is not introduced for three more days. The face of the surface waters have a great deal of work to be done to them (day 2 and 3) before light is introduced in day 4 to *cause light to shine on the earth.*

[5] *Calling to* Isaiah 48:13.

[6] *It*, literally *he*, and so throughout for the expression *And it (he) is becoming morning, and it (he) is becoming evening.*

[7] *Evening* similar to the word *Raven.*

[8] *Morning* similar to the word *Ox.* Without the accent marks, the account would equally read, *And he is becoming Raven, and he is becoming Ox—day One.*

and between the waters which, from-above[9] to the space: and it[10] is becoming so. ⁸ And he is calling—God—to the space 'Heavens;' and it is becoming evening, and it is becoming morning—day second.

⁹ And he is saying—God—'They flow together[11], the waters, from under[12] the heavens toward one place, and she is seen—the dryness:' it is becoming so. ¹⁰ And he is calling—God—to the dryness 'Earth,' and to the collection of the waters he calls 'Seas.' And he is seeing—God—that *as* good.

¹¹ And he is saying—God—'She causes to vegetate, the earth, vegetation; herbage sowing seed; fruit tree making fruit to his species whose seed of him *is* in him on the earth;' and it is becoming so. ¹² And she is yielding forth—the earth—vegetation; herbage sowing seed to his species, and fruit-making tree whose seed of him *is* in him to his species. And he is seeing—God—that *as* good. And it is becoming evening, and it is becoming morning—day third.

¹⁴ And he is saying—God—'He becomes light-bearers in the space of the heavens, to cause[13] to separate between the day and between the night. And they become for signs[14], and for appointments[15], and for days and years[16]. ¹⁵ and they become for light-bearers in space of the heavens to cause to light on the earth;' and it is becoming so.

¹⁶ And he is making—God—**two** of the light-bearers: the great ones: the **light bearer**, the great one, to ruling of the day, and the

---

[9] *From above* similar to the word *Offense*.

[10] *It*, literally *he*, and so throughout for the expression *And it (he) is becoming so*.

[11] *They flow together* or *They expect (wait for)*, as one gathers together one's disparate thoughts when expecting something.

[12] *From under*; the Hebrew expression connotes the *taking away from under* the heavens.

[13] *Cause to*, a complex expression; literally *to to-separate*. The sense is the set-up for an action, hence active causality. Similarly throughout the chapter except verse 11, which is literally *she shall cause*.

[14] *Signs*; this word has both the sense of an omen and that which signals the omen, as a beacon.

[15] *Appointments*, as a cyclic formal gathering or festival.

[16] *And years*, or *and two*; the sense of the changing process of beings in the revolutions of time.

light bearer, the small one, to ruling of the night—and the **stars**[17]. [17] And he is giving—God—**them** in the space of the heavens to cause to light on the earth, [18] and to cause to rule in the day and in the night, and to cause to separate between the light and between the darkness. And he is seeing—God—that *as* good. [19] And it is becoming evening, and it is becoming morning—day fourth.

[20] And he is saying—God—'They roam the waters; roamers of living soul and flier flies over the earth on face of space of heavens. [21] And he is creating—God—the **monsters**, the great ones, and **all of** the living soul, the moving, they who roam the waters to their species, and **all of** flier of wing to his species. And he is seeing—God—that *as* good. [22] And he is blessing **them**—God—to cause to say, 'You—fruitful! and you—increase! and you—fill the **waters** in the seas! and the flier, he increases in[18] the earth.' [23] And it is becoming evening, and and it is becoming morning—day fifth.

[24] And he is saying—God—'She *brings* forth—the earth—living soul to her species; beast and moving *ones* and animal of him to her—earth's—species;' and it is becoming so. [25] And he is making—God—**animal** of the earth to her species, and the **beast** to her species, and **all of** moving *ones* of the ground to his species. And he is seeing—God—that *as* good.

[26] And he is saying—God—'We do Adam in image[19] of us, as likeness of us, and they descend in fish of the sea, and in flier of the heavens, and in the beast, and in all of the earth, and in all of the moving, the moving one on the earth.'

[27] And he is creating—God—the **Adam** in his image; in image of God he creates **him**: male and female he creates **them**. [28] And he is blessing **them**—God—and he is saying to them—God—'You —fruitful! and you—increase! and you!—fill the **earth**, and you

---

[17] *Stars;* a centrally focused burning compression which endures.
[18] *In the earth*, not 'over' the earth or 'on'' the earth. For a discussion of this expression, see Appendix XIV.
[19] *Image*: properly, *shadow*, from a root that means *to shade*, thus a representation, figure, resemblance; used most often for idols and molten images.

1:28—2:28

—subdue her! and you!—descend in fish of the sea, and in flier of the heavens, and in every animal, the moving one on the earth.'
²⁹ And he is saying—God—'Behold! I give to you **all of** herb seeding seed, that on the face of all of the earth, and **all of** the tree which, in him, fruit of tree seeding seed for you; he is becoming for food, ³⁰ and for **all of** animal of the earth, and for **all of** flier of the heavens, and for **all of** moving *ones* on the earth, which in him *has* living soul, breath of life, **all of** green herbage for food:' and it is becoming so.
³¹ And he is seeing—God—**all of** *that* which he has done, and behold! very good. And it is becoming evening, and it is becoming morning—day of the sixth.
2 And they are being finished—the heavens and the earth and all of their assembly. ² And he is finishing—God—in the seventh day his work which he does; and he is ceasing in the seventh day from all of his work which he does. ³ And he is blessing—God—the **seventh day**, and he is making holy, **him**, that in him he ceases from all of his work which he creates—God—to cause to do.

2:4—2:5

⁴ These:[20] Generations of the heavens and the earth in creation of them in the day of the doing of Jehovah God—earth and heavens.

⁵ And all of the field's[21] impulse[22]. he is restrained[23] in the earth, and all of of the field's herb[24], he is *not* yet sprouting, that he caused it *to* not rain[25]—Jehovah God—on the earth, and *there* is

---

[20] Without the accent marks, *These* also reads *Eloah*.

[21] *Field*; from *spread out*, with the sense of being flat; neither a prepared space nor a wild space, but a large spread in which a prepared place (such as the Garden or a flock) can be placed. See note 2:11 for *Land, Earth*. See also Appendix XIV. Note also that *field* in Chaldean (used instead of Hebrew in Daniel 2:4 to the end, Ezra 4:8-6:18, and Jeremiah 10:11) without the accent marks is the same as the Hebrew word *create*. Thus one sense of this introductory verse is *And all impulses of creations are arising in the Field* (as their birthplace).

[22] *Impulse*; word used only twice in Genesis and twice in Job, though in 24:63 Isaac goes out to *meditate* in the *field*; the word for meditate being identical but for the accent marks. It is an effort in a specific direction, whether conception of that effort as in *meditate* or physical as in *flight*.

[23] *He is restrained*; literally *before he is becoming*, yet this rare use of *before* has the sense of a universal arresting of action, somewhat stronger than a hesitation. It is the same word as '*not* yet' regarding the herbs in the verse.

[24] *Herb*; literally, *physical reestablishment to the original form*, thus usually translated *herb* as an annual plant that returns. This is parallel with *impulse* earlier in the verse, indicating the field is being held in temporary check from reestablishing his ecosystem until the new element of the Adam was in place.

[25] *Caused it to not rain*; the thought is more than rain not happening yet; it is the deliberate holding back of rain.

2:5—2:9

no Adam to cause to serve the **ground**. ⁶ And Ad[26]!—he is ascending from the earth, and he waters **all of** face of the ground.
⁷ And he is forming—Jehovah God—the **Adam**, dust from the ground[27], and he is blowing in his nostrils breath of life. And he is becoming—the Adam—to living soul.
⁸ And he is planting—Jehovah God—Garden, in Eden[28], from east[29], and he is placing there the **Adam** whom he forms. ⁹ And he is causing *to* sprout[30]—Jehovah God—from the ground, all of tree

---

[26] *Ad*; powerful extension of purpose, as the arm and hand reaching out to do something. This is the first subject made emphatic by grammar in scripture. *Ad* is used only here and in another form in Job—also in connection with control of water. Ad is contrasted with Adam by the lack of the blood element (see following note) yet shares the element of singularity of power. There is more than a casual connection between Ad and the "one" place to which the waters were gathered on the first half of the third day—the only day in which two separate occasions are declared good; *Ad* is *One* without the middle letter. This suggests that the retelling of creation that starts in 2:4 picks up from the third day of chapter one, the first time that the earth was seen. The other mention of Ad in Job 36:27 is: *That he is shrinking to nothing tributaries of the water; they are refining rain for his Ad, that they are burping up cloud-seeds, they are dumping over Adam increasingly.*

[27] *Adam, Ground*: A series of Hebrew words differentiated only by the accent marks are all related. *Adam* variously reads *Man, Ground, Red, Flushed, Ruddy,* and *Ruby*. The common element is *dam*, Hebrew for *blood*, which is related to the primitive root *damam*, to be dumb, to perish, to be cut off; and to *daham*, to be dumbfounded. The sense must be derived from the use of *Create* in which a center of God's purposes—that is separate from God—is established (see note 1:1). Life is placed into *Adam* (man) who is taken from the *Adam* (ground) and in becoming a living soul with *Dam* (blood) being his life-force, his countenance is *adam* (flushed), *adam* (ruddy), and *adam* (red). But unlike angelic beings (re: Ezekiel 1:20), this life-force (*dam*) is separate from God, thus defined by being dumbfounded (*daham*) and ready to perish and be cut off (*damam*). Adam's name and the ground from which he was taken—as well as his appearance—all have references to mortality.

[28] *Eden*: Delight.

[29] *From east*; this does not mean in the west nor in the east. 'From' means that the east is being left behind. A similar expression is used for the location of Babel in 11:2.

[30] *Causing to sprout*; in 1:11 it was the *earth* that brought forth trees and vegetation. The Garden is a special work of God that has a parallel to Adam being a special formation. Note that in verse 5 the sprouting of the field is deliberately held back by God until his Garden and his Adam are in place.

being desirable to sight and good for food, and tree of the life in middle of the Garden, and tree of the knowledge of good and evil,[31] [10] and stream, issuing from Eden to cause to irrigate the **Garden**. And from there he is being parted, and he becomes to four heads[32]: [11] name of the one: Pison[33]; he *is* the one surrounding **all of** land[34] of the Havilah[35] which, there...the gold[36]. [12] And gold of the land, even he—good; there the pearl[37] and the stone of the onyx[38]. [13] And name of the stream, the second: Gihon[39], he *is* the one surrounding **all of** land of Cush[40] [14] And name of the stream, the third: Hiddekel[41], he *is* the one going east of Asshur[42]. And the stream the fourth: he *is* Phrat.[43]

[15] And he is taking—Jehovah God—the **Adam**, and he is reposing[44] him in Garden of Eden, to cause to serve her and to cause to guard her.

[16] And he is instructing—Jehovah God—on the Adam, to cause to say, 'From any of tree of the Garden, eating you eat; [17] but from tree of knowledge of good and evil, you eat not from him, that in Day of your eating from him—dying you die.'

---

[31] *Good and Evil*, also *Good one and Associate thereof.*
[32] *Four heads*, four generative powers.
[33] *Pison*: Increase; spreading influence; acting proudly.
[34] *Land*, literally *Earth* and so throughout. The fact that the earth (the 'dryness') is covered in water and *passively* appears in chapter one is instructive when considering that the heavens (the 'space') *actively* divide the same waters. Thus the relationship between the Heavens and the Earth are established at the onset of God''s actions.
[35] *Havilah*: Anguish; to twist or writhe painfully; a circumlocutory dance; virtual energy.
[36] *Gold* has the sense of the perfect reflection of light, especially the light of the eye.
[37] *Pearl* has the sense of the dividing of the light, as Job 38:24.
[38] *Stone of the onyx* has the sense of gathering and purification, as the Philosophers' Stone.
[39] *Gihon*: the breaking forth, as a stream; determined motion.
[40] *Cush*: black, terror, fire-like.
[41] *Hiddekel:* propagation of the (date) palm; riddle of nimbleness; quick and prickly.
[42] *Asshur*: a step (forward); from *going forward straight*; *honest.*
[43] *Phrat*; or *Euphrates*: fruitfulness, fertilizing.
[44] *Reposing*; to deposit for safekeeping; the sense is laying something aside to rest.

2:18—2:24

¹⁸ And he is saying—Jehovah God—'Not good to be being, the Adam, to his aloneness; I make for him helper—as his counterpart.'

¹⁹ And he is forming—Jehovah God—from the ground all of animal of the field, and **all of** flier of the heavens, and he is bringing to the Adam, to cause to see what ? he calls to him. And all which he is calling to him—the Adam⁴⁵—living soul—his name. ²⁰ And he is calling—the Adam—names to all of the beast, and to flier of the heavens, and to all of animal of the field; and for Adam he finds not helper, as his counterpart.⁴⁶

²¹ And he is causing to fall—Jehovah God—deep sleep on the Adam, and he is sleeping⁴⁷, and he is taking one from his enclosures, and he is closing flesh under her.

²² And he is building⁴⁸—Jehovah God—the **enclosure** which he takes from the Adam, into Woman, and he is bringing her to the Adam. ²³ And he is saying—the Adam—'This one *is* the one!⁴⁹ bone from my bone, and flesh from my flesh!⁵⁰' To this one he calls Woman, for from ♂man⁵¹ she is taken, this one. ²⁴ On this he is leaving, ♂man, his **father** and his **mother** and he adheres in his

---

⁴⁵ *He the Adam*; the expression connotes that the names given were expressions of their relationship to Adam himself.

⁴⁶ *As his counterpart*, literally "as in front of him". The words have the sense both of an *opposite* and a bold manifestation, as an announcement... also a *reflection*, but not that of a mirror; a *transforming* reflection per II Corinthians 3:18.

⁴⁷ *Sleeping*; different word from *deep sleep*. This is normal sleep, *deep sleep* could be translated *distilled blood* or *a trance*. The repetition of the idea accentuates God''s action and Adam''s reaction being paired, a theme throughout the account until interrupted by the knowledge of good and evil.

⁴⁸ *Building*, without accent marks reads *Understanding*.

⁴⁹ *This one is the one*, or *This is the [proper] step*.

⁵⁰ *Bone, flesh*; connoting substance, shape.

⁵¹ *Woman, man* or *female, male*. Male/man and female/woman in Hebrew are *ish* and *isha*. They carry the sense of *intellectual faculty* and *active faculty* in relationship.

2:24—3:6

wife[52], and they are to flesh, One.[53][54] 25 And they are, two of them, naked ones, the Adam and his wife, and they are not self-shaming.

3 And the serpent[55] becomes crafty[56] from all of animal of the field which he—Jehovah God—does. And he is saying to the woman, 'Indeed? that he says—God—you eat not from all of *the* tree*s* of the Garden?' And she is saying—the woman—to the serpent, 'From fruit of *the* tree*s* of the Garden we are eating; but from fruit of the tree which *is* in the middle of the Garden, he says —God—'You eat not from him, and you touch not in him, lest you die.' And he is saying, the serpent to the woman, 'Not in dying you die; but One knowing—God—that in day of your eating from him and opening[57] those, your eyes, and you become as God, ones apprehending of good and evil.'

⁶ And she is seeing—the woman—that good *is* the tree for food, and that yearning he *is* to the eyes, and being desired the tree to

---

[52] Woman and wife are the same word in Hebrew (as well as Greek); additionally, so are *man, male,* and *husband*. See previous note.

[53] *On this... ...One.* This is a rare "aside" in the text, in which it is ambiguous as to whether Adam is still speaking, or God is speaking without telling us so. This device is used to force the reader to pay attention and inquire further. Matthew 19:4-5 suggests that it is God speaking, which raises the question as to whom he was speaking. It is not to Adam as in the previous instructions in which he used "you", not "he". This leads to more than one mystery; see following note.

[54] Adam as of yet did not know that he was incomplete (naked) and did not as of yet have the knowledge of good and evil. Seeing that the animals were complete, and possibly assuming that mere reception of the woman completed him, he goes forward on the strength that he could satisfy God's edict to fill and subdue the earth using only himself and his wife... that is without God (leaving his father). While this leads to the eating of the tree of the knowledge of good and evil, it is not 'original sin'—a concept which occurs nowhere in scripture—but 'original faith'... see note 3:6.

[55] *Serpent*: the sense here is of a coiled serpent eager to strike rather than the fleeing serpent of Job 26:13 or the crooked serpent of Isaiah 27:1. More than a mere snake, it suggests all inner darkness caused by contained vehemence, the image is of the heart being coiled about by self-occupation to the point of self-destruction; the opposite of the meaning of *Asshur* as noted in 2:14.

[56] *Crafty*, or more exactly, *Blindly passionate*.

[57] *Opening*, as *opening to the light*.

3:6—3:14

causing intelligence.⁵⁸ And she is taking from his fruit, and she is eating, and she is giving even to her ♂man with her, and he is eating. ⁷ And they are being opened, *the* eyes of two of them, and they are knowing that they *are* naked ones, and they are raising a tent of mourning, and they are making for them*selves traveling girdles.*⁵⁹

⁸ And they are hearing **voice** of Jehovah God walking in the Garden at wind of the day, and he is self-hiding—the Adam and his wife—from face of Jehovah God in middle of *the* trees of the Garden.   ⁹ And he is calling—Jehovah God—to the Adam, and he is saying to him, 'Where—you?' ¹⁰ And he is saying, 'Your **voice** I hear in the Garden, and I am fearing that I *am* naked, and I am hiding.'

¹¹ And he is saying, 'Who tells to you that—naked you *are*? From the tree which I instruct you, so as not to eat of him . . . you eat?'

¹² And he is saying, the Adam, 'The woman whom you do give with me—she gives to me from the tree, and I am eating.'

¹³ And he is saying—Jehovah God—to the woman, 'What *is* this you do?' And she is saying—the woman—'The serpent—he seduces me, and I am eating.'

¹⁴ And he is saying—Jehovah God—to the serpent, 'That you do this, you *are* being cursed from all of the beast and from all of animal of the field. On your belly⁶⁰ do you go, and dust you eat all

---

⁵⁸ Being Adam's 'opposite', 'counterpart', and 'helper', Eve fulfills her role admirably by looking for—and believing that she has found—a way to make the declaration '*on this he is leaving his father and mother*' into reality. Urged by the serpent who knew better, she is tricked into believing that the knowledge of good and evil—which God has and they have not—will supply the missing element necessary to be able to subdue the earth *on their own* and present it to God. This is necessarily, in her unfinished condition, a supreme act of faith, albeit misguided. Note that she is assessing the desirability of the fruit for the sake of its suitability to her husband''s purposes; not, as many have claimed, for her own indulgence. See note 4:6 for the extension of this idea in Cain as he attempts to extend the same action, but in a completely different manner.

⁵⁹ *Traveling girdles*; the sense of the word is of a belt one puts on for war, or a traveling skirt put on for a journey.

⁶⁰ *Belly*; similar to *serpent* and *crafty* (notes verse 1), *belly* connotes an utter helpless wallowing in those qualities that previously had been operated by choice. It has the sense of a constant breaking forth in an untoward

3:14—3:19

of *the* days of your life. ¹⁵ And enmity I am setting between you and between the woman, and between your seed and her seed; head—he overwhelms you; and heel—you overwhelm him.'

¹⁶ To the woman he says, 'To increase, I am increasing your vexation and your pregnancy, in pangs you birth sons, and to your husband your impulse[61], and he rules[62] in you.'

¹⁷ And to Adam he says, 'That you listen to voice of your wife, and you are eating from the tree which I instruct you, to cause to say, 'You eat not from him,' the ground *is* being cursed[63] for your sake; in vexation you eat her all of days of your life, ¹⁸ And thorn and thistle[64] she sprouts for you, and you eat **herbage** of the field[65]; ¹⁹ In sweat[66] of your nostrils you eat bread until you are caused to return to the ground; that from her you are taken; that dust[67]—you—and to dust you return.'

---

    direction, as well as to *groveling*.
[61] *Impulse* does not quite do the word justice. It is a drawn-out longing that produces desire manifested in impulsive rather than considered behavior.
[62] *Rule*; a repetitive, almost automatic or symbolic manner of behavior. Also rendered *quote* when without accent marks.
[63] *Cursed*: bitterly cursed; execrated.
[64] *Thorn and thistle*: the former has the sense of outward harm, as in pricking; the latter has the sense of enveloped layers of harm, as a thistle would catch in the hair or clothing, or a weed would need rooted out. There are parallels here to both *field/Garden* and *onyx/pearl*.
[65] *Herbage of the field* in contradistinction to *fruit* of the Garden. Note Cain''s offering in 4:3.
[66] *Sweat* here being the result of agitation; there is the sense of an irritated shaking motion. Think gnats. *Nostrils* here also has the sense of agitation; the rapid breathing through the nostrils; hence the sweating of the whole face; stress.
[67] *Dust* also has the element of *spiritual element* apart from corporeal manifestation. As such, *"...such spiritual element art thou, and toward the spiritual element wilt thou rise again."*

3:20—3:24

²⁰ And he is calling—the Adam—name of his wife Eve[68]: for she becomes mother of all of living[69].

²¹ And he is doing—Jehovah God—for Adam and for his wife coats of skin[70], and he is clothing them.[71]

²² And he is saying—Jehovah God—'Behold! The Adam becomes as one from us, to cause to know of good and evil. And now, lest he is stretching his hand, and furthermore he takes from tree of the life, and he eats, and he lives to *the* Age . . .' ²³ And he is sending him—Jehovah God—from the Garden of Eden to cause to serve **the ground** from which, there, he is taken. ²⁴ And he is driving out the **Adam**, and he is causing to tabernacle from east, to Garden of Eden, the **Cherubim**[72] and **flame** of the sword; the one turning herself[73] to cause to guard **way** of, tree of the life.

---

[68] *Eve*; life-giver... with the additional senses of *elemental existence, to declare or show,* and by extension, *a village.* Note that this naming of his wife gives the last recorded words of Adam... Man falls silent for the duration until the promised Seed; and the Woman, though subjugated by a 'silent partner', is put on to the stage. The necessity for *faith* has been crystallized; Man can no longer proactively *do*, only reactively *believe*; all action must now proceed from God''s word. But the woman, not being in the position of responsibility, has an element of freedom from this reactivity... which tragically is subjugated by her impulsive desire toward her husband. This 'tragedy' in the Greek sense of the word sets the stage for all women from Sarah to Mary.

[69] Equally, *all of living one.*

[70] *Coats of skin*: there are many subtle references here. When used together, and with the phrase following, the sense of these two words can be taken to mean *shapes of their bodies.* See following note.

[71] *He is clothing them*: or, *he is enveloping them (with new shapes and skin, re previous note).* There is also a Hebraism that uses this expression that would translate, *He is wiving them.* The fact that this whole statement appears at the nexus of the Genesis 2 through 4 account invites the readers'' investigation. Compare Second Corinthians 5:1-4 and Romans 7:1-4.

[72] *Cherubim*: innumerable spiritual force associated directly with the presence of God.

[73] *Turning herself,* or *Turning round on herself* as Ezekiel 1:4, *infolding herself.* The *flame of the sword* and the *Way* guarded both have references back to *tabernacle from East,* and thus the both the 'turning' and the 'flame' are operative with the Earth itself; specifically the *wind of the day* in 2:8. Compare Second Samuel 22:11, Job 37: 12, 27, Isaiah 27:8, Ezekiel 19:11-14.

4:1—4:7

4 And the Adam—he knows **Eve** his wife, and she *is becoming* pregnant, and she is birthing **Cain**[74], and she is saying, 'I acquire a ♂man . . . Jehovah!'[75] **2** And she adds to cause to birth his **brother, Abel**[76]. And he is becoming—Abel—flock-shepherding, and Cain, he becomes ground-serving.[77]

3 And it is becoming from end of days[78]; and he is bringing—Cain—from the fruit of the ground, present to Jehovah. **4** And Abel, he brings, he also, from firstlings of his flock, and from their fat. And he is heeding—Jehovah—to Abel and to his present, **5** but to Cain and to his present he heeds not. And he is heating to excess —Cain—and it is falling—his face.

6 And he is saying—Jehovah—to Cain, 'To what? it heats to you; and to what? it falls—your face? **7** *Is* not, if you are *do*ing well, dignity? And if you *do* not well, to the portal! Sin crouches, and to you his impulse[79], and you rule in him.'[80]

---

[74] *Cain*: fabricator, smith. The strong who references all to himself.

[75] *I acquire Male . . . Jehovah*: this expression indicates Eve's faith in not only believing God's word to the serpent regarding her seed, but seeing that the seed spoken of would necessarily be Jehovah himself, as was the Christ. She was, however, some 4000 years premature.

[76] *Abel*: tenuousness, and by extension, meditation. *Abel* has a sense of giving in whenever contrasted with the assuming-all-to-himself quality of *Cain*. In English, *Who knows what this one is about; we'll have to think about it.*

[77] Note that *ground-serving* is likewise *Adam-serving* (see note 2:7 and Luke 15:29).

[78] *From end of days*; with few exceptions (Ezekiel hiding his girdle, and Elijah hiding out in a cave) this expression is always used for a very specific time period. We don''t know how old Adam was when Cain and Able were born, but he was 130 when he begot Seth. There is a great deal of leeway here for exactly what "'from end of days" might mean. If we are to take the parallel from Shem''s son Asshur (see chart Appendix XII), this was a time of establishing the two camps of activity: Cain''s (relating to Nimrod) attempting to establish man as intrinsically valuable to God on his own, and Abel''s (relating to Asshur) attempting to access God's favor through a transformative process, in this case the recognition of the place of death. It is evident that what is going on here had been building up for quite some time, and now 'proof' of his 'enlightened' path is being sought out by Cain, who initiates this whole procedure.

[79] *Impulse*: Longing desire, as 2:16.

[80] *To you his desire, and you rule in him*: Here we have the exact reverse of what was spoke to Eve. She inherited a drawn-out longing for her husband. Cain, in contrast, inherits—as a wife if we are to keep the accounts parallel

4:8—4:15

⁸ And he is communicating⁸¹—Cain—to Abel his brother, and he is causing them to be in the field, and he is rising—Cain—to Abel his brother, and he is killing him.

⁹ And he is saying—Jehovah—to Cain, 'Where ? Abel your brother?' And he is saying, 'I know not. The one guarding my brother—I?'

¹⁰ And he is saying, 'What *do* you do? Voice of your brother's bloods⁸²—ones crying to Me from the ground! ¹¹ And now, you *are* being cursed from the ground which—she opens wide her **mouth** to cause to take of **bloods** of your brother from your hand. ¹² That you are serving the **ground**, she adds not to give of her strength to you⁸³; one staggering and one wandering you are in⁸⁴ the earth.'

¹³ And he says—Cain—to Jehovah, 'Great my depravity without help⁸⁵. ¹⁴ Behold, you drive out **me** to-day from on face of the ground, and from your face I am concealed; and I become one staggering and one wandering in the earth, and it becomes, every of one finding of me, he kills me.'

¹⁵ And he is saying to him—Jehovah—'Therefore, every of one killing of Cain, sevenfold he rises⁸⁶;' and he is placing—Jehovah

---

—sin personified as a beast crouching 'at the portal', i.e., between the inner and outer earth where the Garden is located, which sin-beast itself has a long drawn-out desire for him. Thus there is always calling to Cain the attractiveness of what the Adam had been driven from—rather than, as Abel, the moving forward into God''s original edict to subdue and fill the earth, the surface outside of the 'field' in which was the Garden ...now occupied by a 'sin-beast'.

⁸¹ *Communicating*: the sense here is of declaring his intentions. Abel, as we have seen, does not resist him, as James 5:6.

⁸² *Bloods*: In the plural this carries also the sense of future children of Abel. It can just as easily be read as singular, much as the 'mass nouns' of Greek. Likewise for *faces, waters, lives*, and others.

⁸³ Blood pollutes the ground (Numbers 35:33) because as the substance from which Adam is taken, she has a vested interest in his progeny.

⁸⁴ *In the earth:* the land of exile for murderers and demigods alike is traditionally in the earth, as explained in Appendix XIV.

⁸⁵ *Without help*; literally, *from to lift up of,* as *without me being able to bear it.*

⁸⁶ *Sevenfold he rises*: this is the key to not resisting evil. The words carry the sense that if one attempts to slay Cain that he will rise again seven times stronger. Without Mosaic law, which limited justice to an eye for an eye so as to stay the multiplying of evil, vengeance begets seven times what it

—for Cain, token, to cause to smite not of **him** every of one finding him.

¹⁶ And he is *go*ing forth—Cain—from toward face of Jehovah. And he is dwelling in the earth—exile; east of Eden, ¹⁷ And he is knowing—Cain—his **wife**, and she is *becom*ing pregnant, and she is birthing **Enoch**[87]; and he is building city, and he is calling name of the city, as the name of his son—Enoch.

¹⁸ And he is being born to Enoch **Irad**[88]; and Irad, he generates **Mehujael**[89]; and Mehujael, he generates **Methusael**[90]; and Methusael, he generates **Lamech**[91].

¹⁹ And he is taking for him—Lamech—two of wives; name of the one, Adah; and name of the second, Zillah[92].

²⁰ And she is birthing—Adah—**Jabal**[93]; him, he becomes father of him of tent dwelling and acquisitions[94]. ²¹ And the name of his brother, Jubal[95]; he becomes father of all of one*s* handling of harp and reed[96].

²² And Zillah—also she—she births **Tubal-Cain**[97], one forging of all of artificer of copper and iron. And sister of Tubal-Cain, Naamah[98].

---

attempts to destroy; as such, vengeance belongs to God alone.
[87] *Enoch*: dedicated; to institute, to found.
[88] *Irad:* a wild donkey; the meaning has the sense of extreme passion within an orderly body.
[89] *Mehujael*: smooth out by God; demonstrate with force.
[90] *Methusael*: they died inquiring; strong yawning pit of death.
[91] *Lamech*: strong cohesion dissolved; unto bringing low.
[92] *Adah and Zillah*: Adah: ornament, periodic order. Zillah shadiness, a depth to which light cannot penetrate. This introduces the woman outside of God''s influence, and is given as a dual character: the dependable ornament of a wife, and the inexplicable depths to her character. Note that until Sarai Abram''s wife, no women on Seth''s side are ever named; including, peculiarly enough, Noah''s wife; who like Eve was mother of all subsequent generations.
[93] *Jabal*: a stream, the overflowing, the plenty.
[94] *Acquisitions*: as livestock and cattle. Jabal''s character here is that of a traveling merchant.
[95] *Jubal*: Jubilation, thriving, being carried.
[96] *Harp and reed*: these carry the sense of *bright conception* and *love worthy*; i.e., useful and pleasing arts.
[97] *Tubal-Cain*: result of Cain''s path; mutual yielding to the central might.
[98] *Naamah*: becoming united; sociableness; pleasant aggregation.

4:23—4:26

²³ And he is saying—Lamech—to his wives,
'Adah and Zillah, you listen! My voice!
Wives of Lamech, you give ear! My saying!:
For ♂man I have slain for my splitting,
And progeny for my fraternity[99];
²⁴ That sevenfold he is being raised—Cain—
And Lamech seventy and sevenfold[100].'
²⁵ And he is knowing—Adam—again his **wife**[101], and she is birthing son, and she is calling his **name** Seth[102], 'That he set for me—God—seed after reducing of Abel,' for he killed him—Cain. ²⁶ And to Seth—also he—he is born son, and he is calling his **name** Enosh[103]; then he is wedging open *hope*, causing to call on, in name of, Jehovah.[104]

---

[99] *For man I have slain for my splitting, and progeny for my fraternity*: 'Man' here is *ish*; male or intellectual man; thus *individual man*, or individuality. Lamech is making a declaration of the power of society, as to which his wives, sons, and daughter attest. The 'splitting', often translated 'wound' refers to this individuality. He is proclaiming the death of the individual man by the power of society over him, and the prevention of future progeny becoming individuals by the power of this fraternity.

[100] *Seventy and sevenfold*: see note verse 15; Lamech is confident that the power of society is 11 times stronger than that of the individual; that a well-regulated society (fascism) is the perfect response to the freedom of the individual. Ironically, there is in his speech the sense given that his actions were individuated by his own will; which particular character is always found at the top echelons of a fascist society.

[101] *His wife*: there is a touch of irony here on the part of the writer in emphasizing 'wife'; it is contrasting her and Adams continuing steadfastness with Lamech's two wives and impetuous actions.

[102] *His name Seth*: the emphasis of the naming itself over the name is remarkable. Seth means appointed, set, the site. The name carries with it two ideas; that of duration in movement, and that of reciprocity; and thus *a stable foundation*; yet a universal foundation upon which can be built both the good and bad. It is related to the number 6, *to allow*.

[103] *Enosh*: mortal man. This word is used to read 'man' throughout the scriptures along with *Adam* (universal man), *Ish* (male, intelligent, individual), and later we will find *Gibbor* (mighty man, hero). Enosh is often used to express weakness and mortality; in its full meaning it connotes tranquil power and gentle movement in the context of the patient endurance of mortality.

[104] *Wedging open hope, causing to call on—in name of—Jehovah*: this is a rather difficult passage to translate without straying from the actual words.

5 This: Scroll of genealogies of Adam.

In Day[105] of causing to create—God—Adam, in likeness of God he does him: ² male and female he creates them[106]. And he is blessing **them**, and he is calling their **name** Adam, in Day of causing them to be created.

Note that the previous two emphases on the word *name* rather than the names themselves have been leading up to this conclusion. It is not merely calling on Jehovah, which endeavor may or may not succeed, but calling on —in name of—Jehovah; the which endeavor is dignified by the character of the calling itself whether or not one receives the desired reply. The word 'hope', while not expressly stated, has its sense from the contrast between helpless mortal man and the proactive movement forward of grasping for anything—in this case His name—which would provide the necessary stability to proceed without the despair of mortality. This issue continues to rise in scripture, and we next see it with the naming of Noah.

[105] *Day* here without the article is contrasted with Year, also missing the article, in the remainder of this passage. The Day is originally set by God to be Year—that is, a 1000 year day—but is interrupted by death.

[106] *Likeness of God...male and female*: the only time that the Adam is spoken of as being in the image or likeness of God is when both the male and female are spoken of being made. In 2:7 when Adam is made first individually there is no mention of it. Here it is simply 'likeness' without the 'image' as man's relationship to his wife has changed. This does not stop Adam from passing the new relationship on to his son as the next verse shows, once again using 'image and likeness' for Adam''s son. Yet the word 'son' is conspicuously absent there; it is less about progeny—the Seed —for Adam than about passing on the newly established relationship with his wife. This is a major contributor to the trial of Womankind that did not end until the resurrection of Jesus, and Mary''s interchange with him, which could not occur until *all* the disciples "left him and fled". It is only when man completely and formally steps out of the way that woman can be addressed by God; see Appendix V.

5:3—5:14

³ And he is living—Adam—thirty and hundred of Year.[107] And he is generating—in likeness of him, as image of him. And he is calling his **name** Seth. ⁴ And they are becoming—days of Adam—after causing to generate him—Seth—eight hundred Year; and he is generating sons and daughters. ⁵ And they are becoming, all of days of Adam which he lives, nine hundred Year and thirty Year, and he is dying.

⁶ And he is living—Seth—five years and hundred of Year, and he is generating **Enosh**. ⁷ And he is living—Seth—after his causing to generate **Enosh** seven years and eight hundreds Year. And he is generating sons and daughters. ⁸ And they are becoming, all of days of Seth two ten Year and nine of hundreds Year, and he is dying.

⁹ And he is living—Enosh—ninety Year, and he is generating **Cainan**[108]. ¹⁰ And he is living—Enosh—after his causing to generate **Cainan** five of ten Year and eight hundreds Year. And he is generating sons and daughters. ¹¹ And they are becoming, all of days of Enosh five years and nine of hundreds Year, and he is dying.

¹² And he is living—Cainan—seventy Year, and he is generating **Mahalaleel**[109]. ¹³ And he is living—Cainan—after his causing to generate **Mahalaleel** forty Year and eight hundreds Year, and he is generating sons and daughters. ¹⁴ And they are becoming, all of days of Cainan ten years and nine of hundreds Year, and he is dying.

---

[107] *Of Year*: the Hebrew is perfectly capable of expressing plural 'years' as we saw in 1:14. What is being emphasized here is the *portion* of a 1000-year lifespan that has been achieved. The number 1000 represents the achievement of complete power... an endeavor impossible to those who *dying do die*. The ages of these patriarchs are given as a proportions of it. Note that five of the years of Seth before begetting Enosh, and seven of the years after are not part of this proportion; the text uses the word "years" instead of "year" as well as several years from Enosh and Cainan. When scripture varies in small details like this, it is useful to pay attention. For an example of how to explore these distinctions, see Appendix XII.

[108] *Cainan*: their smith; influence of the self to others.

[109] *Mahalaleel*: praise of God; mighty rising up; brightness.

5:15—5:29

¹⁵ And he is living—Mahalaleel—five years and sixty Year, and he is generating **Jared**[110]. ¹⁶ And he is living—Mahalaleel—after his causing to generate **Jared** thirty Year and eight hundreds Year, and he is generating sons and daughters. ¹⁷ And they are becoming, all of days of Mahalaleel five and ninety Year and eight hundreds Year, and he is dying.

¹⁸ And he is living—Jared—two and sixty Year and hundred of Year, and he is generating **Enoch**[111]. ¹⁹ And he is living—Jared—after his causing to generate **Enoch** eight hundred Year, and he is generating sons and daughters. ²⁰ And they are becoming, all of days of Jared two and sixty Year and nine of hundreds Year, and he is dying.

²¹ And he is living—Enoch—five and sixty Year, and he is generating **Methuselah**[112]. ²² And he is walking—Enoch—with the **God** after his causing to generate **Methuselah** three of hundreds Year, and he is generating sons and daughters. ²³ And he is becoming, all of days of Enoch five and sixty Year and three of hundreds Year. ²⁴ And he is walking—Enoch—with the **God**, and he is not, that he takes **him**—God.

²⁵ And he is living—Methuselah—seven and eighty Year and hundred of Year and he is generating **Lamech**[113]. ²⁶ And he is living—Methuselah—after his causing to generate **Lamech** two and eighty Year and seven of hundreds Year, and he is generating sons and daughters. ²⁷ And they are becoming, all of days of Methuselah nine and sixty Year and nine of hundreds Year, and he is dying.

²⁸ And he is living—Lamech—two and eighty Year and hundred of Year, and he is generating son. ²⁹ And he is calling his **name**

---

[110] *Jared*: the steadfast one; the descender/the ascender. It is the action that is shown here, not its direction.

[111] *Enoch*: dedicated; to institute; to found. In the context of his fathers and progeny, there is the additional thought of *the panging one.*

[112] *Methuselah*: man of the dart; eager shaft of death. This in contrast with *Methusael*, strong yawning pit of death. The two types of death here are contrasted; in Cain's line it is a wide eager pit toward which one heads, in Seth's line it is an inevitable result of mortality which heads towards one.

[113] *Lamech*: strong cohesion dissolved; unto bringing low. In the context of his fathers and progeny, there is an absence of a necessary act of will here.

Noah[114] to cause to say, 'This one—he consoles[115] us from our labor and from wear of our hands from the ground which he makes her *a* curse—Jehovah.' ³⁰ And he is living—Lamech—after his causing to generate **Noah** five and ninety Year and five of hundreds Year, and he is generating sons and daughters. ³¹ And he is becoming, all of days of Lamech, seven and seventy Year and seven of hundreds Year, and he is dying.

³² And he is—Noah—son of five of hundreds Year, and he is generating—Noah—**Shem**, **Ham**, and **Japheth**.

6 And he is becoming that he dissipates—the Adam—to cause to be multiplied on face of the ground[116], that daughters, they are generated[117] to them. ² and they are seeing—sons of the God—**daughters** of the Adam that they. . . good ones! and they take for them women from all whom they favor[118].

³ And he is saying—Jehovah—'He strives not—my Spirit—in the Adam forever.[119] Altogether he is flesh; and they become—days of him—hundred and twenty Year.'

⁴ The Nephilim—they become in the earth in the days, even those; and even afterward so. Whom they are coming—sons of the God—to daughters of the Adam, and they birth for them—they—the >men[120] who from *the* age, •men[121] of the name.

⁵ And he is seeing—Jehovah—that exponential evil of the Adam in the earth, and all of imagination of[122] designs of his heart but

---

[114] *Noah*: rest; movable. The idea here is a rest that is the result of the interrelationship of all things.

[115] *Consoles*; to sigh or breathe strongly; to release.

[116] This multiplying of the Adam resulted in the dissipation of mankind''s moral strength; answered in Cain's line via Lamech by a social fraternity, and in Seth''s line via Noah by a family.

[117] *They are generated*; the context here implies intent to plentifully gender daughters.

[118] *Favor* is not quite strong enough; the force is of a directed and vehement passion.

[119] *Forever*: for eon; for the age.

[120] *>Men*: Gibborim from *Gibbor*; mighty men; men of renown.

[121] *•Men*: a frail mortal; *Anash, or Enosh*. This depreciating word is deliberately set between *Gibbor* (heroes) and *Hashem* (the name)—two words denoting great might—to emphasize the nature of these crossbreeds from celestial and terrestrial unions.

[122] *Imagination of*: forms of.

evil all of the day. ⁶ And he is sorrowing[123]—Jehovah—that he does the Adam in the earth, and he is grieving to his heart. ⁷ And he is saying—Jehovah—'I wipe *away* the Adam whom I create from on face of the ground; from Adam unto beast unto moving, and unto flier of the heavens, for I sorrow that I do them.' ⁸ But Noah—he finds grace in eyes of Jehovah.

---

[123] *Sorrowing*: to sigh, to breathe strongly. Same word as 5:26 regarding Noah, "This one will *console* us..." Likewise *grieve* in this verse is from the same comment by Lamech; "concerning the *wear* on our hands..." This verse is a reflection on the part of God to the lamentation of Lamech. Yet *he is grieving to his heart* also implies a deliberate withdrawal of empathy on His part.

6:9—6:17

⁹ These[124]: Genealogies of Noah:

Noah: righteous ♂man; flawless he is in his generations[125]; *with* the **God** he walks—Noah. ¹⁰ And he is generating—Noah—three sons: **Shem**[126], **Ham**[127], and **Japheth**[128].
¹¹ And she is being spoiled—the earth—to face of the God, and she is being filled—the earth—!violence. ¹² And he is seeing—God—the **earth**, and behold! she is spoiled; for he spoils—all of flesh—his **way** on the earth. ¹³ And he is saying—God—to Noah, 'End of all of flesh, coming to My face, for full, she—the earth—violence through their **face**; and behold me!, spoiling of them—*with* the **earth**.
¹⁴ 'Do you!—for you—ark of wood of solidarity; *with* chambers you do the **ark**, and you shelter **her** from inside and from outside with the protecting. ¹⁵ And this, how you do **her**: three of hundreds of cubit[129], the length of the ark; fifty cubit width of her, and thirty cubit rise of her. ¹⁶ Gathering-light[130] you do for the ark, and to cubit you finish her from uppermost; and opening of the ark in side of her you place,—lowermost, two, and threefold[131] you do her.
¹⁷ 'And I, behold me! bringing the **Deluge** of waters over the earth to cause to spoil all flesh—in which in him spirit of life—from under heavens; all which *is* in the earth, he expires.

---

[124] *These*: again, without the accent marks, *these* reads *Eloah*.
[125] *Generations*: properly, circles of influence (of any kind).
[126] *Shem*: a name; elevation by dignity; lofty.
[127] *Ham*: obstacle; tumult; fatigue; down-bent; the gloomy one.
[128] *Japheth*: extended and wide; solution; simplification; spread out.
[129] *Cubit*: similar word to *her mother*. *Cubit* is a restricted sense of the word for something upon which all things take their reference and depend.
[130] *Gathering-light*: usually translated a *window*.
[131] *Threefold*, an apparent reference to the top of the three stories of the ark, is literally *thirty*, possibly a simultaneous reference to the ark's height of 30 cubits.

6:18—7:10

¹⁸ 'And I establish My **covenant**¹³² *with* you, and you come¹³³ to the ark; you, and your sons, and your wife, and wives of your sons *with* you. ¹⁹ And from all of the living, from all of flesh, two from all you bring to the ark, to cause to live of you¹³⁴; male and female they are. ²⁰ From the flier for his species, and from the beast for her species; from all of moving *ones* of the ground for species of him; two from all they come to you, to cause to live.
²¹ And you! You fetch for you from all of food which, he is being eaten; and you gather for you; and he becomes for you and for them for food.' ²² And he is doing—Noah—as all which he instructs him—**God**—so he does.

7 And he is saying—Jehovah—to Noah, 'Come you! You and all of your house to the ark, that **you** I see righteous to My face in this the generation. ² Of all the beast, the pure! you fetch to you seven: seven ♂male and his female; and from the beast which *is* not pure—he—two; ♂male and his female. ³ Moreover, from flier of the heavens seven: seven male¹³⁵ and female, to cause to live seed, on face of all of the earth. ⁴ For to days more, seven, I cause rain on the earth: forty Day and forty Night, and I wipe **all of** the standing substance which I do from over face of the ground.'
⁵ And he is doing—Noah—as all which he instructs him—Jehovah. ⁶ And Noah—son of six hundreds Year; and the Deluge, he becomes waters on the earth.
⁷ And he is entering—Noah—and his sons, and his wife, and wives of his sons *with* him, to the ark from face of water of the Deluge.   ⁸ From the beast, the pure, and from the beast which, she is not pure, and from the flier, and all of that moving on the ground. ⁹ Two, two¹³⁶ they come to Noah, to the ark; male and female, as which he instructed—God—**Noah**. ¹⁰ And it is becoming to seven of the days, and water of the Deluge, they are on the earth.

---

¹³² *Covenant*: this word has the sense of *creative authority* wherever it appears. It is God sharing the process of dealing with the earth.
¹³³ *And you come*: the word means to both to come or to go; it is the action that is in focus, not the direction.
¹³⁴ *Live of you*: live on account of you, live with you; both senses.
¹³⁵ *Male*; this word, *zakar*, is different from *Ish* in the previous verse; it is strictly 'male' with no reference to individuality or intelligence.
¹³⁶ *Two, two*: The sense is two pairs, that is two males and two females.

7:11—7:16

¹¹ In year of six of hundreds Year to life of Noah, in the new moon, the second, in seven-ten day to the new moon, in the day, even this, they are unleashed¹³⁷—all of springs of Abyss—vast! And the hidden crevices¹³⁸ of the heavens, they are unfastened. ¹² And he is becoming, the water-mass¹³⁹ over the earth forty Day, and forty Night.

¹³ In the very substance of¹⁴⁰ the day, even this, he enters—Noah and Shem and Ham and Japheth, sons of Noah, and wife of Noah, and three of wives of his sons *with* them to the ark. ¹⁴ They and all of the animal for her species, and all of the beast for her species, and all of the moving, the one moving on the earth for his species, and all of the flier for his species, all of bird¹⁴¹ of all of wing. ¹⁵ And they go in to Noah to the ark, two, two; from all of¹⁴² the flesh in which in him *is* spirit of life. ¹⁶ And the ones coming, male and female from all of flesh they come as that he instructed **him**—God. And he is shutting out—Jehovah—about him¹⁴³.

---

¹³⁷ *Unleashed*: made unrestricted. It is less of a sending forth the springs of the Abyss than releasing their bonds as Proverbs 8:29 and Job 38:8-11.

¹³⁸ *Hidden crevices*: a network, a series of pigeon roosts; from the root word *to lurk*.

¹³⁹ *Water mass*: rain not distinguished by individual drops; the root connotes a thing continual, palpable, thick, and obscure.

¹⁴⁰ *Very substance of*: properly, *in the bone of the day*.

¹⁴¹ *Bird*: this is the first time the Hebrew word for 'bird' has been used; previously it was 'flier' as the ancients divided up animal species not according to their composition (mammal, reptile, etc.) but according to their mode of locomotion. 'Bird' here is from the root 'to hop about'.

¹⁴² *From all of*: it would be good to reiterate here that the Hebrew pronoun *from* is far more forceful than its English equivalent. It means to utterly leave whatever or wherever it is coming from, and to take up new residence or position.

¹⁴³ *He is shutting out—Jehovah—about him*: or *behind him*. This peculiar expression has little application to the ark, but the stance that Jehovah takes to proceed with allowing Deluge to have his sway over the earth. The same expression is used in Judges 3:23 when Ehud locked Eglon in his bathroom behind him as he escaped, and in Second Kings 4:21 when the great woman of Shunam locked her dead son into the upper chamber in preparation for Elisha's arrival. The parallels with God `forsaking` Jesus on the cross are remarkable.

7:17—7:22

¹⁷ And he is becoming—the Deluge—forty Day on the earth. And they are increasing¹⁴⁴, the waters, and they are bearing the **ark**, and she is rising high¹⁴⁵ from on the earth. ¹⁸ And they are dominating, the waters, and they are increasing exceedingly on the earth; and she is going—the ark—on face of the waters¹⁴⁶.
¹⁹ And the waters, they dominate utterly exceedingly¹⁴⁷ on the earth, and they are being plumbed¹⁴⁸, all of the mountains, the lofty¹⁴⁹ ones which *are* under all of the heavens. ²⁰ Five of ten of¹⁵⁰ cubit from over-above they dominate—the waters—and they are being plumbed—the mountains. ²¹ And he is expiring, all of flesh, the one moving on the earth: in the flier, and in the beast, and in the animal, and in all of the roaming, the roaming one on the earth . . .and all of the Adam. ²² All who breathe of spirit of life in his nostrils—from all—which *is* in the drained¹⁵¹—they die.¹⁵²

---

¹⁴⁴ *Increasing*: both intensity and duration.

¹⁴⁵ *Rising high*: there is an element of lifting ones self up in addition to being lifted up; thus the use of *rising high* instead of *she is raised high*.

¹⁴⁶ *On the face of the waters*: note the contrast with the Spirit of God in 1:2.

¹⁴⁷ *Utterly exceedingly*; literally *exceedingly exceedingly*; the Hebrew could not put more emphasis than it has here.

¹⁴⁸ *They are being plumbed*: the initial idea is to measure, but with a strong sense of *overwhelm* and *cover*.

¹⁴⁹ *Lofty ones*; also, *haughty ones*.

¹⁵⁰ *Five of ten of*: the implication here seems to be 15, not 50. It could read, *five, ten*. There is, however, room for consideration.

¹⁵¹ *The drained*: this is not the 'dry land' so often spoken of. The word is used here for the first time and means *drained off land*; i.e., reference to its previous condition of being covered with water. It is used of the land that Israel crossed when the Jordan was stopped, and again when Elijah smote the waters with his mantle and walked over on *drained land*. The imagery being evoked is from the second Day, when the waters were drained from the surface of the earth to make room for life... and as that process was not finished until Deluge had completed his way with the earth, the second Day was not declared 'good' as were the others. This hints that whatever caused the earth to be covered with water at the introduction of the text did not end until this event.

¹⁵² *They die*; this is the correspondent to God's instruction to Adam, *dying you die*. Adam''s genealogies to this point had each ended in "and he dies." When we get to chapter 11 and see the genealogies from Noah to Abram, the expression is pointedly missing. After the Deluge, life itself is given new hope; while *dying you die* still has reign over the Adam, it is not the looming end-all that it is before the Deluge. Noah, in effect, is seen as

7:23—8:3

²³ And he is wiping **all of** the standing, that on face of the ground; from Adam to beast, to moving, and to flier of the heavens; and they are being wiped from the earth. And he is remaining[153]; yes! Noah and whom *are* with him in the ark. ²⁴ And they are dominating—the waters—over the earth fifty and hundred of Day.
8 And he is remembering[154]—God—**Noah**, and **all of** the animal, and **all of** the beast which *are with* **him** in the ark, and he is causing to pass over[155]—**God**—Spirit over the earth; and they are checked[156]—the waters ² And they are surrendering—springs of Abyss and hidden crevices of the heavens—and he is being forbidden—the water mass from the heavens.
³ And they are repenting[157]—the waters—from *being* on the earth, to go and to return[158]. And the waters are abating[159] from end of fifty and hundred of Day.

---

moving into a new arena in which there are available to the Adam new elements which supersede death, i.e., faith, judgment, and mercy. This is established by God`s covenant with Noah, as the text will show.

[153] *Remaining*: the word has the implication of Noah being redundant to the process that just occurred.

[154] *Remembering*: to mark something out as special; the word connotes 'be a male.' In today''s English we might say, *And God made Noah his pal*.

[155] *Causing Spirit to pass over—God—over*; there are a number of subtle images here; the *passing over* means to cross and go beyond; it also implies mastery over, and is used in the sense of a man being over a woman when making love.

[156] *Checked*: Again we have a reference to the the first verse of Genesis. It was the shutting away of God`s Spirit in 7:16 that removed the constraints on the waters, and now God`s *remembering*, or taking note of, the earth returns his attention, and thus his Spirit, to the place where the forces of water are once again held in abeyance.

[157] *Repenting*; restoring themselves a before; to *cause to turn back*.

[158] *To go and to return*: a back and forth movement; the Chaldean has *going and returning alternatively*.

[159] *Abating*; to lack, fail, want, lessen. There is a strong sense of experiencing sorrow and contrition; to bereave. This is a continuation of the sense of *repenting* earlier in the verse; here it is more *to fully reflect upon*, to consider all angles while diminishing as a result of that consideration; see note of the next verse.

8:4—8:7

⁴ And she is resting—the ark—in the seventh new moon, in the seven-ten day to the month, on mountains of Ararat[160]. ⁵ And the waters become to go and to abate[161] till the tenth new moon; in the tenth, in one to the new moon, they appear, the heads[162] of the mountains.

⁶ And he is becoming, from end of forty Day, and he is opening[163], Noah , **window**[164] of the ark which he did[165], ⁷ and he sends forth

---

[160] *Mountains of Ararat*: Mountain of *manifested light*, referring both to the rainbow of which ours today are mere shadows and the 'seven colors' of the covenant God there iterated to Noah. This mountain is today located near the town of Nasar in Turkey 2 miles north the Iranian border, 10 miles southeast of Dogubayazit, where the remains of the ark can be seen. (The Durupinar site, as it's called, is GPS 39° 26.470' and 44° 14.110' E at 6,148.3 feet altitude at its lower end, to 39° 26.391' N and 44° 14.049" E at 6,269.7 feet altitude at its upper end).

[161] *To go and to abate* is contrasted with verse 3, *to go and to return, and the waters are abating*. The back and forth movement of *to return* in verse three is missing here. *Abating* has the sense of a circular movement, as the whirlpool of a sink or tub drain.

[162] *Heads*, properly *shaking [heads]*.

[163] *Opening*: to open wide; release; let go free.

[164] *Window,* emphatic. There is a much deeper play on words here. Just as God called to the light—which he had just called into being—Day, and to the darkness—which was already there—Night, so we have Noah following a similar path. The word *window* has the sense of a *night-light*, that is, to send light *out* of the ark rather than to let it in. The picture here is of one sending out a beacon into the chaotic darkness to signal the recommencement of the evening and morning cycles.

[165] *The ark which he did* (or made): a most peculiar expression, especially as found at this juncture of the narrative. Noah is proactively taking up his part of the covenant mentioned in 6:18—the which will not be iterated until chapter 9—and is proceeding to do his part in establishing order; thus it is no longer the ark as ordered by God, but the ark which Noah made. The lesson here is that the terms of the promised covenant will be determined by the faith Noah demonstrates in taking part in God''s restoration of the earth; so it is vital to understand the significance of Noah's actions here.

8:7—8:9

the **raven**[166], and he is going forth! to go forth and return![167] till to dry of the waters from over the earth[168].
⁸ And he sending the **dove**[169] from *with* **him**[170] to cause to see ?are they slight?—the waters[171], from over face of the ground? ⁹ And she finds not—the dove—rest[172] for sole of her foot[173], and she she is returning to him, to the ark; that waters *are* on face of all of

---

[166] *Raven*, without the accent marks, the same word as 'evening' from chapter 1; a sad veil of dimness that devours.

[167] *To go and return*; this is a continuation of the back-and-forth theme of the waters abating in verse 5. The Raven, or as the text is hinting, the *Evening* released from the ark, becomes a cyclic event. Evening and morning are here being reestablished by Noah. It is evident that he knew exactly what he was doing by sending out a *nightlight*, or *beacon*.

[168] *From over the earth* has reference to the waters above the space of the heavens in 1:7; the same word is used connoting *to offend*.

[169] *The dove*, emphatic. This word, as the bird which bears its name, is of great symbolic significance in all ancient cultures. It means the gentle and generative process of creation; a fertile and easily worked land; in short, the beauty in the process of creation before a thing is fully formed. It also has the sense of *the one tyrannizing,* as the vital power of the process of growth can be fearsome; the dandelion can push up through concrete. And just as the evening put a dark veil over each of the days of Creation so that the morning could expose the generative power of God`s work, so the Raven, or the Nightshade was sent out by Noah to initiate the rhythms of growth (the dove). Note also that one of the roots of Dove is to efflovesce; wine, or intoxication; as we shall see in chapter 9.

[170] *From with him*; here is the correspondent action to Eve giving the fruit to her husband *with* her. Noah, in the place of Adam here, is sending it out again to see if what she gave him has a place of rest, and by proxy, whether he does. This is an ultimate act of humility on Noah`s part; unlike Cain who resented what had happened, Noah is accepting his condition, and saying in effect, *Is there a place for me in God`s work, who find myself unfinished?*

[171] *The waters*: this would be a good place to mention the symbolism employed by the Hebrew for *waters*. It is, in short, *'the word of...[context]'*. The Red Sea was the word that Pharaoh uttered regarding them not leaving; thus it stood as a wall to them on their right hand and left; there was but one way of passing that word; follow Moses. The Jordan, overflowing its banks in flood season, stood up in an imposing heap that formed when the priests' feet touched the water; the word was the book of Deuteronomy spoken shortly before to all of Israel: be faithful to the law and nothing can touch you. Elijah when leaving for heaven smote the Jordan with his cloak and the waters scattered "hither and thither", which was the nation''s constant

the earth. And he is stretching[174] his hand, and he is taking her, and he is bringing **her** to him, to the ark.

[10] And he is writhing[175] still more seven of days[176], difficult ones, and he is adding to send away the **dove** from *being a part of*[177] the ark. [11] And she is coming to him—the dove—to time of evening[178], and behold!, leaf of olive[179], ripped off in her beak. And he is knowing—Noah—that they are slight—the waters—

---

reaction to his word; there had been no continuity of reaction during his life. So we find that the movements of the waters always follow the authority of the word. Here Noah is tenuously checking to see if the unleashed power of the Word of judgment on the earth has fully spent itself, but more: is there a new word? Without a new word from God, he will not leave the ark, as we will see, he uncovers the ark, sees that the land is dry, but stays until the word from God instructs him to leave it. Thus the dove returning although trees are already growing.

[172] *Rest*: Ma-Noah.

[173] *Sole of her foot*: or by implication, *place of generation.* With a common bird, this would mean a nesting place; with the wider meaning here of generative creation, the earth is not yet prepared to countenance progenerative behavior so soon after the judgment enacted on the misuse of the same. It is not until the 27th (the meaning of which number is progeneration) of the 2nd (a couple) new moon in the 601st (meaning the first act of allowance after repentance) year of Noah''s life that the way is cleared, as we will see in verse 13.

[174] *Stretching*: the implication is a protective gesture; reassurance of ownership. Creative vitality was to be kept on the ark under Noah''s command for another week. *Taking* and *bringing* her in the verse have the same connotations.

[175] *Writhing*: while a weakening of the word could be translated *waiting*, the text here is expressing extreme agitation in expectation. The word means to twist or whirl in a circle; to writhe with pain.

[176] Note that ever since sending out the beacon (nightlight) and subsequently the raven (evening), events are proceeding once again in a cyclic manner. The seven days here are a new establishment of cycles contrasted with the months, years, and symbolically cycle-breaking numbers thus far, such as 150 days of the Deluge dominating, 40 days of water-mass descending, and the like. Though it is stretching the limits of his patience, Noah is determined to establish order on the earth.

[177] *From being a part of*: this is necessary to insert to provide the sense that in sending the dove, Noah is giving up part of himself. Throughout this passage there is an underlying theme of extreme agitation on the part of Noah; the ark, in becoming the only safe haven in the world, had effectively *become* the world. Now that world needed broken apart and spread out, and

from on the earth. ¹² And he is waiting still more seven of days, difficult ones, and he is sending¹⁸⁰ the **dove**, yet she adds¹⁸¹ not to cause to return to him still more.

¹³ And he is becoming in one of and six hundreds Year, in the first, in one to the new moon, they waste¹⁸², the waters, from on the earth. And he is taking away—Noah—the **covering** of¹⁸³ the ark, and he is seeing, and behold, it wastes, face of the ground. ¹⁴ And in the new moon, the second, in seven and twenty Day to the new moon, she is dry¹⁸⁴—the earth.

¹⁵ And he is orating—God—to Noah, to cause to say, 'You! Issue from the ark; you, and your wife, and your sons, and wives of your sons *with* **you**. ¹⁶ All of the living that *is with* **you**, from all of flesh in the flier, and in the beast, and in all of the moving, the one moving on the earth, issue with you! ¹⁷ And they swarm in the earth, and they are fruitful, and and they increase on the earth.¹⁸⁵'

¹⁸ And he is issuing forth—Noah and his sons, and his wife, and wives of his sons *with* **him**. ¹⁹ All of the animal, all of the moving one, and all of the flier; all of one moving on the earth to their families¹⁸⁶, they issue from the ark.

²⁰ And he is building—Noah—altar¹⁸⁷ to Jehovah, and he is taking from all of the beast, the pure, and from all of the flier, the pure,

---

the process is taking great emotional toll on Noah.

[178] *To time of evening*: or, *leaving (being finished with) the raven*.

[179] *Leaf of olive*: or *ascending of illumination*. With *ripped off in her beak* reads, *rising light torn to shreds by the edges of her force (blowing)*.

[180] *Sending*: same word as *stretching*, verse 9.

[181] *She adds*: response to him *adding* to send her out again in verse 10.

[182] *Waste:* a strong word meaning to be destroyed by drought.

[183] *Covering of*: same word as *plumbed* when the the mountains were *plumbed (covered)* by the waters in 7:19.

[184] *Dry*: also, ashamed or confused.

[185] *Swarm in the earth... increase on the earth*: The Hebrew is exceedingly precise in its use of prepositions for in/on, see Appendix XIV.

[186] *Families*: the word is feminine and has a strong sense of exposure and spreading out.

[187] *Altar*: Note scripture's habitual introduction of a formal word which subsequently characterizes an entire section. We have just finished a section in which the *ark* has been foremost; the setting to which all other scenery refers, now the Text introduces the *altar* in the same manner. Thus the *altar* is the necessary transitional element from *ark* to *covenant*.

8:20—9:5

and is raising ascents[188] in the altar. ²¹ And he is breathing—Jehovah the restful fragrance; and he is saying—Jehovah—to His heart, 'I add not to cause to slight[189] of any more the **ground** on the Adam's account. That, form of the Adam's heart—evil from his youth[190]; and I add not to still more cause to smite of **all of** living, as which I have done. ²² During all of days of the earth, seed and reaping, and cold and heat, and harvest and winter, and day[191] and night[192], they rest not.'

9 And he is blessing[193]—God—**Noah** and his sons, and he is saying to them, 'You!—fruitful, and You!—increase, and You!—fill the **earth**. ² And the fear of you and awe of you is on all of animal of the earth, and all of flier of the heavens, in all of which she is gliding *on* the ground, and in all of fishes of the sea—in your hand they are given. ³ All of moving whom—he is alive—he is becoming for food; as the green herb I give to you **all**. ⁴ Yes, flesh in his soul—his blood—you eat not. ⁵ And yes, your **blood**,

---

[188] *Raising ascents*: in English we would add a great many words to capture the concentration of ideas here. The idea presented is the energetic raising up of something which rises and sublimates on its own; to spend great care to trigger a process which, once activated, undergoes a process of its own energetic nature; in short, to *spiritualize*.

[189] *Slight*: same word as in verse 8.

[190] *Evil from his youth*; the implication of *youth* is his first impulses. *Evil* connotes a bending, twisting, or missing from what is laid out before him in maturity. God is here relegating this 'evil' to the growth process itself, that is, opening a way in his heart to treat of the evil without destroying the entire earth in the process.

[191] *Day*: heat, time of work; not merely day, but a time of events. See Amos 5:8 for the use of these two terms.

[192] *Night*: to twist away from the light; to fold back; not merely night, but a time of adversity.

[193] *Blessing*: to lay the hands over someone with paternal affection. God here blesses them in preparation for his covenant with them (and all the animals) in verse 8. He must deal with the ease with which the serpent approached Eve, thus the fear and dread upon all animals. He must address the fact that they have eaten of something for which they were not ready, thus the permission to eat animals (and not just clean ones). He must address Cain's slaying of his brother and the fact that blood defiles the ground, thus the edict against eating blood. He must deal with Lamech's seventy-and-seven claim, thus the edict regarding consequences for murder.

your souls, I inquire[194]; from hand of all of animal I inquire him, and from hand of the Adam; from hand of ♂man of his brother I inquire **soul** of the Adam. ⁶ One shedding of blood of the Adam, in the Adam his blood he sheds[195]: that in image of God he does the Adam. ⁷ And you! Fruitful—you! and increase—you! Roam you! in the earth, and increase you! in her.'

⁸ And he is saying—God—to Noah and unto his sons *with* **him** to cause to say, ⁹ 'And I, behold me!—raising up My **covenant**[196] *with* **you**, and *with* your **seed** after you, ¹⁰ and *with* **all of** soul, the living, that *with* **you**; in the flier, in the beast, and in all of animal of the land with **you**; from all of ones issuing of the ark—for all of animal of the earth. ¹¹ And I raise up My **covenant** *with* **you**, and he is not cut off, all of flesh, still more from water of the Deluge, and he is not still more—Deluge—to cause to spoil the earth.'

¹² And he is saying—God—'This sign of the covenant which I give between me and between you, and between all of living soul which *with* **you**, for generations of eon. ¹³ My **bow**[197] I have given in the cloud, and she is for sign of a covenant between me and between the earth; ¹⁴ and he becomes, in my causing to cloud over the earth, and she appears—the bow—in the cloud[198]. ¹⁵ And I remember my **covenant**, that between me and between you, and between all of living soul in all of flesh; and he becomes not, still more, the waters for Deluge to cause to spoil of all of flesh. ¹⁶ And she becomes the bow in the cloud, and I see her—to cause

---

[194] *Inquire*: this seems a strange word for God to use to use; yet the text says neither 'require' nor 'avenge'. It is the word used for inquiring of the word of God to a priest or a prophet; and indeed, it is exactly what God did with Cain when he slew his brother. Thus it is the male brother upon whom the responsibility for retribution falls.

[195] *In the Adam his blood he sheds*: it would be a mistake to simplify this verse beyond how the text puts it. There are several layers of meaning here; it does not simply mean *by man shall his blood be shed*.

[196] *Covenant*: this word has the sense of *creative authority* wherever it appears. It is God sharing the process of dealing with the earth. In this case it corresponds to Noah sending a beacon of light out of the ark after the chaos; God gives a token of light in the sky after the cloud.

[197] *Bow*: this has reference both to the bending of a bow, and a severe effort made in doing so.

[198] *Cloud, bow*: note that God is sending both the cloud and the bow.

to remember covenant of eon between God and between all of living soul in all of flesh which, on the earth.'

¹⁷ And he is saying—God—to Noah, 'This, the sign of the covenant which I raise up between me and between all of flesh which—on the earth.'

¹⁸ And they are, sons of Noah issuing from the ark, Shem and Ham and Japheth; and Ham, he *is* father of Canaan.[199]

¹⁹ Three these, sons of Noah; and from these she scatters—all of the earth.

²⁰ And he releases[200]—Noah—♂man of the ground[201], and plants a vineyard, ²¹ and he is drinking of the wine, and he is being drunk; and he self-reveals in the middle of his tent. ²² And he is seeing—Ham, father of Canaan—the **nakedness** of his father, and he is announcing[202] to two of his brothers in the outer enclosure. ²³ And he is taking—Shem and Japheth—the **garment**, and they are placing on the shoulder, two of them, and they are going backward, and they are covering **nakedness** of their father; and their faces—backward, and nakedness of their father they see not.

²⁴ And he is awaking—Noah—from his wine, and he knows **what** he did to him, his son, the small one. ²⁵ And he is saying,

'Being cursed—Canaan; Servant of servants he is for his brothers.'

²⁶ And he is saying,

'Being blessed—Jehovah, God of Shem, And he is—Canaan—servant to him.

---

[199] *Canaan*: humiliated; physical existence becoming nothing.

[200] *Releases*: same word as when Enosh *wedged open hope* in 4:26.

[201] ♂*Man of the ground*: the thought here is implied that Noah is with great effort releasing *Ish*—man as an intellectual being—from the mere toil of the ground. A *vineyard* has the sense of spiritual heights; what is lofty; art, philosophy, and mysteries.

[202] *Announcing*: boldly proclaiming publicly. With the preceding thought, the idea is that Noah revealed secrets while 'outside' of himself; intoxicated in his mind like the prophets of old; things that ought to have remained secret; and that Ham revealed them publicly. The fact that Noah did this in the middle of his tent puts the onus on Ham.

9:27—9:29

²⁷ He beautifies[203]—God—Japheth, and he tabernacles in tents of Shem, and he is—Canaan—servant to him.'

²⁸ And he is living—Noah—after the deluge three hundreds Year and fifty Year. ²⁹ And they are becoming, all of days of Noah, nine of hundreds Year and fifty Year, and he is dying.

---

[203] *Beautifies*: or *entices* or *enlarges* (spread out). The ideas are related by the thought of a long process by which God brings Japheth to fruition.

10:1—10:5

10 And these: Genealogies of sons of Noah; Shem[204], Ham[205], and Japheth[206].

And they are being born, to them, sons—after the Deluge.
² 'Sons of Japheth: Gomer[207], and Magog[208], and Madai[209], and Javan[210], and Tubal[211], and Meshech[212], and Tiras[213]. ³ And sons of Gomer: Ashkenaz[214], and Riphath[215], and Togarmah[216]. ⁴ And sons of Javan: Elishah[217], and Tarshish[218], Kittim[219], and Dodanim[220]. ⁵ From these they are parted—coast-lands of the nations in their lands; ♂man to his tongue, to his families in their nations.

---

[204] *Shem*: a name; elevation by dignity; lofty.
[205] *Ham*: obstacle; tumult; fatigue; down-bent; the gloomy one.
[206] *Japheth*: extended and wide; solution; simplification; spread out.
[207] *Gomer*: full increase of substance; completion.
[208] *Magog*: overstretching; covering.
[209] *Madai*: commensurate abounding; my measure; my garments; what is enough.
[210] *Javan*: see *the dove* in 8:8 and note; that root (the generative process of creation) and *yahyin*, *to* effervesce or wine both contribute to this name which finally settled on to the Greek peoples. It is both what is beautiful and philosophical, and the tyrannizing effects of wine; but properly the relationship between the two.
[211] *Tubal*: sympathetic flowing; to settle outward.
[212] *Meshech*: a drawing out; to speculate and act; a purchase.
[213] *Tiras*: reflection (as in thought) of becoming granular (by grinding); effusing. For a sketch of these seven sons of Japheth, see Appendix VI.
[214] *Ashkenaz*: fire in its self and its effect; caloric.
[215] *Riphath*: the movement of spreading from a center; the active force of the name Jephthah his father. In the negative it is seen as bruising or healing; slander or influence. Centrifugal force.
[216] *Togarmah*: corresponding force to *Riphath* above; centripetal force, gathering from outside resources for inner stability.
[217] *Elishah*: power used to make ductile; in society, propaganda.
[218] *Tarshish*: successive movements for self-honor; periodic military conquest.
[219] *Kittim*: isolationism; beaters down or cutting off of outsiders; nationalism.
[220] *Dodanim*: mutually pleasing and self-sufficient; the *selected*, those mutually in agreement.

10:6—10:11

⁶ And sons of Ham: Cush²²¹, and Mizraim²²², and Phut²²³, and Canaan²²⁴. ⁷ And sons of Cush [are] Seba²²⁵, and Havilah²²⁶, and Sabtah²²⁷, and Raamah²²⁸, and Sabtecha²²⁹. And sons of Raamah: Sheba²³⁰ and Dedan²³¹.

⁸ And Cush, he generates **Nimrod**²³². ⁹ He forces! to cause of becoming Master in the earth. He!—he becomes masterful assailer²³³ to face of Jehovah; on this it is being said, 'As Nimrod, masterful assailer to face of Jehovah.' ¹⁰ And she is the beginning of his dominion²³⁴; Babel²³⁵, and Erech²³⁶, and Accad²³⁷, and Calneh²³⁸, in the land of Shinar²³⁹. ¹¹ ²⁴⁰From the earth, even he—

---

[221] *Cush*: power of fire; combustion.
[222] *Mizraim*: double straightness; subduing, overcoming power; complete oppression. *Shem*: a name; elevation by dignity; lofty.
[223] *Phut*: afflicted; cessation of breath; stifledness.
[224] *Canaan*: humiliated; physical existence becoming nothing.
[225] *Seba*: cyclic flow of production.
[226] *Havilah*: anguish as in travail-pain, but here especially suffering from violence.
[227] *Sabtah*: (occasional) cause and effect.
[228] *Raamah*: both the cause and effect of lightning; often simply *thunder*.
[229] *Sabtecha*: reference to *Sabtah* above, it is the result of the occasional cause and effect, which becomes an extreme oppression; enchaining; an infernal pain. But on its own, simply *determined motion*.
[230] *Sheba*: reference to *Seba* and *Raamah* above, restoring rest; settling into the place previously devastated by lightning and thunder.
[231] *Dedan*: unanimity of judgment; agreement of terms.
[232] *Nimrod*: self-ruling will, arbitrary proclivities, anarchy, despotism. Properly, *to give over to one''s own impulse; to shake off any restraining yoke.*
[233] *Masterful assailer to face of Jehovah*: This is in the same sense that Satan appears in Job as the Accuser.
[234] *Beginning of his dominion*: or *source of his lordly power.* The next five elements can equally be read, not as cities founded, but as the qualities by which Nimrod became great: empty pride, slackness, selfishness, all-engrossing desire, and civil revolution against God.
[235] *Babel*: confusion, empty pride.
[236] *Erech*: slackness.
[237] *Accad*: selfishness.
[238] *Calneh*: the wail is complete; all-engrossing desire.
[239] *Shinar*: tooth of the city; civil revolution.
[240] *From the earth itself*: Note the sudden change in tone. This parenthetical nature of this verse is indicated by the lack of '*and*' beginning it, and demonstrates the principal of *order within disorder*; the which was the bane

he issues—Asshur²⁴¹—and he is building **Nineveh**²⁴², and **Reheboth-city**²⁴³, and **Calah**²⁴⁴, ¹² and **Resen**²⁴⁵, between Nineveh and between Calah; he—the city²⁴⁶—the great.

¹³ And Mizraim²⁴⁷, he generated **Ludim**²⁴⁸, and **Anamim**²⁴⁹, and **Lehabim**²⁵⁰, and **Naphtuhim**²⁵¹, ¹⁴ and **Pathrusim**²⁵², and **Casluhim**²⁵³, (which they issued from there—Philistines²⁵⁴,) and **Caphtorim**²⁵⁵.

¹⁵ And Canaan, he generated **Sidon**²⁵⁶ his first-born, and **Heth**²⁵⁷ ¹⁶ and the **Jebusite**²⁵⁸, and the **Amorite**²⁵⁹, and the **Girgashite**²⁶⁰, ¹⁷ and **the Hivite**²⁶¹, and the **Arkite**²⁶², and the **Sinite**²⁶³, ¹⁸ and the **Arvadite**²⁶⁴, and the **Zemarite**²⁶⁵, and the **Hamathite**²⁶⁶. And

---

of Nimrod's efforts. Inserted in the account of Ham, we have Shem's son Asshur building Nineveh, Calah, and Resen to stand against the Babel movement. See note verse 18.

²⁴¹ *Asshur*: a step (forward); from going forward straight; honest.
²⁴² *Nineveh*: home of the growing son; a colonization.
²⁴³ *Reheboth*: infrastructure; public establishments.
²⁴⁴ *Calah*: full age; the growing wise; old men ruling within.
²⁴⁵ *Resen*: a bridle; the state's holding reigns.
²⁴⁶ *The City*: or civil safeguard; a city with watchmen. The city being referenced here is Nineveh.
²⁴⁷ *Mizraim*: overcoming power; see verse 6.
²⁴⁸ *Ludim*: to the firebrands; travailing, pregnancies.
²⁴⁹ *Anamim*: affliction of the waters; material heaviness.
²⁵⁰ *Lehabim*: flames; glittering blades.
²⁵¹ *Naphtuhim*: openings; hollowed caverns.
²⁵² *Pathrusim*: reduced and dispersed; broken into crowds
²⁵³ *Casluhim*: forgiven ones; tried for atonement.
²⁵⁴ *Philistines*: a wallowing; slighted; dispersal.
²⁵⁵ *Caphtorim*: the converted (as translated from one belief to another).
²⁵⁶ *Sidon*: ensnaring foe; deceptive enemy.
²⁵⁷ *Heth*: terror; surprised reaction; stupefaction resulting from an useless effort.
²⁵⁸ *Jebusite*: inward crushing; to crush with the foot to extract liquid.
²⁵⁹ *Amorite*: a sayer; outward wringing.
²⁶⁰ *Girgashite*: rumination; continual contractual labor; endless chewing.
²⁶¹ *Hivite*: natural living; animalistic lives.
²⁶² *Arkite*: my gnawing; brutish appetites.
²⁶³ *Sinite*: thorn; bloody disposition of rage.
²⁶⁴ *Arvadite*: greed for plunder.
²⁶⁵ *Zemarite*: thirst for domination.
²⁶⁶ *Hamathite*: enclosure of wrath; covetous desire; violent cravings.

afterwards²⁶⁷ they are scattered, families of the Canaanite. ¹⁹ And he is becoming—border of the Canaanite—from Sidon to your coming Gerar-ward²⁶⁸, as far as Gaza²⁶⁹; to your coming Sodom-ward²⁷⁰, and Gomorrah²⁷¹, and Admah²⁷², and Zeboim²⁷³, as far as Lasha²⁷⁴. ²⁰ These: sons of Ham, to their families, to their tongues, in their lands, in their nations.

²¹ And to Shem²⁷⁵, he also generates, he—Father of all of sons of Eber, Brother of Japheth the Great²⁷⁶.

²² Sons of Shem: Elam²⁷⁷, and Asshur²⁷⁸, and Arphaxad²⁷⁹, and Lud²⁸⁰, and Aram²⁸¹. ²³ And sons of Aram: Uz²⁸², and Hul²⁸³, and

---

²⁶⁷ *And afterwards* is contrasted with the description of the borders following. The text implies that an event occurred to the sons of Cush, Mizraim, and Canaan (Phut is left out); Nimrod attempted to organize them and take over by force, and the cities of Nineveh, Rehoboth-city, Calah, and Resen were the defenses raised by God who stood against Nimrod—cities built by Asshur the son of Shem. The collective was then scattered "afterwards", leaving just remnants of these three plundering nations in the land of Canaan as described. The possibility is suggested by parallel that the defeating of Nimrod''s power was concurrent with God''s dealings with the Tower of Babel.

²⁶⁸ *Gerar*: dragging away; ruminating; self-crushing.

²⁶⁹ *Gaza*: strength of her; stiffness.

²⁷⁰ *Sodom*: fettered; hidden wiles; silent contamination.

²⁷¹ *Gomorrah*: thrashing into heaps; oppressing.

²⁷² *Admah*: psychopathic; unmerciful; insensate.

²⁷³ *Zeboim*: troops; trained hyenas (as soldiers).

²⁷⁴ *Lasha*: blindness; the swallowing up of resources for social cohesion.

²⁷⁵ *Shem*: a name; elevation by dignity; lofty.

²⁷⁶ *Japheth the Great*: or *Japheth the eldest*. From the genealogy in the next chapter, we see that Shem was born two years after Japheth, as a chronology of the Deluge will show. As per First Chronicles 5:1-2, we see that genealogical order is listed variously by birth order or blessing depending on the context. Since the sons of Eber are the focus of the Text, Shem is consistently listed first despite being the middle child. See Appendix VIII.

²⁷⁷ *Elam*: eternity; the age; hidden events ready to be manifested.

²⁷⁸ *Asshur:* a step (forward); from going forward straight; honesty, order; enlightened government leading to prosperity.

²⁷⁹ *Arphaxad*: healing of productive nature; restoring of Providence.

²⁸⁰ *Lud*: productive power; travailing with pregnancies.

²⁸¹ *Aram*: exalted; collective invigoration.

²⁸² *Uz*: counsel; to provide (aught of) substance.

²⁸³ *Hul*: to have pain; writhing in effort.

Gether[284], and Mash[285] ²⁴ And Arphaxad, he generates **Shelach**[286], and Shelach, he generates **Eber**[287]. ²⁵ And to Eber, he generates two of sons; name of the one, Peleg[288], that in his days she is split, the earth; and name of his brother: Joktan[289]. ²⁶ And Joktan, he generates **Almodad**[290], and **Sheleph**[291], and **Hazarmaveth**[292], and **Jerah**[293], ²⁷ and **Hadoram**[294], and **Uzal**[295], and **Diklah**[296], ²⁸ and **Obal**[297], and **Abimael**[298], and **Sheba**[299], ²⁹ and **Ophir**[300], and **Havilah**[301], and **Jobab**[302]; all of these, sons of Joktan. ³⁰ And he is becoming, their seat, from Mesha[303], to your coming Sephar-ward[304]; mountain of the east. ³¹ These; sons of Shem, to their families, to their tongues, in their lands, to their nations.

---

[284] *Gether*: abundance from pressing (as juice from grapes).
[285] *Mash*: harvest of fruits, as in those produced by the previous three names.
[286] *Shelach*: variously 'Salah' or 'Shelah' in other translations; inspiration; 'eureka!'; luminous flash.
[287] *Eber*: from beyond the other side; figuratively connoting here the bringing of spiritual truth to mortals.
[288] *Peleg*: a channel; cleft; dividing.
[289] *Joktan*: made small; here, the lessening of evil.
[290] *Almodad*: given to achieve full measure.
[291] *Sheleph*: a drawing out; meditation; realization from reflection.
[292] *Hazarmaveth*: distinguishing the elements of mortality; sanctification by death.
[293] *Jerah*: lunar; seeing our brothers.
[294] *Hadoram*: public honor and splendor.
[295] *Uzal*: purified fire; desire communicated (in the sense of 'letting go' without concern).
[296] *Diklah*: becoming a song.
[297] *Obal*: accumulating full understanding.
[298] *Abimael*: my father is God; absolute fullness.
[299] *Sheba*: *Sheba*: restoring rest; settling into the place previously devastated. See verse 6, *Sheba* of Ham''s lineage.
[300] *Ophir*: in the negative, reducing to ashes; here, becoming gold; substantiation achieved.
[301] *Havilah*: previously (in verse 7) anguish; to twist or writhe painfully; here, virtual energy through trial.
[302] *Jobab*: triumphant shout.
[303] *Mesha*: bringing deliverance; (spiritual) harvest-fruits.
[304] *Sephar*: enumeration; census; literally book, as in this very book of Moses; thus *a spiritual record*.

10:32—11:6

³² These: families of sons of Noah, to their genealogies, in their nations; and from these they are parted³⁰⁵: —the nations in the earth—after the Deluge.

11³⁰⁶ And it is—all of the earth—one language³⁰⁷ and united matters³⁰⁸. ² And it is becoming, in their causing to journey from east³⁰⁹... and they are finding Valley in land of Shinar, and they are dwelling there. ³ And they are saying, ♂man to his fellow, 'Give help!³¹⁰ We mold bricks and we burn to burning:' and she is becoming to them, the brick, for stone; and the bitumen³¹¹, he becomes to them for the mortar. ⁴ And they are saying, 'Give help! We build for us city and tower; and its top³¹² in the heavens, and we make for us Name³¹³, lest we are scattering³¹⁴ over face of all of the earth.'

⁵ And he is descending—Jehovah—to cause to see of the **city** and the **tower** which they build—the sons of the Adam. ⁶ And he is saying—Jehovah—'Behold! The people, one; and language, one to all of them. And this? To their forcing open ability to do? And now it is not restrained from them; all they devise to be able to

---

³⁰⁵ *From these they are parted*: the force of the Hebrew here goes beyond simply saying that people spread out. The preposition *from*, especially when used with *parted* indicates a deliberate leaving and utter separation. The word '*from*' here has the additional sense of execration; a curse. And here we have that rare but specific expression '*in the earth*', i.e., the breach between inner and outer earth is here solidified.

³⁰⁶ 11:1-8 is somewhat of an explanatory and parenthetical section, as the previous section is formally closed, and the following section is formally introduced.

³⁰⁷ *Language*: literally, 'lip'.

³⁰⁸ *Matters*: words, acts, doings, etc.

³⁰⁹ *From east*; see 2:5; the same expression is used of the Garden of Eden.

³¹⁰ *Give help*: literally, *Grant you.*

³¹¹ *Bitumen*: or *slime*. From the root word 'to boil up'; used for everything from stomach gas to tar pits.

³¹² *Top*: shaking head. This is the same word as the tops of the mountains being seen in the Deluge of chapter 8.

³¹³ *Name*: without the accent marks, this word is the same as both 'there' (as in verses 7, 8, and twice in 9) and 'Shem'. The word is used twice in 4:17 regarding the first city (Enoch) that Cain built.

³¹⁴ *Scattering*: this word has also the sense of dashing into pieces, as with verse 9.

do. ⁷ Give help! We descend and we overload there their language, whose language they hear not—♂man his fellow.'

⁸ And he is scattering—Jehovah—**them** from there[315], over face of all of the earth, and they are leaving off to build of the city. ⁹ On this he calls her name Babylon[316], that there he overwhelms—Jehovah—language of all of the earth. And from there he scatters them—Jehovah—over face of all of the earth.

---

[315] *There*: this normally unnecessary word occurs also in the previous and next verses, indicating that there was something about that location which was contributed to the danger Jehovah saw.

[316] *Babylon*: there is no difference between the word here translated 'Babel' and elsewhere translated 'Babylon'.

11:10—11:23

¹⁰ These: Genealogies of Shem

Shem: son of hundred of Year. And he is generating **Arphaxad** *two* years after the Deluge. ¹¹ And he is living—Shem—after his causing to generate **Arphaxad** five of hundreds Year. And he is generating sons and daughters.

¹² And Arphaxad, he lives five and thirty Year[317], and he is generating **Shelach**. ¹³ And he is living—Arphaxad—after his causing to generate **Shelach** three years and four hundreds Year, and he is generating sons and daughters.

¹⁴ And Shelach he lives thirty Year, and he is generating **Eber**. ¹⁵ And he is living—Shelach—after his causing to generate **Eber** three years and four of hundreds Year, and he is generating sons and daughters.

¹⁶ And he is living—Eber—four and thirty Year, and he is generating **Peleg**. ¹⁷ And he is living—Eber—after his causing to generate **Peleg** thirty Year and four of hundreds Year, and he is generating sons and daughters.

¹⁸ And he is living—Peleg—thirty Year, and he is generating **Reu**[318]. ¹⁹ And he is living—Peleg—after his causing to generate **Reu** nine years and *two* hundreds Year, and he is generating sons and daughters.

²⁰ And he is living—Reu—two and thirty Year, and he is generating **Serug**[319]. ²¹ And he is living—Reu—after his causing to generate **Serug** seven years and *two* hundreds Year, and he is generating sons and daughters.

²² And he is living—Serug—thirty Year, and he is generating **Nahor**[320]. ²³ And he is living—Serug—after his causing to generate **Nahor** *two* hundreds Year, and he is generating sons and daughters.

---

[317] *Year/years*: the Hebrew distinctions between plural *years* and singular *Year* have been maintained; see note in 5:3. In general the plural is accumulative amount of years and the singular is in proportion to a larger time-frame at hand.

[318] *Reu*: transformation of work to idea; physical translation.

[319] *Serug*: intertwined; circling to strike; turning to the orchard.

[320] *Nahor*: restraining the wind; rebuking of freedom.

²⁴ And he is living—Nahor—nine and twenty Year, and he is generating **Terah**³²¹. ²⁵ And he is living—Nahor—after his causing to generate **Terah** nine of ten of³²² Year and hundred of Year, and he is generating sons and daughters

²⁶ And he is living—Terah—seventy Year, and he is generating **Abram**³²³, **Nahor**, and **Haran**³²⁴.

---

³²¹ *Terah*: steadfastness; determined laborer.
³²² *Nine of ten of*: nineteen.
³²³ *Abram*: father is exalted; efficient determination increasing; sublime generating force.
³²⁴ *Haran*: fresh breath; swift sword stroke.

11:27—12:5

²⁷ <u>And these: genealogies of Terah</u>

Terah, he generates **Abram**, **Nahor**, and **Haran.** And Haran, he generated **Lot**; ²⁸ And he is dying—Haran—over face of Terah his father, in land of his birth, in Ur[325] of the Chaldeans[326].

²⁹ And he is taking—Abram and Nahor—to themselves wives; name of Abram's wife: Sarai[327], and name of Nahor's wife: Milcah[328], daughter of Haran father of Milcah and father of Iscah[329]. ³⁰ And she is—Sarai—**barren**; to her is no child.

³¹ And he is taking—Terah—**Abram** his son, and **Lot**, son of Haran; son of his son, and **Sarai** his daughter-in-law, wife of Abram his son, and they are *go*ing forth from Ur of the Chaldeans, to cause to go Canaan-land-ward. And they are coming as far as Haran, and they are dwelling there. ³² And they are becoming—days of Terah—five years and *two* hundreds Year, and he is dying—Terah—in Haran.

12 And he is saying[330]—Jehovah—to Abram, 'Go you! for you; from your land, and from your kindred, and from house of your father, to the land which I show you. ² And I make you to great nation, and I bless you, and I make great your name; and be you! —blessing. ³ And I bless ones blessing of you, and one making light—you—I curse; and they are blessed in you: all of families of the ground.'

⁴ And he is going—Abram—as what he speaks to him—Jehovah —and he is going *with* him—Lot. And Abram: son of five years and seventy Year in his causing to go from Haran. ⁵ And he is taking—Abram—**Sarai** his wife, and **Lot** his brother's son, and

---

[325] *Ur*: light, ardor, that which burns.
[326] *Chaldeans*: satisfaction of study; spiritual abundance.
[327] *Sarai*: my princess; ready liberation; spiritual openness; melody; poem; universal harmony.
[328] *Milcah*: queen; perfection in place; oratory performance; complete propriety.
[329] *Iscah*: he will anoint her; spiritual conformity; keeping one's place.
[330] *Is saying*; there is no reason to change the text to read past tense perfect here in order to reconcile Acts 7. Stephen mentions that Abram was given a similar instruction when he was in Ur, and here the additional phrase is used, "*from house of your father*". See Appendixes VIII and IX for the time line.

12:5—12:13

all of their goods which they have, and the **soul** which they make in Haran; and they *go* forth to cause to go towards land of Canaan; and they are coming towards land of Canaan. ⁶ And he is passing—Abram—in the land as far as place of Shechem³³¹, as far as Oak of Moreh³³²; and the Canaanite, then in the land.

⁷ And he is appearing—Jehovah—to Abram, and he is saying 'To your seed I give the **land**, even this.' And he is building there, altar to Jehovah—the one appearing to him. ⁸ And he is removing from there, towards the mountain, from east to Bethel³³³, and he is pitching his tent, Bethel from sea³³⁴, and the Ai³³⁵ from east, and he is building there, altar to Jehovah, and he is calling in name of Jehovah.

⁹ And he is journeying—Abram—to go and to journey the rim-ward³³⁶.

¹⁰ And it³³⁷ is becoming famine in the land. And he is descending—Abram—towards Egypt³³⁸ to cause to sojourn there; that, heavy the famine in the land. ¹¹ And it is becoming, as which he nears to cause to come towards Egypt, and he is saying to Sarai his wife, 'Behold! Please! I know that... woman, enticing³³⁹ appearance—you. ¹² And it becomes that they are seeing **you**—the Egyptians—and they say, 'His wife, this one!' and they kill **me**, and **you** they keep alive. ¹³ Say you! Please! My sister—you; so that it is well for me in your sake, and she lives—my soul—because of you.'

---

³³¹ *Shechem*: back, shoulder blade, mountain slope; same word as Japheth and Shem putting the cloak on their *backs* to cover Noah's nakedness.

³³² *Moreh*: teacher; former rain; actions of a helpmate. *Oak of Moreh*: towards indolence; delicate force of movement.

³³³ *Bethel*: house of God; powerful family.

³³⁴ *From sea*: a Hebraism meaning *on the west*, the Mediterranean Sea being to the west.

³³⁵ *Ai*: false growth; patient endurance.

³³⁶ *Rim-ward*: a Hebraism meaning *the south*, referring to the lower rim of Judah that borders the desert. Directions of this kind are centric to the land of Israel, as we see in 13:1, Abram travels *north* from Egypt "rim-ward"; i.e. to the south of what one later becomes the land of Israel.

³³⁷ *It is becoming*: "he is becoming"; characteristic in the Hebrew.

³³⁸ *Egypt*: gathered home together; suckling the stream; settled into place.

³³⁹ *Enticing*: without the accent marks, this is the same word as the name Japheth.

12:14—13:7

¹⁴ And it is becoming, as coming to—Abram—Egypt-ward and they are seeing—the Egyptians—the **woman** that *s*he—exceedingly lovely³⁴⁰. ¹⁵ And they are seeing **her**, chiefs of Pharaoh³⁴¹, and they are praising **her** to Pharaoh, and she is taken—the woman—*to* Pharaoh's house. ¹⁶ And to Abram he is good because of her; and it is becoming to him flock, and herd, and donkeys, and servants, and maids, and she-donkeys, and camels.

¹⁷ And he is touching—Jehovah—**Pharaoh**, plagues, great ones! And his **house** over matter of Sarai Abram's wife. ¹⁸ And he is calling—Pharaoh—to Abram and he is saying, 'What? This you do to me, What? You told not to me that—your wife—she. ¹⁹ To what ? say you, My sister, *s*he, and I take **her** to me for wife? And now, behold! Your wife; take you! And go you!' ²⁰ And he is instructing over him—Pharaoh—•men³⁴² and they are sending away **him**, and his **wife**, and **all of**, which *is* to him.

13 And he is *go*ing up—Abram—from Egypt; he and his wife, and all which, to him; and Lot with him, the rim-ward. ² And Abram—exceedingly weighty in the cattle, in the silver, and in the gold. ³ And he is going to his journeyings from the rim and as far as Bethel, as far as the place³⁴³ which—it is there—his tent in the commencement³⁴⁴, between Bethel and between the Ai ⁴ to place of the altar which he does there at the first, and he is calling there—Abram—in name of Jehovah.

⁵ And moreover to Lot, the one going with Abram, there is flock and herd and tents. ⁶ And he bore **them** not, the land, to cause to dwell together, for it is—their property—vast, and they *are* unable to cause to dwell together. ⁷ And it is becoming *a* contest between ones grazing of Abram's cattle, and between ones

---

³⁴⁰ *Lovely*: the word goes beyond appearance and includes demeanor; or properly, life-force.
³⁴¹ *Pharaoh*: the generator of all physical reality.
³⁴² *Men*: 'enoshim', plural of Enosh; weak mortal men. It is used here to contrast with Pharaoh.
³⁴³ *The place*; the word also include a condition of mind.
³⁴⁴ *Commencement*; at the forcing of something open; see 4:26, 11:6 and notes.

grazing of Lot's cattle. And the Canaanite and the Perizzite[345] then dwelling in the land.

⁸ And he is saying—Abram—to Lot, 'No, Please! she is becoming quarreling between me and between you and between my shepherding ones and between your shepherding ones; for •men—brothers, we. ⁹ ?Not all of the land to face of you? Be parted, you! Please!—from on me. If the left, then I go right; and if the right, then I go left.'

¹⁰ And he is lifting—Lot—his **eyes**, and he is seeing **all of** the Jordan's circuit that all of her, watered to face of[346] Jehovah's causing to ruin **Sodom** and **Gomorrah**; as Jehovah's garden, as Egypt's land, your coming to Zoar. ¹¹ And he is choosing—Lot—**all of** the Jordan's circuit; and he is journeying—Lot—from east, and they are being parted, ♂man from over his brother[347]: ¹² Abram, he dwells in land of Canaan, and Lot, he dwells in cities of the circuit; and he is tenting as far as Sodom. ¹³ And •men of Sodom—evil ones and sinful ones to Jehovah—exceedingly.

¹⁴ And Jehovah, he says to Abram after causing to be parted of Lot from with him, 'Lift you! Please! Your eyes and see you! from the place which you, there: northward, and rim-ward, and eastward, and seaward; ¹⁵ for **all of** the land which you *are* seeing, to you I am giving her, and to your seed—to eon. ¹⁶ And I determine your **seed** as dust of the earth, so that, if he is able—♂man—to cause to number **dust** of the earth, even your seed, he is numbered. ¹⁷ Rise you! Walk you! in the land to her length and to her width; for to you I am giving her.

¹⁸ And he is tenting—Abram—and he is coming and he is dwelling in Oaks of Mamre, which, in Hebron, and he is building there, altar to Jehovah.

---

[345] *Perizzite*; agreeable production; pastoral. This is the first mention of the Perizzites who peopled the plains and lived in unwalled villages. The other time they are paired with the Canaanite is in Judges 1:4, the first people attacked after the death of Joshua, by Judah and Simeon. The are mentioned here because they would have been the other competitors for grazing land with Abram and Lot.

[346] *In face of*; the implication here is that this area was opposed to God; in his face.

[347] *Man from over his brother*: the implication is that oppression was active personally from Lot to Abram.

14:1—14:4

14 And it is becoming, in days of Amraphel[348] king of Shinar[349], Arioch[350] king of Ellasar[351], Chedorlaomer[352] king of Elam[353], and Tidal[354] king of Goyim[355], ² they do war: **Bera**[356] king of Sodom[357] and **Birsha**[358] king of Gomorrah[359], Shinab[360] king of Admah[361], and Shemeber[362] king of Zeboim[363], and the king of Bela[364]; he—Zoar[365]. ³ All of these, they join to Vale of the Siddim[366]; he—Sea of the Salt. ⁴ Two ten-of Year they serve **Chedorlaomer**, and three of ten of[367] Year they revolt.[368]

---

[348] *Amraphel*; ruler of the royal metropolis; restorer of sacred mysteries.
[349] *Shinar*: tooth of the city; civil revolution.
[350] *Arioch*; lion like; self-satiation; to move toward a purpose with planning and intent.
[351] *Ellasar*; powerful independence; driving rebellion.
[352] *Chedorlaomer*; industrious in-gathering; swallowing up for self-sufficiency. The image is that of a spider who gathers paralyzed prey for breeding.
[353] *Elam*; eternity; the age; hidden events ready to be manifested. In this context it implies an impending unification.
[354] *Tidal*; cast down from above; the idea is using superior knowledge to gain possession of and subjugate a groaning people.
[355] *Goyim*; a collective organization; used consistently in the Hebrew to mean *nations* with the sense of *other* nations. Here it has the additional aspect of coercion.
[356] *Bera*; potential for showing self. Normally used for manifesting crooked purposes, thus often translated *in the evil*.
[357] *Sodom*; to close into homogeneity; used for scorching into a molten mass; the idea of a hand clenching its contents into one.
[358] *Birsha*; to make inner intentions concrete in action, especially ones that wrong; used for *in wickedness* elsewhere.
[359] *Gomorrah*; bondage; to heap up bedazzlement. There is hardly a more apt Hebrew word for today''s *television* than this.
[360] *Shinab*; hatred of father; mutation of fruit-bearing.
[361] *Admah*; ground; red; likeness... see note in 2:7.
[362] *Shemeber*; chief's headdress; Name (dignity) power, conception and active production; the CEO of operations.
[363] *Zeboim*; the splendid disgusting ones; armies of disgust. A similar idea to today's movie stars who are at the same time revered for their glamor and scandalized in the tabloids.
[364] *Bela*; devouring; vanity of materialism.
[365] *Zoar*; predetermined path; irresolute running to and fro; vanity or monotony of the daily grind. Used later as synonymous with *small*.
[366] *Siddim*; spread out; the fields; the provision of nature.
[367] *Two of ten of, Three of ten of*; twelve and thirteen.

14:5—14:8

⁵ And in four of ten of Year he comes—Chedorlaomer and the kings who *are* with him, and they are smiting **Rephaim**[369] in Ashteroth Karnaim[370], and the **Zuzim**[371] in Ham, and the **Emim**[372] in Shaveh Kiriathaim[373], ⁶ and the **Horites**[374] in their mountain, Seir[375], as far as El-Paran[376], that on the wilderness. ⁷ and they are returning and they are coming to En-Mishpat[377]; he—Kadesh[378], and they are smiting **all of** field of the Amalekite[379], and moreover the **Amorite**[380], the one dwelling in Hazezon-Tamar[381].

⁸ And he is *go*ing forth—king of Sodom, and king of Gomorrah, and king of Admah, and king of Zeboim, and king of Bela; he—

---

[368] Note that this revolt coincides with the length of time Abram had spent in Canaan. This would mean that the subjugation of Canaan by Chedorlaomer coincided with Abram''s move to the area when Terah died in Haran. The text strongly implies that the impetus for the revolt was the supposition—only partly correct—that Abram would repel the control from these Babylonian nations. Chedorlaomer and his crew pointedly avoided the area of Mamre where Abram was staying... yet Abram did not involve himself until it was learned that his charge Lot, who may have boasted of Abram''s prowess to Bera, was taken. As an example of this prowess, note that any threat from giants is missing among all the troubles Abram encountered in the land.

[369] *Rephaim* is the generic word for giants and other halfbreed humans; as the *Zuzim, Emim, Horites* and others. *Rephaim* means 'those that regenerate powerfully', i.e., difficult to kill. The land of Canaan was a renown land of giants, yet ruled by Chedorlaomer who held the secrets to their weaknesses.

[370] *Ashteroth Karnaim*; Composition for determined self-purpose of force; here a space set aside for breeding purposes reserved for war.

[371] *Zuzim*; the shining ones; vibrating.

[372] *Emim*; monsters; giants; the word implies *a disordered will*; *beings who have left their nature.*

[373] *Shaveh Kiriathaim*; stronghold of the shout of terror.

[374] *Horites*; barren or burnt caverns; cave dwellers.

[375] *Seir*; safeguard of reverence; shaggy; hairy; goat-like; it is used for both hairy goats and devils and satyrs as in Isaiah 13:21 and 34:14, the root meaning *a shudder of horror* or *an opening.*

[376] *El-Paran*; ornamental grove of oaks; glorious shout; the word implies a very distinctive and specific spot, such as the place of a monument.

[377] *En-Mishpat*; eye, or fountain of justice.

[378] *Kadesh*; enduring summit; sanctuary.

[379] *Amalekite*; lesson of nations; original instruction.

[380] *Amorite*; a sayer; outward wringing.

[381] *Hazezon-Tamar*; defensive shelter of virtuous arrows.

14:8—14:17

Zoar; and they are arraying them; battle! in Vale of the Siddim; ⁹ **Chedorlaomer** king of Elam, and Tidal king of Goyim, and Amraphel king of Shinar, and Arioch king of Ellasar; four kings with five. ¹⁰ And Vale of the Siddim... wells! Wells of asphalt; and they are fleeing—king of Sodom and Gomorrah—and they are falling toward there, and the ones remaining, they flee mountain-ward.

¹¹ And they are taking **all of** substance of Sodom and Gomorrah, and **all of** their food, and they are going. ¹² And they are taking **Lot** and his **substance**—son of Abram's brother—and they are going; for he dwells in Sodom.

¹³ And he is coming—the one escaping—and he is declaring to Abram the Hebrew, and he, tabernacling among the oaks of Mamre the Amorite, brother of Eshcol[382], and brother of Aner[383], and they—possessors of covenant of Abram. ¹⁴ And he is hearing —Abram—he is captured—his brother—and he is unsheathing his **initiated ones**, ones born of his house; eight-ten and three of hundreds[384]; and he is pursuing as far as Dan[385].

¹⁵ And he is being apportioned over them—night!, he and his servants, and he is smiting them, and he is pursuing them as far as Hobah[386], which, from left, to Damascus[387]. ¹⁶ And he is restoring **all of** the substance, and moreover **Lot** his brother and his substance he restores, and moreover the **women** and the **people**.

¹⁷ And he is *com*ing forth—king of Sodom—to cause to meet him after his causing to return from causing to smite **Chedorlaomer**,

---

[382] *Eshcol*; fullness of strength; unmovable perfection.

[383] *Aner*; consideration; decision; personal motivation.

[384] *Eight-ten and three of hundreds*; 318. Hebrew has a variety of ways to express numbers and days, for which reason the original expression is characteristically provided.

[385] *Dan*; to judge in the sense of *dissension* or *debate*. It is judgment from an ability to *morally part* from the whole. The writer uses this anachronistic expression—as well as the first mention of a land named from the sons of Jacob—to put the later possessing of the land into the present faith of Abram in God''s word that he would possess it.

[386] *Hobah*; pit of potential life; the hiding of what could have been.

[387] *Damascus*; assimilation into homogeneity; that which seeks out and possesses disparate elements into a whole; banally used for *sackcloth weaver*.

14:17—15:3

and the **kings** who *are* with him, to Vale of Shaveh[388]—he, Vale of the King. [18] And Melchizedek[389] king of Salem[390], he *brings forth*[391] bread and wine; and he—priest to God Supreme[392]. [19] And he is blessing him, and he is saying, 'Being blessed! Abram! to God Supreme, owner of heavens and earth. [20] And being blessed! God Supreme!, whom, he delivers your opponents in your hand.' And he is giving to him tenth of all.[393]

[21] And he is saying—king of Sodom—to Abram, 'Give you! to me the soul, and the substance take you! for you.' [22] And he is saying—Abram—to king of Sodom, 'I raise my hand to Jehovah, God Supreme, owner of heavens and earth,[23] if from thread and unto sandal lacing, and if I am taking from any of *that* which is to you, and you say not, 'I—I enrich **Abram**,' apart from me. [24] But which they eat—the young men—and the portion of the •men whom—they go with me—Aner, Eshcol, and Mamre—they, they take their portion.'

15 After the matters, these happenings[394], he becomes—word of Jehovah—to Abram in the vision to cause to say, 'As to nothing, you are fearing, Abram; I—shield to you, reward of you: to increase exceedingly.' [2] And he is saying—Abram—'My Lord Jehovah, ?what do you give to me, and I am going heirless[395], and son of acquiring of[396] my house is Damascus Eliezer[397].' [3] And he

---

[388] *Shaveh*; equilibrium; conformable; compensation; see verse 5.
[389] *Melchizedek*; King of righteousness; this agrees with Hebrews 7:2.
[390] *Salem*; tranquil gathering; peace. This is an early name for Jerusalem.
[391] *Brings forth*; English does not have an expression for 'forthing' as the Hebrew; thus the constant use of 'bringing' or 'coming' forth put into italics. '*Issuing*' has also been used frequently for this expression.
[392] *God Supreme*; El Elyon; often translated 'God Most High'.
[393] Understatement is a favorite Hebrew device. In giving to Melchisedek a tenth of all, volumes are stated regarding both Abram''s position as a sojourner in the land, and Chedorlaomer''s attempt to usurp it. The land of Israel had always been God''s land—whether or not Israel possessed it—and Melchisedek was a testimony to that, in the middle of the Canaanites and their warrior-giants attempts to own it, as well as Chedorlaomer''s attempt to control it in imitation of Abram''s call.
[394] *These happenings*; literally, *the these*.
[395] *Heirless*; or childless; used only here, Leviticus 20:20 & 21, and Jeremiah 22:30.

15:3—15:11

is saying—Abram—'Behold! to me you give no seed, and behold!, son of my house occupies[398] **me**.'

⁴ And behold!, word of Jehovah to him, to cause to say, 'He occupies you not—this one—but rather he who *comes* forth from your bowels; he!—he does occupy you.' ⁵ And he is *bring*ing forth **him** to outside, and he is saying 'Look you! Please! towards the heavens, and number you! the stars, if you are *be*ing able to cause to number **them**.' And he is saying to him, 'Thus he is—your seed.' ⁶ And he believes in Jehovah, and he is reckoning[399] —her[400]—to him, righteousness.

⁷ And he is saying to him, 'I—Jehovah whom, I *brought* you forth from Ur of the Chaldeans, to cause to give to you the **land**, even this, to cause to occupy it.' ⁸ And he is saying, 'My Lord, Jehovah, in what ? I know that I occupy her?'

⁹ And he is saying to him, 'Take you! for Me, heifer being three, and she-goat being three, and ram being three, and turtle-dove[401], and fledgling[402].' ¹⁰ And he is taking for him **all of** these, and he is dividing **them** in the middle, and he is giving, ♂man[403], his divided *part* to cause to meet his fellow, but the **bird** he divides not. ¹¹ And he is descending—the bird of prey—over the carcasses, and he is turning back **them**—Abram[404].

---

[396] *Acquiring of*; harvester of possessions, also has the sense of running to and fro. Used only here.

[397] *Eliezer*; God my help. *Damascus Eliezer*; comptroller by God's help.

[398] *Occupies*; to occupy by driving out the previous tenant; to make destitute.

[399] *Reckoning*; this has the sense of a mental process and effort; *contrive*; *devise*.

[400] *Her* refers to the belief.

[401] *Turtle-dove*; has the sense of affection; the *rows* of the cheek in Song of Songs 1:10, the *turn* of each maiden in Esther 2:12 & 15, and often *to search out*. In the masculine it is *bullocks* or *oxen*, though only in Ezra and Daniel.

[402] *Fledgling*; a young bird who has just gotten its first feathers; used only here and Deuteronomy 32:11.

[403] ♂*Man*; or *each*.

[404] ♂*Man... ...Abram*; in characterizing Abram as *Ish*, an individual intellectual man, at the onset of this experience, the writer is introducing a new role for Abram; one representing all *Ish* from here forward in his relationship with God. The covenant thus becomes more than a personal event with Abram; it is presented as the path for all men.

15:12—15:21

¹² And he is becoming—the sun—to cause to set; and deep sleep[405], she falls on Abram. And behold!, dreadful darkness, great![406] falling upon him. ¹³ And he is saying to Abram, 'To know, you are knowing: that sojourner he becomes—your seed—in land not theirs; and they serve them, and they humiliate **them** four of hundreds Year. ¹⁴ And moreover, the **nation** which they are serving I judge, and so after they *go* forth in great substance. ¹⁵ And you—you come to your fathers in peace; you are buried in grey haired goodness[407]. ¹⁶ And generation—fourth—they return to here, that not made equitable—depravity of the Amorite—until to here.'[408]

¹⁷ And it is becoming: the sun—she set, and dusk[409]—he becomes; and behold!, furnace of smoke and torch of fire, which, he passes between the divided *parts*—these!

¹⁸ In the day, He! He cuts—Jehovah—**Abram,** covenant to cause to say 'To your seed I give the **land**, this! from River of Egypt as far as the River, the great river of Euphrates, ¹⁹ the **Kenite**[410], and the **Kenizzite**[411], and the **Kadmonite**[412], ²⁰ and the **Hittite**[413], and the **Perizzite**[414], and the **Rephaim,** ²¹ and the **Amorite**, and the **Canaanite**, and the **Girgashite**, and the **Jebusite**.[415]'

---

[405] *Deep sleep*; a trance; a stupor; used just seven times in scripture, including the deep sleep that fell on Adam, and the deep sleep of instruction that Elihu speaks of in Job.

[406] *Great*; in the sense of a tumultuous frenzy.

[407] *Grey-haired goodness*; Hebraism for a good old age.

[408] *That not made equitable... until to here*; the idea seems to be that piecemeal requiting of the Amorite was an undesired option; that until a full presence of God's people could take the land, the depravity currently in it could not be addressed.

[409] *Dusk*; used only here and three times in Ezekiel 12:6-12.

[410] *Kenite*; vehemence or usurping to themselves. The Kenite was an ancient people living between Egypt and Israel in the same general regions as the Amalekites; Moses' father-in-law was a Kenite.

[411] *Kenizzite*; spreading appropriation; this appears to be an ancient nation of Japheth's lineage, possibly the son of Magog.

[412] *Kadmonite*; same word as e*astern ones* and *ancient ones*; likely the Canaanite nation dispossessed by the invading Philistines shortly before Israel's taking of the land.

[413] *Hittite*; terror; to break down by violence; constant degradation.

[414] *Perizzite*; see 13:7.

16:1—16:11

16 And Sarai Abram's wife—she births not for him, and to her, handmaid, Egyptian, and her name: Hagar[416]. ² And she is saying—Sarai—to Abram, 'Behold! Please! He restrains me—Jehovah—from causing to birth. Come you! please! to my maid; perhaps I am built from her.' And he is listening—Abram—to Sarai's voice[417].

³ And she is taking—Sarai Abram's wife—**Hagar** the Egyptian, her handmaid, from end of ten years to cause to dwell—Abram—in land of Canaan; and she is giving **her** to Abram her husband, to him to wife. ⁴ And he is coming to Hagar, and she is *becom*ing pregnant; and she is seeing that she *is* pregnant, and she is making light—her mistress—in her eyes.

⁵ And she is saying—Sarai—to Abram, 'My damage on you; I—I give my maid in your bosom, and she is seeing that she *is pregnant*, and I am being made light in her eyes. He judges—Jehovah—between me and between you.' ⁶ And he is saying—Abram—to Sarai, 'Behold! your maid, in your hand; do you! to her the good in your eyes.' And she is humiliating her—Sarai—and she is *flee*ing[418] from her face.

⁷ And he is meeting her—angel of Jehovah—on fountain of the waters in the wilderness, on the fountain in way of Shur[419]; ⁸ and he is saying, 'Hagar, Sarai's maid, where ? from this come you, and to where ? are you going?' And she is saying, 'From face of Sarai my mistress, I flee.'

⁹ And he is saying to her—angel of Jehovah—'Return you! to your mistress, and humble yourself! under her hands.' ¹⁰ And he is saying to her—angel of Jehovah—'To increase I increase your **seed**, and he is not numbered from multitude.' ¹¹ And he is saying

---

[415] Note that in keeping with "...from River of Egypt as far as the River, the great river of Euphrates," the ten peoples in this list make a spiral starting at the River of Egypt, circling north along the Mediterranean, west across the Hittite empire, south through the Amorites, then looping eastward again through the Canaanites and Girgashites, finally ending the spiral in Jerusalem with the Jebusites.

[416] *Hagar*; the sojourner; stirring journey; moving discourse.

[417] There is a continuation of the theme here of Adam listening to his wife in 3:17 which is again addressed in 21:12.

[418] *Fleeing*; to flee suddenly; to bolt.

[419] *Shur*; being directed; broadly, *music* as in modulating the voice.

to her—angel of Jehovah—'Behold you! Pregnant! and you birth son, and you call his name Ishmael[420], that he hears—Jehovah—to your humiliation. ¹² And he is becoming wild ass of man; his hand in the all, and hand of all in him—and over face of all of his brothers he tabernacles.'

¹³ And she is calling name of Jehovah, the one speaking to her, 'You! God of Sight[421]', that she says, 'Even to here I see—following—of one seeing.' ¹⁴ On this he[422] calls to the well, 'Well of the Living, Seeing.[423]' Behold! —between Kadesh[424] and between Bered[425].   ¹⁵ And she is birthing—Hagar—for Abram, son. And he is calling—Abram—name of his son, whom she births—Hagar—Ishmael.   ¹⁶ And Abram: son of eighty Year and six years in causing birth of Hagar—**Ishmael**—for Abram.

17 And he is becoming—Abram—son of ninety Year and nine years, and he is appearing—Jehovah—to Abram; and he is saying to him, 'I—God Providence[426]; walk you! to my face; and become you! perfect. ² And I am giving My covenant between Me and between you, and I am increasing **you**—in exceedingly, exceedingly!

³ And he is falling—Abram—on his face, and he is speaking *with* **him**—God—to cause to say, ⁴ 'I—behold! My covenant *with* **you**, and you become to father of multitude of nations. ⁵ And he is not still called—your **name**—Abram; but he becomes—your name—Abraham[427]; that father of multitude of nations I give you. ⁶ And I *make* fruitful **you**—in exceedingly, exceedingly! And I give you to *become* nations, and kings; from you they issue.

---

[420] *Ishmael*; God always hears.
[421] *God of Sight*; El-Rai.
[422] *He calls*; the 'he' (or 'they') in these cases is nonspecific in Hebrew; as in English, "*They* call that..." This device is even more pronounced in Hebrew.
[423] *Well of the Living, Seeing*; Beerlahairoi; see 24:62, 25:11.
[424] *Kadesh*; sactuary.
[425] *Bered*; sons of nature; hail.
[426] *God Providence*; El-Shaddai; often translated *God Almighty*.
[427] *Abraham/Abram*; Abram had meant *exalted father* with the sense of *determination increasing* and *sublime generating force*; having fulfilled that role, he is given a new one: *Abraham* means *father of a glorious family*, the sense of *glorious* being of those that fascinate or dazzle the eyes. Perhaps we would say, *father of the shining ones*.

17:7—17:16

⁷ 'And I raise up My **covenant** between Me and between you, and between your seed after you for their generations, for covenant eternal, to cause to become to you, for God, and to your seed after you. ⁸ And I give to you, and to your seed after you, **land** of your sojournings; **all of** land of Canaan for possession forever, and I become to them, for God.'

⁹ And he is saying—God—to Abraham, 'And you—My **covenant** you keep; you and your seed after you, for their generations. ¹⁰ This My covenant which you keep between Me and between you, and between your seed after you: To be circumcised, to you, every male[428]. ¹¹ And you circumcise **flesh** of your foreskin[429], and he becomes for sign of covenant between Me and between you.

¹² 'And son of eight of days, he is circumcised to you; every male for your generations, one born of house, or acquisition of silver from any of foreigner's son, he who *is* not from your seed. ¹³ To be circumcised, he is circumcised; one born of your house and acquisition of your silver; and she becomes My covenant in your flesh, for covenant of age[430]. ¹⁴ And uncircumcised male whom, he is not being circumcised, **flesh** of his foreskin, and she[431] is cut —the soul, the same—from her peoples; My **covenant** he annuls.'

¹⁵ And he is saying—God—to Abraham, 'Sarai your wife—you call not her **name** Sarai, for Sarah[432], her name; ¹⁶ and I bless **her**,

---

[428] *Male*; not *ish*, the individual intellectual male as previously, but *zacher*; the male of any species. The word connotes remembrance, and the root has the sense of a 'mark'.

[429] *Foreskin*; prepuce. As much as the word 'penis' may seem to apply, the sense is strictly the covering on its end. There is no specific word for the penis in Hebrew; the word 'flesh' is used instead... which has all the other meanings of flesh as well.

[430] *Age*; 'olam' is variously translated throughout, *eternal, forever, to the age, eon*, etc. according to context.

[431] *She*; the 'soul' spoken of in these verses is feminine.

[432] *Sarai/Sarah*; Sarai had meant *my princess; ready liberation; spiritual openness; melody; poem; universal harmony*, and was a term of endearment from Abram. This change to Sarah takes all these ideas and moves them from potential beauty and enduring qualities to living beauty and expressive qualities. It is similar to the change from *Isha* (activity for the man) to *Eve* (life giver). In both cases the emphasis turns from her husband (inward) to her gifts (outward).

17:16—18:2

and moreover I give from her, to you, son. And I bless her, and she becomes to nations—kings of peoples; from her they become.'

¹⁷ And he is falling—Abraham—on his face, and he is laughing, and he is saying in his heart, '? To son of hundred Year is he born? and if Sarah—daughter of ninety Year—she births?'

¹⁸ And he is saying—Abraham—to God, 'O that[433] Ishmael lives to your face.' ¹⁹ And he is saying—God—'Surely Sarah your wife *is* bearing for you, son; and you call his **name** Isaac[434], and I raise My **covenant** *with* **him**, for eternal covenant, to his seed after him.   ²⁰ And to Ishmael, I hear you; Behold! I bless **him**, and *make* fruitful **him**, and I increase **him** in exceedingly, exceedingly! two ten[435] princes he generates, and I give him to great nation. ²¹ But My **covenant** I raise *with* **Isaac**, whom she births for you—Sarah—to the appointment, the selfsame time in this next year[436].' ²² And he is finishing to cause to speak *with* **him**, and he is ascending—God—from on Abraham.

²³ And he is taking—Abraham—**Ishmael** his son, and **all of** ones born of his house, and **all of** acquisition of his silver—every male in •men of Abraham's house—and he is circumcising **flesh** of their foreskin, in the very day, the selfsame as which he speaks with him—God.

²⁴ And Abraham: son of ninety and nine Year in his causing to be circumcised, flesh of his foreskin. ²⁵ And Ishmael his son: son of three of ten Year his causing to be circumcised **flesh** of his foreskin. ²⁶ In the very day, the selfsame, he is circumcised—Abraham and Ishmael his son. ²⁷ And all of •men of his house—one born of house, and acquisition of silver from son of foreigner—they are circumcised *with* him.

18 And he is appearing to him—Jehovah—in Oaks of Mamre, and he is sitting, opening of the tent, as warmth of the day. ² And he is lifting his eyes and he is seeing, and behold! three •men

---

[433] *O that*; or *suppose*.
[434] *Isaac*; he is laughing; same word as Abraham laughing in verse 17.
[435] *Two ten*; twelve.
[436] *To the appointment, the selfsame time in this next year*; literally, *to the appointed (time) the this in the year the other.*

18:2—18:16

standing by him, and he sees, and runs to meet them from opening of the tent, and he is self-bowing toward earth.

³ And he is saying, 'My Lord, if please! I find grace in your eyes, not so, please! *that* you are passing from on your servant. ⁴ It is taken, please!, little of water and you wash your feet, and you recline under the tree; ⁵ and I take morsel of bread, and you refresh your heart; afterward you pass, for on this you pass over your servant.' And they are saying, 'So you do as which you speak.'

⁶ And he is hastening—Abraham—toward the tent to Sarah, and he is saying, 'Hasten you! three of measures, meal flour knead you! and make you! cakes[437].' ⁷ And to the herd he runs—Abraham—and he is taking son of herd, tender and good, and he is giving to the lad, and he is hastening to cause to do **him**. ⁸ And he is taking butter and cream, and son of the herd which he does, and he is giving to face of them; and he is standing over them under the tree, and they are eating.

⁹ And they are saying to him, 'Where?—Sarah your wife?' And he is saying, 'Behold!—in the tent;' ¹⁰ And he is saying, 'To return, I return to you, as the season of living, and behold! son to Sarah your wife. And Sarah, you hear!—opening of the tent.' and she *is* behind Him.

¹¹ And Abraham and Sarah: old ones; ones entering in the days—it leaves off to cause to become to Sarah *the* way as of women. ¹² And she is laughing—Sarah—in her center, to cause to say, 'After causing me to fail she is pleasure to me?—And my lord; he *is* old!'

¹³ And he is saying—Jehovah—to Abraham, 'To what? this—she laughs—Sarah—to cause to say, ? Indeed truly I birth—and I—I *am* old? ¹⁴ Is it too wonderful? From Jehovah *this* word: to the appointment I return to you, at the season of living, and to Sarah —son.'

¹⁵ And she is denying—Sarah—to cause to say, 'I laugh not;' for she fears. And he is saying, 'Not? —except you laugh.'

¹⁶ And they are rising from there—the •men—and they are gazing[438] on face of Sodom, and Abraham going with them to

---

[437] *Cakes*; well-baked; well-done; used only here and Numbers 11:8.
[438] *Gazing*; the sense is leaning out of a window to look.

18:16—18:28

cause to send them on. ¹⁷ And Jehovah—he says, '?⁴³⁹ Covering—I—from Abraham that which I do? ¹⁸ Yet Abraham, to become he becomes to nation great and powerful⁴⁴⁰, and they bless in him, all of nations of the earth. ¹⁹ But I know him, on account of whom he appoints his **sons** and his house after him, and they keep Jehovah's way, to cause to do righteousness and judgment, so that he brings—Jehovah—on Abraham *that* which he speaks over him.'

²⁰ And he is saying—Jehovah—'Outcrying⁴⁴¹ of Sodom and Gomorrah—because abundant, and their sin—because she *is* exceedingly heavy, ²¹ I descend, please! and I see ? as her outcrying—the one coming to Me—they do conclude; and if not, I know.'

²² And they are turning to face from there—the •men—and they are going toward Sodom. And Abraham, still him, standing to face of Jehovah.

²³ And he is *com*ing near—Abraham—and he is saying, 'Really? You sweep away righteous one with wicked one? ²⁴ Perhaps there are fifty righteous ones in middle of the city. Really? you sweep away and you bear not to the place on account of fifty—the righteous ones who *are* in her middle? ²⁵ Break open to you from causing to do as this, to cause to kill righteous one with wicked one; and he becomes—as righteous one, with wicked one—break open to you! The One judging all of the earth, does he not *do* judgment?' ²⁶ And he is saying—Jehovah—'If I am finding in Sodom fifty righteous ones in middle of the city, then I bear to all of the place on account of them.'

²⁷ And he is answering—Abraham—and he is saying, 'Behold! please! I yield to cause to speak to my Lord; and I—dust and ashes; ²⁸ perhaps they are lacking—the fifty righteous ones—five. Really? you ruin in the five **all of** the city?' and he is saying, 'I ruin not, if I am finding there forty and five.'

---

⁴³⁹ *?*; the prefix *hem* on the word *Covering* (*kawsaw*) has the sense of the burden of a decision. Often in English a Hebrew word is most clearly expressed with punctuation; so throughout the text.

⁴⁴⁰ *Great and powerful*; the first word is an outer growing force, the second an inner closing-in force.

⁴⁴¹ *Outcrying*; the root here is to shriek from pain or danger, as with verse 21.

18:29—19:8

²⁹ And he is adding further to cause to speak to Him, and he is saying, 'Perhaps they are being found there, forty.' And he is saying 'I do not, on account *of* the forty.'

³⁰ And he is saying, 'As not, please! it is angering to my Lord and I am speaking: perhaps they are being found there thirty.' And he is saying, 'I do not, if I am finding there thirty.'

³¹ And he is saying, 'Behold! please! I yield to cause to speak to my Lord: perhaps they are being found there twenty?' And he is saying, 'I ruin not on account of the twenty.'

³² And he is saying, 'As not, please! it is angering to my Lord, and I speak, yes, this once: perhaps they are being found there ten?' and he is saying, 'I ruin not on account of the ten.'

³³ And he is going—Jehovah—as when he finishes to cause to speak to Abraham. And Abraham, he returns to his place.

19 And they are coming—two of the angels—toward Sodom in the evening. And Lot, sitting in gate of Sodom, and he is seeing—Lot—and he is rising to cause to meet of them, and he is self-bowing, nose earthward⁴⁴². ² And he is saying, 'Behold! please! my lords, turn you aside, please! to house of your servant; and you lodge! and you wash! your feet, and you rise early and you go to your way.' And they are saying, 'No, but in the broad place we lodge.'

³ And he is urging in them exceedingly, and they are turning aside to him, and they are coming to his house; and he is doing for them a feast, and unleavened he bakes; and they are eating.

⁴ Not yet they are lying *down*, and •men of the city—•men of Sodom—they surround over the house, from lad and as far as aged; all of the people from extremities. ⁵ And they are calling to Lot and they are saying to him, 'Where ? the •men whom, they come to you this night? You *bring* them forth ! to us, and we know **them**.'

⁶ And he is *go*ing forth to them—Lot—toward the opening and the door he closes after him. ⁷ And he is saying, 'Must not *be*, please! my brothers, you are *do*ing evil. ⁸ Behold! please! To me, two of daughters, whom—they know not ♂man; I *bring* forth,

---

⁴⁴² *Nose earthward*; when this expression is used rather than *face earthward* it connotes a rushing; the nostrils being an allusion to heavy breathing and effort.

19:8—19:15

please! **them** to you, and you do! to them as the good in your eyes; but to the •men, these, must not *be* you are doing *this* thing, that on this they come in shadow of my roof.'

⁹ And they are saying, 'You approach! To yonder!⁴⁴³' And they are saying, 'This one, he comes to cause to sojourn, and he is judging to judge! Now we *do* evil to you with them.' And they are pressing⁴⁴⁴ in the ♂man—in Lot—exceedingly, and they are approaching to cause to break the door.

¹⁰ And they are sending—the •men—their **hand**, and they are *bring*ing in **Lot** to them toward the house, and the **door** they shut.

¹¹ And the •**men**—who, opening of the house—they smite with blindnesses⁴⁴⁵, from small one and to great one, and they are wearying *themselves* to cause to find the opening.

¹² And they are saying—the •men—to Lot, 'Still any? to you here? —in-law and your sons also and your daughters and all whom *are* to you in the city, you *bring* forth! from the place.

¹³ For ones spoiling—we—this the **place**, that she *is* great—their outcry—with face of Jehovah. And he is sending us—Jehovah—to cause to ruin her.'

¹⁴ And he is *go*ing forth—Lot—and he is speaking to his in-laws, ones taking of his daughters, and he is saying, 'Rise you! *Go* forth you! from this the place, for ruining, Jehovah, the **city**.' And he is as one making sport in eyes of his in-laws.

¹⁵ And as the dawn—he ascended, and they are pressing—the angels—in Lot to cause to say, 'Rise you! take you! your **wife**,

---

⁴⁴³ *You approach! To yonder!*; there are a number of meanings in the language here; *you approach* is a euphemism for lying with a woman; it is also used for starting an argument, and when used as a reversal, *stand back.* The same word is used when they *approach* to break down the door. *Yonder* has the idea of scattering afar, but also *thus far no further* as in drawing a line in the sand.

⁴⁴⁴ *Pressing*; also meaning *pecking at.*

⁴⁴⁵ *Blindnesses*; this is not the normal word *ivver* for blindness; it is *anurim* used only here and in Second Kings 6:18. It has more the sense of 'moonstruck'; a bedazzling light that spreads and confuses.

19:15—19:24

and **two** of your daughters, the ones being found[446], lest you are swept away in the perversity of the city.'

[16] And he is lingering[447], and they are seizing—the •men—in his hand, and in hand of his wife, and in the hand of two of his daughters, in compassion of Jehovah over him, and they are *bring*ing him forth, and they are depositing him beyond the city[448].

[17] And it is becoming, as to their *coming* forth—**them**—toward the outside, and he is saying, 'Escape you! over your soul; must not *be* you are looking[449] behind you, and must not *be* you are standing in all of the circuit toward the mountain; escape you! lest you are swept away.'

[18] And he is saying—Lot—to them, 'No, please! lord; [19] behold! please! he finds—your servant—grace in your eyes, and you are increasing your kindness which you do with me to cause my **soul** to live, and I am not able to cause to escape toward the mountain, lest she is overtaking me, the evil[450], and I die. [20] Behold! please! The city, this one, *is* near to cause to flee toward there, and she *is* little. I escape please! toward there—?*Is* she not little?—and she lives, my soul.'

[21] And he is saying to him, 'Behold! I lift your face also to this the word, so as to cause my not overturning the **city** which you mention. [22] Hasten you! escape you! toward there, for I am not able to *be* doing of *any*thing until your coming there.' On this he calls name of the city Zoar[451].

[23] The sun—he issues over the earth, and Lot—he comes toward Zoar, [24] and Jehovah—he causes rain over Sodom and over

---

[446] *Two... being found*; the text clearly implies that Lot had other children who were not with him in the house. Abraham certainly knew the size of Lot's family, so it is suggestive that Abraham stopped with ten when interceding with Jehovah.

[447] *Lingering*; to question or hesitate.

[448] *Beyond the city*; the Hebrew is *from outside of to the city*. The expression means 'beyond the immediate outside of the city'.

[449] *Looking*; looking with regard or respect to; looking favorably.

[450] *She is overtaking to me, the evil*; lest nature dissipate me back with calamity.

[451] *Zoar*; small; ignoble; directed toward destitution; heading nowhere.

19:24—19:34

Gomorrah: sulfur and fire from **Jehovah**, from the heavens[452]. ^{25} And he overturns the **cities**, even these, and **all of** the circuit, and **all of** inhabitants of the cities and the ground's sprouting. ^{26} And she is scanning—his wife—from behind him, and she is becoming pillar[453] of salt.

^{27} And he is rising early—Abraham—in the morning to the place where he stands there with face of Jehovah. ^{28} and he is gazing[454] over face of Sodom and Gomorrah, and over all of face of land of the circuit, and he is seeing, and behold! he ascends—the fume[455] of the land, as fume of the smelting furnace.

^{29} And it is becoming, in causing to ruin—God—**cities** of the circuit, and he is remembering—God—**Abraham**, and he is sending **Lot** from middle of the overturning, in causing to overturn of the **cities** which, he lived in them—Lot.

^{30} And he is ascending—Lot—from Zoar, and he is living in the mountain, and two of his daughters with him; for he fears to cause to live in Zoar. And he is living in the cave—he and two of his daughters.

^{31} And she is saying—the first-born—to the younger, 'Our father, he *is* old, and there is no ♂man in the earth to cause to come over us, as path of all of the earth. ^{32} You go! We *cause to* drink, our father, wine; and we lie with him, and we *cause to* live from our father—seed.'

^{33} And they *cause to* drink, their father, wine—he—in the night; and she is coming, the first-born, and she is lying with her father, and he knows not her causing to lie *down* and her causing to rise.

^{34} And it is becoming from morrow, and she is saying—the first-born—to the younger, 'Behold! I lay last night with my father: we *cause* him *to* drink wine also the night, and you go! lie you! with

---

[452] *The sun, he issues... Lot, he comes... Jehovah, he causes*; note the subject leading the verb, as well as the lack of '*and*' initiating it. Both connote extreme emphasis in Hebrew.

[453] *Pillar*; a monument; the idea is a stationary expression of the height of action; a frozen yelp.

[454] *Gazing*; as 18:16, as from out a window.

[455] *Fume*; used only here and twice in Psalms; extremely hot fumes that distort the background and bring change. Psalm 119 uses this word to describe the heat used to temper a skin bottle to be watertight. *Smelting furnace* refers to a set-up distinct from a mere oven or fire, used to transform materials.

19:34—20:6

him, and we *cause to* live from our father—seed.' ³⁵ And they *cause* to drink also in the night, the same—**father** of them, wine, and she is rising—the younger—and she is lying with him, and he knows not her causing to lie *down* and in her causing to rise.

³⁶ And they are *becom*ing pregnant, two of Lot's daughters from their father. ³⁷ And she is birthing—the first-born—son, and she is calling his name Moab⁴⁵⁶; he, father of Moab unto this day. ³⁸ And the younger also she; she births son, and she is calling his name Ben-Ammi⁴⁵⁷: he, father of sons of Ammon⁴⁵⁸ unto this day.

20 And he is journeying from there—Abraham—toward the Negev⁴⁵⁹ land, and he is dwelling between Kadesh⁴⁶⁰ and between Shur⁴⁶¹, and he is sojourning in Gerar⁴⁶²; ² And he is saying—Abraham—to Sarah his wife, 'She *is* my sister;' and he is sending —Abimelech⁴⁶³ king of Gerar—and he is taking **Sarah**.

³ And he is coming—God—to Abimelech in the dream, the night, and he is saying to him, 'Behold you! dying over the woman you take, and she being possessed of husband⁴⁶⁴.'

⁴ And Abimelech, he comes not near to her, and he is saying, 'My Lord, ? nation also righteous you are killing? ⁵ ? Says not he himself to me, She *is* my sister? and she—also she herself—says, He *is* my brother. In integrity of my heart, and in cleanness of my palms I do this.'

⁶ And he is saying to him—the God in the dream—'Also I—I know that in integrity of your heart you do this, and I am restraining—also I—**you** from causing to sin to Me. On this, in no

---

⁴⁵⁶ *Moab*; from father; from mother to father. It gives the sense of an easily influenced person; a passive father.
⁴⁵⁷ *Ben-Ammi*; son of my people. Ammi also has the sense of an enduring nation.
⁴⁵⁸ *Ammon*; tribal; indolent people; being corrupted by pleasures.
⁴⁵⁹ *Negev*; the south of Israel, called this because of its drought. We encountered this first as the ''rim-land' in 12:9, which is the same word.
⁴⁶⁰ *Kadesh*; enduring summit; sanctuary.
⁴⁶¹ *Shur*; being directed; broadly, *music* as in modulating the voice; see 16:7. Abraham is near where the God spoke to Hagar.
⁴⁶² *Gerar*: dragging away; ruminating; self-crushing. Gerar was at the Canaanite border; see 10:19.
⁴⁶³ *Abimielech*; my father is king; father of king.
⁴⁶⁴ *Possessed of husband*; the same word is used here; *being possessed of possessor,* or *mastered of master*.

way I am giving you: to cause to touch, to her[465]. ⁷ And now restore you! the ♂man's wife, for prophet, he. And he prays over from under[466] you, and you live! And if no one—you—*is* one restoring, know you! that to die, you die; you, and all of, which, to you.'

⁸ And he is rising early—Abimelech—in the morning, and he is calling to all of his servants, and he is speaking **all of** the words, even these, in their ears; and they are fearing—the •men—exceedingly. ⁹ And he is calling—Abimelech—to Abraham, and he is saying to him, 'You do what ? to us? And what? I sin to you, that you bring on me, and on my kingdom, a great[467] sin? Doings which are not done you do with me.' ¹⁰ And he is saying—Abimelech—to Abraham, 'You see what ? that you do the thing, even this?'

---

[465] *On this... her*; this is multi-layered. Literally it is '*On so not I give you to to touch of to her.*' The first layer is *to touch of*, which is left dangling without a prepositional object. The second layer is *not I give you to (to touch of)*, for which phrase we use *in no way I am giving you: to cause (to touch)*, which moves the *of* at the end into a causal relationship with touching, eliminating the dangle while maintaining the hierarchy, and shows that what was prevented by not being given wasn''t him touching her, but him finding any cause to be able to approach the matter in the first place. God wasn''t slapping his hand away, he was locking the outer door to the building. We change *not* to *in no way* to give it sense in English for the context. The next layer is *On so thusly*: *On this* (*in no way I am giving you: to cause (to touch)*). The next layer is *restraining you from to sin of to me... ...to her*, thusly: *restraining—also I—***you** *from causing to sin to Me; (on this, (in no way I am giving you: to cause (to touch))), to her*. The sense, then, is "I restrained you from even being able to be sinning to me or to her; I did not give you any way to arrange things so that you would ever be able to get into a position in which you could consider touching her in the first place, and the reason I did this was for me and her, not you." This is somewhat more involved than a simple, "*Therefore I suffered thee not to touch her*" which makes it sound like God was rewarding Abimelech for his integrity.

[466] *Over from under*; this is a rare preposition (*bod; beth-ayin-daleth*) meaning *in from out, out from in, off from on, on from off, over from under, under from over* etc. It occurs but thrice in Genesis, here, verse 18, and in 26:8 when Abimelech looked *out from in* a window. Throughout God''s communication to Abimelech, unusually rich language is employed.

[467] *Great*; great and terrible. The word is always used to describe calamity or terror.

20:11—21:7

¹¹ And he is saying—Abraham—'That I say, 'But fear of God is not in the place, even this; and they kill me over matter of my wife.   ¹² And also, truly; my sister, daughter of my father[468]—she. Yes—not daughter of my mother; and she is becoming for me to wife.   ¹³ And it is becoming, as when they[469] cause *to* stray—God—from my father's house, and I am saying to her, This your kindness which you do with me to all of the place*s* which we are coming toward there: say you! for me, my brother he *is*.'

¹⁴ And he is taking—Abimelech—flock and herd and servants and maids, and he is giving to Abraham, and he is restoring to him **Sarah** his wife. ¹⁵ And he is saying—Abimelech—'Behold! my land to your face; in the good in your eyes, you dwell!'

¹⁶ And to Sarah he says, 'Behold! I give thousand of silver to your brother; behold! it, for you, covering of eyes, for all of *those* who are with you, and **all**.' And *she is* one being reproved.

¹⁷ And he is praying—Abraham—to the God, and he is healing—God—**Abimelech**, and his **wife**, and his maids, and they are birthing: ¹⁸ for to restrain he restrains—Jehovah—in from out, all of womb to house of Abimelech over matter of Sarah, Abraham's wife.

21 And Jehovah, he visits **Sarah** as which he says, and he is doing—Jehovah—for Sarah as which he speaks[470]. ² And she is *becoming* pregnant, and she is birthing—Sarah—for Abraham, son for his old *age*, to the appointment which he speaks *with* **him**—God. ³ And he is calling—Abraham—**name** of his son, the one being born to him, whom she births for him—Sarah—Isaac. ⁴ And he is circumcising—Abraham—**Isaac** his son, son of eight of days, as which he instructs **him**—God.

⁵ And Abraham: son of hundred of Year in causing to be born to him **Isaac** his son. ⁶ And she is saying—Sarah—'Laughter he did for me—God. All of the one hearing me—he is laughing for me.' ⁷ And she is saying, 'Who? he declares[471] to Abraham, 'She suckles sons—Sarah!' that I birth son for his old *age*?'

---

[468] By adoption; see Appendix IX.
[469] *They*; the *he* and the *they* here are non-specific, a common Hebraism, as in English, *they* say.
[470] *Says... speaks*; the senses of declaring and arranging respectively.

21:8—21:16

⁸ And he is growing—the boy—and he is being weaned. And he is making—Abraham—feast, great, in day of causing to be weaned—**Isaac**. ⁹ And she is seeing—Sarah—Hagar the Egyptian's **son** whom she births for Abraham, mocking⁴⁷². ¹⁰ And she is saying to Abraham, 'Drive out you! this maidservant, even this, and her **son**; that he inherits not—son of the handmaid, even this—with my son, with Isaac.'

¹¹ And it is being evil—the word—exceedingly Abraham's eyes, over causes of his son. ¹² And he is saying—God—to Abraham, 'As not, it is *be*ing evil in your eyes over the lad, and over your maidservant: all which she is saying to you—Sarah—listen you! in her voice; that in Isaac—he is called to you 'seed'. ¹³ Moreover, the maidservant's **son**, to nation I place him; that seed of you—he.'

¹⁴ And he is rising early—Abraham—in the morning, and he is taking bread, and flask⁴⁷³ of waters, and he is giving to Hagar, placing over her shoulder⁴⁷⁴, also the **boy**, and he is sending her away. And she is going, and she is wandering in the wilderness of Beer-Sheba⁴⁷⁵. ¹⁵ And they are consuming the waters from the flask, and she is throwing the **boy** under one of the shrubs.

¹⁶ And she is going, and she is sitting to her*self*⁴⁷⁶ from opposite, removed as they shoot *a bow*, that she says, 'Not so, I am looking

---

⁴⁷¹ *Declares*; as an oration; a public or poetic discourse; used five times in the positive and five in the negative in scripture.

⁴⁷² *Mocking*; or *making sport*. Similar word to Isaac, laughter; same word as Lot seeming to make sport to his in-laws, and the same word as Isaac *sporting* with his wife in 26:8. Thus Ishmael can just as easily be seen as laughing *along with* Isaac rather than mocking.

⁴⁷³ *Flask*; unusual word found only thrice in this account and once in Habakkuk. It is a skin used for alcoholic beverages or poison, and the same word as *fury*. To carry it around for water would be a public sign of disgrace... and the deleterious effects of whatever had last been in the skin until Hagar could clean it out at the well shown to her by the angel is left as an open possibility by the text. In any case, the text puts an unusual emphasis on this item.

⁴⁷⁴ *Shoulder*; there is a play on words here, *shoulder* being almost identical to *he is rising early*.

⁴⁷⁵ *Beer-Sheba*; well of oath; showing of promise; complete revelation. It is named in verse 31, as well as again in 26:33.

⁴⁷⁶ *Sitting to herself*; also *sitting indefinitely*.

21:16—21:30

in the boy's death.' And she is sitting from opposite, and she is lifting her **voice** and she is weeping.

[17] And he is hearing—God—**voice** of the lad. And he is calling—angel of God—to Hagar from the heavens, and he is saying to her, 'What ? to you, Hagar? As nought, you are fearing; for he listens—God—to the voice of the lad in where—he—there. [18] Rise you!, lift up you! the **lad** and encourage you! your **hand** in him, for to nation great I set him.'

[19] And he is opening—God—her **eyes**, and she is seeing well of waters; and she is going, and she is filling *with* the **flask** waters, and she is *giv*ing drink—the **lad**. [20] And he is—God—with the lad, and he is growing, and he is living in the wilderness, and he is becoming one increasing *the* bow. [21] And he is living in wilderness of Paran, and she is taking for him—his mother—wife from land of Egypt.

[22] And it is becoming in the same season, and he is saying—Abimelech and Phichol[477] head of his army—to Abraham, to cause to say, 'God *is* with you in all which you do. [23] And now, swear you! to me in God; behold! here: you are not becoming false to me, or to my progenitor, or to my offspring; as the kindness which I do with you, you do with me and with the land in which, in her you sojourn.' [24] And he is saying—Abraham—'I —I swear.'

[25] And he reproves[478]—Abraham—**Abimelech** over occasions of well of the waters which they snatched—Abimelech's servants. [26] And he is saying—Abimelech—'I know not who ? he does the **thing**, even this, and also you—you confront not to me, and also, I—I hear not except today.'

[27] And he is taking—Abraham—flock and herd, and he is giving to Abimelech, and they are cutting, two of them, covenant. [28] And he is setting—Abraham—**seven**[479] ewe-Lambs of the flock to themselves. [29] And he is saying—Abimelech—to Abraham, 'What ? they—these the seven ewe-lambs which you set to themselves?' [30] And he is saying, 'That **seven** ewe-lambs you take

---

[477] *Phichol*: mouth of all; concluding speaker; the final word.
[478] *Reproves*; same word as 21:16 with Sarah.
[479] *Seven*; this is in reference to Abraham saying *I swear*, the word for *swear* also meaning 'seven'' from the tradition of repeating an oath seven times.

from my hand, so you become to me witness that I dig[480] the well, even this.' ³¹ On this he calls to the place 'Beer-Sheba[481],' that there they swear, two of them.

³² And they are cutting covenant in Beer-Sheba, and he is rising—Abimelech and Phichol head of his host—and they are returning to the land of the Philistines[482]. ³³ And he is planting grove[483] in Beer-Sheba, and he is declaring there in name of Jehovah, Eternal God[484]. ³⁴ And he is sojourning—Abraham—in land of the Philistines many days.

22 And it is becoming after the matters, even these, and the God, he tries[485] **Abraham**, and he is saying to him, 'Abraham!' and he is saying, 'Behold me!' ² And he is saying, 'Take you! please! your **son**, your **only**[486] one, whom you love—**Isaac**—and go you!

---

[480] *Dig*; also meaning *to search out* as Joshua 2:2 to *search out* the land.

[481] *Beer-Sheba*; well of oath; showing of promise; open disclosure. It is first mentioned in 21:14, as well as named again by Isaac in 26:33.

[482] *Philistines*; this is the first mention of Abimelech's bloodline. His kingdom was on the border of the Canaanites; Canaan's brother was Mizraim, from which came Casluhim who produced the Philistines. The text does not mention that Abimelech was the king of the Philistines until 26:8 with Isaac. This slow introducing of an important subject is characteristic in the text; eventually the reader must put as much effort into uncovering all the meanings, as the scribe spent in layering them. For a history of Mizraim's as seen in his seven sons (and thus insight into Abimelech's character) see Appendix VI.

[483] *Planting a grove*; grove is *ashel*, 'enduring true path', often translated 'tamarisk'. The word for 'planting' occurs only here, God''s planting of the Garden, and Noah's planting of his vineyard (see note indicating actual meaning of vineyard in 9:20). *Grove* occurs only here, where Saul hung out in First Samuel 22:6, and where the men of Jabesh Gilead buried the bodies of Saul and his sons in the last verse of First Samuel. The idea presented is peculiar; that of an unchanging tabernacle, that is a *transient* place of *permanent* energy. Physically it would have been a geometric arrangement of specific species of trees that any traveler would recognize as sacred. The *planting* idea has the sense of initiating a path, thus a *map of life*.

[484] *Eternal God*; El Elyon; used only here, though 'Jehovah King of Eternity' is used in Psalm 10:16 and Jeremiah 10:10; likewise 'God (Elohim) of Eternity' in Isaiah 40:28.

[485] *Tries*; probes; to lead someone around in a circle; an uncertain guide.

[486] *Only*; this has the sense of united (with him), lonely, beloved ...in short, a euphemism for *soul*, as used in Psalm 22:20-21. Used 11 times in scripture, including Jephthah's daughter in Judges 11:34.

22:2—22:12

—for you to land of the Moriah[487], and ascend you him! there for ascent on one of the mountains which I say to you.'

³ And he is rising early—Abraham—in the morning, and he is saddling his **donkey**, and he is taking **two** of his youths with him, and **Isaac** his son. And he cleaves wood of ascent[488], and he is rising and he is going to the place which he speaks to him—the God.

⁴ In the day, the third, and he is lifting—Abraham—his eyes, and he is seeing the **place** from afar. ⁵ And he is saying—Abraham—to his youths, 'Sit you! for you here with the donkey, and I and the youth, we go further thus and we worship, and we return to you.'

⁶ And he is taking—Abraham—**wood** of the ascent, and he is placing on Isaac his son, and he is taking in his hand the **fire**, and the **knife**; and they are going, two of them, together.

⁷ And he is saying—Isaac—to Abraham his father, and he is saying, 'My father.' And he is saying, 'Behold me! my son.' And he is saying, 'Behold! the fire and the wood, and where ? the lamb[489] for ascent?' ⁸ And he is saying—Abraham—'God, he sees to him the lamb for ascent, my son;' and they are going, two of them, together.

⁹ And they are coming to the place which he says to him—the God. And he is building there—Abraham—the **altar**, and he is arranging the **wood**, and he is binding **Isaac** his son, and he is placing **him** on the altar from above to the wood. ¹⁰ And he is stretching out—Abraham—his **hand**, and he is taking the **knife** to cause to slaughter his **son**.

¹¹ And he is calling to him—angel of Jehovah—from the heavens, and he is saying, 'Abraham, Abraham!' And he is saying, 'Behold me!' ¹² And he is saying, 'Not so, you are stretching out your hand to the youth, and not so you are doing to him anything, for now I know that one fearing of God—you, and you keep not back your **son**, your **only** one, from Me.'

---

[487] *Moriah*; tyrant-God; seen of Jehovah; impulsive divine life. Only here and Second Chronicles 3:1 where Solomon built the temple.

[488] *Ascent*; used throughout here as *offering*. Commonly translated both *offering* and *burnt-offering* in the law.

[489] *Lamb*; any young member of a flock.

22:13—22:22

¹³ And he is lifting—Abraham—his **eyes**, and he is seeing, and behold! ram behind, being seized in the thicket in his horns. And he is going—Abraham—and he is taking the **ram**, and he is ascending him for ascent instead of his son. ¹⁴ And he is calling—Abraham—name of that place, the same, 'Jehovah-Jireh[490],' where it is being said today, 'In the mountain of Jehovah he is seen.'

¹⁵ And he is calling—angel of Jehovah—to Abraham double from the heavens, ¹⁶ and he is saying, 'In Myself I swear—the revelation of Jehovah—that because which you do the word, even this, and keep not back your **son**, your **only** one, ¹⁷ that to bless, I bless you, and to increase, I increase your **seed** as stars of the heavens, and as the sand which *is* on the sea-shore; and he occupies—your seed—**gate** of ones hating him. ¹⁸ And they bless themselves in your seed, all of nations of the earth, because that you listen to My voice.'

¹⁹ And he is returning—Abraham—to his youths, and they are rising, and they are going together to Beer-Sheba; and he is living —Abraham—in Beer-Sheba.

²⁰ And it is becoming after these matters, even these, and it being declared to Abraham, to cause to say, 'Behold! she births—Milcah—even she—sons for Nahor your brother: ²¹ **Uz**[491] his firstborn, and **Buz**[492] his brother; and **Kemuel**[493] father of Aram[494], ²² and **Chesed**[495], and **Hazo**[496], and **Pildash**[497], and **Jidlaph**[498], and

---

[490] *Jehovah-Jireh*; Jehovah, He sees.
[491] *Uz*; counsel; to provide (aught of) substance. Also a grandson of Shem; see 10:23.
[492] *Buz*; contempt; rising above others and disdaining them. If Jeremiah 25:23 is referring to the same person, he left and settled in a distant land.
[493] *Kemuel*; rise in strength; the idea is something that is established, physical, and stable transforming into something powerful and spiritual.
[494] *Aram*; exalted; collective invigoration. A son of Shem; see 10:23.
[495] *Chesed*; harrower; rising to devastate.
[496] *Hazo*; his vision; (prophetic) contemplation, especially of judgment.
[497] *Pildash*; privileged propagation; noble birth.
[498] *Jidlaph*; he will weep; responsibility; it is the idea of ability or administration returning to itself.

22:22—23:4

Bethuel[499]. 23 And Bethuel, he generates **Rebecca**[500].' These eight she births—Milcah—for Nahor, Abraham's brother. 24 And his concubine—and her name, Reumah[501]—and she is birthing, even she—**Tebah**[502], and **Gaham**[503], and **Thahash**[504], and **Maachah**[505].

23 And they are becoming—life of Sarah—hundred Year and twenty Year and seven years[506]—years of life of Sarah. 2 And she is dying—Sarah—in Kirjath-Arba[507]—he: Hebron[508], in land of Canaan[509]. And he is going—Abraham—to cause to lament for Sarah, and to cause to mourn her.

3 And he is rising—Abraham—from over face of his dead one, and he is speaking to sons of Heth[510], to cause to say, 4 'Sojourner

---

[499] *Bethuel*; point you out God; house of great sorrow; house of grand intentions.

[500] *Rebecca*; tying; fettering (by beauty); alluring; shocked into action; motivated by necessity; the idea is movement toward grandeur, but through a vague sense of fear or necessity.

[501] *Reumah*; raised up; obedience; conforming to what pleases the eye.

[502] *Tebah*; slaughter for supply, as butcher.

[503] *Gaham*; hot devastator; accumulating violence; the idea is rushing to gather more and more things to burn up.

[504] *Thahash*; arduous or riled he-goat.

[505] *Maachah*; pressure; conformed to the schedules of life.

[506] *Year... years*; see notes in 5:1 & 5:3. *Year* (capitalized in this text) refers to a proportion of some greater period—the reader is forced to discern what it is a proportion for himself—and *years* refers to the numeric accumulation... which may or may not include the amount of the ''Year'. It is typical in the Text to find numbers arranged in ways that demand attention to grammatical detail... in fact, one cannot be explored without the other; see Appendix XII.

[507] *Kirjath-Arba*; city of four; the sign of self-knowing (*Kirjath*) with a vigorous exclamation or effort (*Arba*), i.e., satisfaction that you have gone as far as you can go.

[508] *Hebron*; seat of association; communion; a deep hidden love against the background of the murmur of all the elements of life.

[509] *Kirjath-Arba... Hebron... Canaan*; as with Rachel in 35:19, the careful description of the place of his wife's death provides a unique emphasis.

[510] *Heth*; terror; surprised reaction; stupefaction resulting from an useless effort. Heth was the second son of Canaan (10:15).

23:4—23:9

and a guest I, with you; give! to me possession[511] of tomb with you, and I entomb my dead one from before my face.'

⁵ And they are answering—the sons of Heth—**Abraham**, to cause to say to him, ⁶ 'Hear[512] you us! my lord; prince of God—you—in our midst; in choice of our tombs you entomb your **dead one**: ♂man from us his **tomb** forbids not from you, from entombing your dead one.'[513]

⁷ And he is rising—Abraham—and he is bowing himself[514] to people of the land, to sons of Heth. ⁸ And he is speaking with them, to cause to say, 'If it may be your **soul** to cause to entomb my **dead** one from my face, hear you! me, and entreat you! for me with Ephron[515], son of Zoar[516]; ⁹ and he gives to me **cavern** of the Machpelah[517], which to him, which in fringes of his field. In full silver he gives her to me, in your midst, for possession of tomb.'[518]

---

[511] *Possession*; a holding in the sense of something seized; a foothold. The issue here goes far beyond merely buying a tomb; it changed Abraham's status in relation to the local government of the sons of Heth. As a landowner, he would be entitled to certain rights that a mere sojourner was not allowed, and the normal expectation would be that he would be summarily refused. He approaches the matter by appealing to precedent by asking for a piece of land owned by another foreigner—a Hittite—so that none of the natives could later be accused by their compatriots of 'selling out'.

[512] *Hear you us*; pay close attention. When this phrase introduces a discourse, it is saying that there are conditions that need to be met.

[513] *Man from us* means that they were working on Abraham collectively. *Forbids not* means *is not able to forbid*, i.e., they are wryly stating that they know Abraham could take what he wanted by force, as Jacob later did with the parcel he gave to Joseph. Emphasis on *dead one* shows that they felt they had him over a barrel in terms of necessity. *Choice of our tombs* is stating that they wanted a transaction large enough to make a profit, and emphasis on *tomb* is an attempt to limit the purchase to as small—and expensive—a parcel as possible.

[514] *Bowing himself*; this is a formal act that signals his acceptance of their terms.

[515] *Ephron*; he of dust; fawn-like; smooth operator. The idea is a swift calculating mind that transforms opportunity into cash; a *shark*.

[516] *Zohar*; to clamp down tightly, as on one's possessions; a *miser*.

[517] *Machpelah*; a fold; deteriorated treasure. The sense is a wonderful and mysterious place that is long fallen into disarray.

[518] Abraham has skillfully laid out his terms. He first emphasizes *soul* to transform their "we don''t have a choice" to "we would love to help you

23:10—23:15

¹⁰ And Ephron, sitting in middle of sons of Heth, and he is answering—Ephron the Hittite—**Abraham** in ears of sons of Heth to all of ones entering of gate of his city, to cause to say, ¹¹ 'No, my lord, hear you me!: the field I give to you, and the cave which in him, to you I give her; to eyes of sons of my people I give her to you—entomb you!'[519]

¹² And he is bowing himself[520]—Abraham—to face of people of the land, ¹³ and he is speaking to Ephron in ears of people of the land to cause to say, 'Yes—if only that you hear me—I give silver of the field; take you! from me, and I entomb my **dead one** toward there.'[521]

¹⁴ And he is answering—Ephron—**Abraham**, to cause to say to him, ¹⁵ 'My lord, hear you me! land of four hundred shekels of

---

out." He knows that a direct approach to Ephron will meet with disaster, so he asks them to intercede—based on their claim that they were working together—and reiterates their "in our midst" back to them to remind them of the cut (through taxation or whatever) that they would be receiving. None of this is lost on Ephron.

[519] Ephron is saying, "No way buddy; you''ve got to buy the whole field, not just the cave."

[520] *He is bowing himself*; Abraham has just been insulted; Ephron should have bowed in response to his position, and he chooses the arrogant path; inasmuch as to indicate that he thinks he has the upper hand. Abraham, instead of responding to the insult, bows again, keeping the transaction moving smoothly. Yet he makes his point by bowing to the people of the land rather than to Ephron, as protocol otherwise demanded.

[521] Abraham lightly skips over Ephron''s demand for the entire field and puts the emphasis back where it belongs—that he intends to establish an ownership foothold. He is addressing Ephron directly for the first time, and dangles in front of him the only language he understands—silver.

silver[522] between me and between you, what ? is she?—entomb your **dead one**.'[523]

¹⁶ And he is listening—Abraham—to Ephron. And he is weighing —Abraham—for Ephron the **silver** which he arranges in the ears of the sons of Heth: four of hundreds silver shekels, passing to the one merchandising.

¹⁷ And he is rising—field of Ephron which in the Machpelah, which to face of Mamre: the field and the cavern which *is* in him, and all of the tree which *is* in the field, which *is* in all of his border round about—¹⁸ to Abraham for purchase, to eyes of sons of Heth, in all entering ones of gate of his city.

¹⁹ And after, on this, he entombs—Abraham—**Sarah** his wife to the cavern of the field of the Machpelah on face of Mamre—he, Hebron—in land of Canaan. ²⁰ And he is rising—the field, and the cave which in him—to Abraham for possession of tomb from sons of Heth.

24 And Abraham, he *is* old, he enters into days, and Jehovah, he blesses **Abraham** in all. ² And he is saying—Abraham—to his

---

[522] *Four hundred shekels of silver*; about $60,000 in 2013 dollars. Before the advent of the Federal Reserve (1913) and then the Bretton-Woods agreement (1944) which have given governments the ability to manipulate metals, silver throughout history was priced at 1/12th the value of gold. In Judges 17, the yearly wages for a Levite was 10 silver pieces; the value of a slave in Exodus 21 was 30 shekels (Joseph was sold for 20) and variously from 3 to 50 shekels depending on age and gender in Leviticus 27, from which chapter we find a field of farmland (how much one person could plow in one day, from where we get our *acre*) valued at 50 shekels of silver; 1/8th of what Ephron demanded for the same unit. Also for comparison, a thoroughbred from Egypt went for 150 shekels, and a chariot for 600 in First Kings 10, meaning these chariots were equivalent to a 2013 Mercedes CLS.

[523] *Dead one*; this constant emphasis is the key to what Abraham was doing here. As the leader of a thousands-strong community, there would be people dying every day. Yet for his own wife, he requires a memorial place that is not affected by his sojourning. This creates an alliance of sorts with the people of Heth, which could be either helpful or dangerous to them depending on their relationship with Abraham. It also establishes Abraham's intention toward ownership of the entirety of the land. Note that in the last verse, it is from the sons of Heth—not Ephron—that the land is spoken of as being purchased from. Throughout the account it is they, as guardians of the land they considered theirs, who had the final say.

servant, old one of his house, the one ruling in all of which to him, 'Put you! please! your hand under my thigh, ³ and I cause you to swear in Jehovah, God of the heavens, and God of the earth, that you take not wife for my son from daughters of the Canaanite, whom I dwell among him; ⁴ but to my land and to my kindred you go, and you take wife for my son, for Isaac.'

⁵ And he is saying to him—the servant—'Perhaps she is not willing—the woman—to cause to go after me unto the land, even this; ? bring I back your **son** to the land that—from there you *come* forth?'

⁶ And he is saying to him—Abraham—'You beware! to you, lest you are bringing back my **son** toward there. ⁷ Jehovah, God of the heavens whom—he takes me from the house of my father, and from land of my nativity, and whom—he speaks to me and whom —he swears to me to cause to say, 'To your seed I give the land, even this,' he sends his angel to your face, and you take wife for my son from there. ⁸ And if she is not willing—the woman—to cause to go after you, and you are clean from this my oath, still: my **son** you bring not back toward there.'

⁹ And he is placing—the servant—his **hand** under thigh of Abraham, his socket⁵²⁴, and he is swearing to him on the matter, even this.

¹⁰ And he is taking—the servant—ten camels from camels of his lord, and he is going. And all of all the substance of his lord *is* in his hand. And he is rising, and he is going to Aram-Naharaim⁵²⁵, unto city of Nahor⁵²⁶. ¹¹ And he is kneeling the camels from outside to the city to well of the waters to evening-time, to time to *go* forth of the *women* drawing *water*.

¹² And he is saying, 'Jehovah, God of my lord Abraham, cause you meeting!, please! to my face today—and do you! kindness with my lord Abraham: ¹³ behold! I, being stationed on well of the waters, and daughters of •men of the city, ones issuing to cause to

---

⁵²⁴ *Socket*; as Exodus 40:18. This word is normally translated 'lord', though often considered plural (lords) the context is almost always singular. Thus this passage equally reads "*And he is placing—the servant—his **hand** under the thigh of Abraham his lord(s)...*"

⁵²⁵ *Aram-Naharaim*; Aram: 5th son of Shem, exalted; collective invigoration. *Naharaim*; a bustling colony of commerce.

⁵²⁶ *Nahor*: restraining the wind; rebuking of freedom; Terah's father.

24:13—24:23

draw waters; ¹⁴ and it becomes, the maiden whom I say to her, Stretch out⁵²⁷ you! please! your pitcher, and I drink, and she says, Drink you! and also your camels I water—**her** you choose for your servant, for Isaac; and in her I know that you do kindness with my lord.'

¹⁵ And it is becoming, he—before he finishes to cause to speak—and behold! Rebecca *com*ing forth, who—she is born to Bethuel, son of Milcah, wife of Nahor Abraham's brother—and her pitcher on her shoulder. ¹⁶ And the maiden *is* good of appearance exceedingly—virgin, and ♂man he knows her not; and she descends toward the well, and she is filling her pitcher, and she is ascending.

¹⁷ And he is running—the servant—to cause to meet her, and he is saying, 'Cause you me to swallow⁵²⁸, please! little of waters from your pitcher;' ¹⁸ and she is saying, 'Drink you! my lord;' and she is hastening, and she is lowering her pitcher on her hand, and she is *giv*ing him drink.

¹⁹ And she is finishing to cause him to drink, and she is saying, 'Also for your camels I draw until when they finish to cause to drink.' ²⁰ And she is hastening, and she is emptying her pitcher into the trough, and she is running more to the well to cause to draw, and she is drawing for all of his camels.

²¹ And the ♂man, stunned to his core to her, *is* contemplating, to cause to know ? he prospers—Jehovah—his way or not.

²² And it is becoming as when they finish—the camels to cause to drink, and he is taking—the ♂man—ring of gold, bekah⁵²⁹ his weight, and two or bracelets on her hands—ten gold their weight⁵³⁰. ²³ And he is saying, 'Daughter of who ? —you? Declare

---

⁵²⁷ *Stretch out you*; this has the sense of *turn aside from what you are doing and stretch out to help me*.

⁵²⁸ *Swallow*; only used here and Job 39:24. Same without accent marks as bullrushes which suck up water. The servant is emphasizing his extreme thirst.

⁵²⁹ *Bekah*; half a shekel; 5 grams; about $500 of gold in a "shining flower" ornament, as *ring* (nezem) connotes.

⁵³⁰ *Weight*; same word as *shekel*, 10.5 grams. The servant has just put $1500 of jewelry on Rebecca in the metal content alone. The words used indicate that they were exquisitely crafted.

24:23—24:36

you! please! to me. Is your father's house place for us to cause to lodge?'

²⁴ And she is saying to him, 'Daughter of Bethuel—I—son of Milcah, whom she births for Nahor.' ²⁵ And she is saying to him also, 'Straw, also provender aplenty with us, also place to cause to lodge.'

²⁶ And he is bowing[531]—the ♂man—and he is bowing to Jehovah, ²⁷ and he is saying, 'Blessed is Jehovah, God of my lord Abraham, whom, he forsakes not His kindness and His faithfulness from with my lord; —I in the way, he guided me—Jehovah—house of my lord's brothers.'

²⁸ And she is running—the maiden—and she is declaring to house of her mother as the words, even these. ²⁹ And to Rebecca, brother, and his name, Laban[532], and he is running—Laban—to the man, towards the outskirts, to the well. ³⁰ And it is becoming, as to seeing of the **ring** and the **bracelets** on the hands of his sister, and as to his hearing of **words** of Rebecca his sister, to cause to say, 'Thus he spoke to me—the ♂man,' that he is coming to the ♂man, and behold! standing over the camels over the well. ³¹ And he is saying, 'Come you! One being blessed of Jehovah. To what ? you are standing in the outskirts, and I—I turn[533] the house and space for the camels!'

³² And he is coming—the ♂man—toward the house, and he is freeing the camels, and he is giving straw and provender to the camels, and water to cause to wash his feet, and feet of the •men who *are* with him. ³³ And he is being placed to his face to cause to eat. But he is saying, 'I eat not until when I speak my cause.' And he is saying, 'Speak you!'

³⁴ And he is saying, 'Servant of Abraham, I. ³⁵ And Jehovah—he blesses my **lord** exceedingly, and he is increasing; and he is giving to him flock, and herd, and silver, and gold, and servants, and maids, and camels, and donkeys. ³⁶ And she is birthing—

---

[531] *Bows*; this is a different word from the next, which is Abraham bowing to the sons of Heth. This connotes subjection to, agreement with, and thankfulness for the circumstances as they are; the latter is bowing in the presence of divinity or royalty.

[532] *Laban*; passion for self.

[533] *Turn*; prepare; change or turn to meet the new circumstances.

Sarah my lord's wife—son for my lord, after her old age; and he is giving to him **all of**, which to him
³⁷ 'And he is adjuring me—my lord—to cause to say, you take not wife for my son from daughters of the Canaanite, whom I, in his land, *am* dwelling. ³⁸ If not—to house of my father you are going, and to my family, and you take wife for my son.
³⁹ 'And I am saying to my lord, Perhaps she is not going, the woman, after me; ⁴⁰ and he is saying to me, 'Jehovah—whom to his face I walk—he sends His angel with you, and he causes *to* prosper your way, and you take wife for my son from my family, and from house of my father; ⁴¹ then are you clean from my oath, that you come to my family, and if they are not giving to you; and you become clean from my oath.'
⁴² 'And I am coming today to the well, and I am saying, Jehovah, God of my lord Abraham, if you exist, please! prosper my way which I on her *am* going—⁴³ behold! I being stationed over well of the waters, and it becomes, the damsel, the one *go*ing forth to cause to draw, and I say to her, *give* you! me *to* drink, please, little of waters from your pitcher, ⁴⁴ and she says to me, Also you —drink you! and also for your camels I draw—she, the woman whom he chooses—Jehovah—for my lord's son.
⁴⁵ 'I—before I am finishing to cause to speak to my heart, and behold!, Rebecca *com*ing forth, and her pitcher on her shoulder, and she is descending toward the well, and she is drawing; and I am saying to her, *give* you! me *to* drink, please! ⁴⁶ And she is hastening and she is lowering her pitcher from on her, and she is saying, Drink you! and also your camels I water; and I am drinking, and also the camels she waters.
⁴⁷ 'And I am asking **her**, and I am saying, Daughter of whom ? — you? And she is saying, daughter of Bethuel, son of Nahor, whom she births for him—Milcah. And I am placing the ring on her nose, and the bracelets on her hands. ⁴⁸ And I am bowing, and I am bowing[534] to Jehovah, and I am blessing **Jehovah**, God of my lord Abraham, who—he guides me in the way of faithfulness to cause to take **daughter** of my lord's brother for his son.

---

[534] *Bowing*; see verse 26.

24:49—24:61

⁴⁹ 'And now, if you are ones doing kindness and faithfulness with my lord, declare you! to me; and if not, declare you! to me; and I turn on right or on left.'

⁵⁰ And he is answering—Laban, and Bethuel—and they are saying, 'From Jehovah it is proceeding, the matter; we are not *be*ing able to speak of⁵³⁵ to you evil or good; ⁵¹ behold!, Rebecca *is* to your face. Take you! and go you! and she becomes wife for your lords' son, as which he speaks—Jehovah.'

⁵² And it is becoming, as which he hears—Abraham's servant—their words, and he is bowing himself towards earth before Jehovah. ⁵³ And he is *bring*ing forth—the servant takes out vessels⁵³⁶ of silver, and vessels of gold, and garments, and he is giving to Rebecca; treasures⁵³⁷ also he gives to her brother and to her mother.

⁵⁴ And they are eating and they are drinking, he and the •men who *are* with him, and they are lodging. And they are rising in the morning, and he is saying, 'Send you me! to my lord.' ⁵⁵ And he is saying—her brother and her mother—'She lives, the maiden, *with* **us** days or ten, afterwards she goes.'

⁵⁶ And he is saying to them, 'Not so, you are delaying **me**, and Jehovah, he prospers my way. Send you me! and I go to my lord.' ⁵⁷ And they are saying, 'We call to the maiden, and ask *at* her **mouth**.' ⁵⁸ And they are calling to Rebecca, and they are saying to her, '? You go with the man, even this?' And she is saying, 'I go.'

⁵⁹ And they are sending **Rebecca** their sister, and her **one nursing**, and Abraham's **servant**, and his •men. ⁶⁰ And they are blessing **Rebecca**, and they are saying to her, 'Our sister, you; become you! to thousands of ten-thousands, and he occupies—your seed—**gate** of those hating of him.'

⁶¹ And she is rising—Rebecca and her maidens—and they are riding on the camels, and they are going after the ♂man; and he is taking—the servant—Rebecca and he is going.

---

⁵³⁵ *To speak of*; as *to arrange*.
⁵³⁶ *Vessels*; the word is always used for precious vessels; it connotes something finished to perfection.
⁵³⁷ *Treasures*; a precious gift set aside specifically for formal occasions.

24:62—25:4

⁶² And Isaac—he goes from coming of Beerlahairoi⁵³⁸; and he is dwelling in land of the Negev. And he is *go*ing forth—Isaac—to cause to meditate in the field, toward to face of evening, and he is lifting his eyes and he is seeing, and behold! camels—ones coming.

⁶⁴ And she is lifting—Rebecca—her **eyes**, and she is seeing **Isaac**, and is alighting from on the camel. ⁶⁵ And she is saying to the servant, 'Who ? this man, even this the one coming in the field to cause to meet us?' And he is saying, the servant—the same—'He: my lord;' and she is taking the veil, and she is covering herself.

⁶⁶ And he is enumerating—the servant—to Isaac **all of** the matters which he does. ⁶⁷ And he is bringing her—Isaac—toward the tent —his mother Sarah's—and he is taking **Rebecca**, and she is becoming to him for wife, and he is loving her. And he is being comforted—Isaac—after his mother.

25 And he is adding—Abraham—and he is taking wife, and her name, Keturah⁵³⁹. ² And she is birthing for him **Zimran**⁵⁴⁰, and **Jokshan**⁵⁴¹, and **Medan**⁵⁴², and **Midian**⁵⁴³, and **Ishbak**⁵⁴⁴, and **Shuah**⁵⁴⁵.

³ And Jokshan, he generates **Sheba**⁵⁴⁶ and **Dedan**⁵⁴⁷; and sons of Dedan, they become Asshurim⁵⁴⁸, and Letushim⁵⁴⁹, and Leummim⁵⁵⁰. ⁴ And sons of Midian: Ephah⁵⁵¹, and Epher⁵⁵², and

---

⁵³⁸ *Beerlahairoi*; Well of the Living, Seeing; see 16:14, 25:11.
⁵³⁹ *Keturah*; incense; the west wind; whipping stick.
⁵⁴⁰ *Zimran*; their song; music composer.
⁵⁴¹ *Jokshan*; insidious; snare; divided loyalty; subject to change.
⁵⁴² *Medan*; strife; discernment; to fully measure up to one's self.
⁵⁴³ *Midian*; contention; to fully accomplish one's own desires.
⁵⁴⁴ *Ishbak*; to leave forever; a dying old man; substance fading.
⁵⁴⁵ *Shuah*; depression; a pit; inclining or leaning toward.
⁵⁴⁶ *Sheba*; he who is coming; to powerfully reestablish.
⁵⁴⁷ *Dedan*; their love; parting of friends.
⁵⁴⁸ *Asshurim*; a step (forward); from going forward straight; honest; see 10:11.
⁵⁴⁹ *Letushim*; sharpened ones; hammered ones; hidden change.
⁵⁵⁰ *Leummim*; united peoples.
⁵⁵¹ *Ephah*; darkness; covered; obscure; accumulating speech.
⁵⁵² *Epher*; dustiness; abundant progeneration.

25:4—25:11

Enoch[553], and Abida[554], and Eldaah[555]: all of these, sons of Keturah.

⁵ And he is giving—Abraham—**all of**, which to him, to Isaac. ⁶ And to sons of the concubines which to Abraham, he gives—Abraham—gifts, and he is sending them from on Isaac his son, in him still living, eastward, to land of east.

⁷ And these, days of years of life of Abraham which he lived: hundred of Year and seventy Year and five years. ⁸ And he is expiring, and he is dying—Abraham—in grey haired goodness, aged and satisfied, and he is being gathered to his people. ⁹ And they are entombing **him**—Isaac and Ishmael his sons—to cave of the Machpelah, to field of Ephron, son of Zoar the Hittite, which, on face of Mamre, ¹⁰ the field which he buys—Abraham—from sons of **Heth**; toward there he is entombed—Abraham and Sarah his wife.

¹¹ And it is becoming after the death of Abraham, and he is blessing—God—**Isaac** his son. And he is dwelling—Isaac—with Beerlahairoi[556].

---

[553] *Enoch*; dedicated; to institute; to found.
[554] *Abida*; father of knowledge; power of grasping things.
[555] *Eldaah*; knowing God.
[556] *Beerlahairoi*; Well of the Living, Seeing; see 16:14, 24:62.

25:12—25:18

¹² And these: genealogies of Ishmael, Abraham's son, whom she births—Hagar the Egyptian—Sarah's maid, for Abraham:

¹³ And these, the names Ishmael's sons, in their names, to their genealogies: first-born of Ishmael, Nebaioth[557]; and Kedar[558], and Adbeel[559], and Mibsam[560], ¹⁴ and Mishma[561], and Dumah[562], and Massa[563], ¹⁵ Hadar[564] and Tema[565], Jetur[566], Naphish[567] and Kedmah[568]. ¹⁶ These, they; sons of Ishmael; and these their names, in their villages[569], and in their garrisons; two ten[570] princes to their clans.

¹⁷ And these: years of life of Ishmael, hundred of Year and thirty Year and seven years; and he is expiring, and he is dying, and he is being gathered to his peoples. ¹⁸ And they are tabernacling from Havilah as far as Shur, which *is* on Egypt's face, to cause you to go toward Asshur; on face of all of his brothers he fell.

---

[557] *Nebaioth*; prophecies; increasings; heights.
[558] *Kedar*; darkness; proclaiming the times.
[559] *Adbeel*; grieved of God; taken from great abundance.
[560] *Mibsam*; fragrant; self-distinguishing.
[561] *Mishma*; a report; gathering inner strength.
[562] *Dumah*; silence; passive languishing.
[563] *Massa*; a prophecy; a burden; endurance.
[564] *Hadar*; properly, *Hadad*; honor; to be fierce, sharpen; a goad.
[565] *Tema*; southerner; 'the end justifies the means'; moral aggrandizement.
[566] *Jetur*; he will arrange; vain defensiveness; constant inflation.
[567] *Naphish*; refreshing; physical transformation.
[568] *Kedmah*; eastward; anticipate; the main question.
[569] *Villages*; walled villages.
[570] *Two ten*; twelve.

25:19—25:28

¹⁹ And these: genealogies of Isaac, Abraham's son:

Abraham, he generates **Isaac**; ²⁰ and he becomes—Isaac—son of forty Year in his causing to take **Rebecca**, daughter of Bethuel the Aramaean from Padan-Aram, sister of Laban the Aramaean, to him for a wife.
²¹ And he is entreating—Isaac—to Jehovah to torments *of* his wife, that she, barren. And he is being entreated to him—Jehovah—and she is *becom*ing pregnant—Rebecca his wife. ²² And they are bruising themselves—the sons—in her center, and she is saying, 'If so—to what this?—I?' and she is going to cause to inquire of **Jehovah**.
²³ And he is saying—Jehovah—to her,
    'Two of nations in your womb,
    And two of peoples[571] from your bowels, they are parted;
    And people from people he is alert;
    And elder, he serves younger.'
²⁴ And they are fulfilling, her days to cause to birth, and behold!, twins in her womb. ²⁵ And he is *com*ing forth, the first, ruddy[572], all of him as hairy garment, and they are calling his name Esau[573]. ²⁶ And after so, he *comes* forth, his brother, and his hand holding in Esau's heel, and he is calling his name Jacob[574]. And Isaac: son of sixty Year causing to generate **them**.
²⁷ And they are growing, the youths, and he is becoming—Esau—♂man knowing game[575], ♂man of field; and Jacob, ♂man, *of* integrity[576], tent-dwelling. ²⁸ And he is loving—Isaac—**Esau**, that, game in his mouth; and Rebecca loving[577] **Jacob**.

---

[571] *Peoples*; a people united by a common bond.
[572] *Ruddy*; red; seen note 2:7.
[573] *Esau*; doing; making; man of action.
[574] *Jacob*; seizing the keynote; forever supplanting; grasping the heel (as if to trip up or stop); also, prince of potential.
[575] *Game*; this connotes all that has to do with hunting, as well as deceiving and opposition of craftiness.
[576] *Integrity*; complete as to virtue, used also for *gentle*.
[577] *Loving*; in both cases here the sense of loving is the *house of the will* and connotes a mutual appreciation.

²⁹ And he is *mak*ing stew—Jacob—and he is coming—Esau—from the field, and he, languishing. ³⁰ And he is saying—Esau—to Jacob, 'Feed⁵⁷⁸ you me! please! from the red; the red, this stuff; that languishing—I.' On so he calls his name Edom⁵⁷⁹. ³¹ And he is saying—Jacob—'Sell you! as the day, your **birthright** to me.'

³² And he is saying—Esau—'Behold!, I *am* going to cause to die, and to what? this to me—birthright?' ³³ And he is saying—Jacob—'Swear you! to me as the day:' and he is swearing to him, and he is selling his **birthright** to Jacob. ³⁴ And Jacob—he gives to Esau bread and stew of lentils. And he is eating, and he is drinking, and he is rising, and he is going, and he is despising—Esau—the **birthright**.

26 And it is becoming famine in the land, from besides of the famine, the first, which—it was Abraham's days. And he is going—Isaac—to Abimelech king of the Philistines, toward Gerar.

² And he is appearing to him—Jehovah—and he is saying, 'Not so—you are descending toward Egypt. Tabernacle you! in the land which I am saying to you; ³ sojourn you! in the land, even this; and I am with you, and I bless you, that to you and to your seed I give **all of** the lands, even these. And I raise the **oath**⁵⁸⁰ which I swear to Abraham your father. ⁴ And I increase your **seed** as stars of the heavens, and I give to your seed **all of** the lands, even these; and they bless themselves in your seed all of nations of the earth;   ⁵ because which he listens—Abraham—in My voice, and he is keeping My charge⁵⁸¹, My instructions⁵⁸², My statutes⁵⁸³, and My laws⁵⁸⁴.'

---

⁵⁷⁸ *Feed*; to swallow greedily; glut. Used only here.

⁵⁷⁹ *Edom*; red, but with a sense of *conformed to Adam* in terms of what caused Adam to become mortal.

⁵⁸⁰ *Oath*; different word from *covenant* used with Noah and Abraham.

⁵⁸¹ *My charge*; that which is drawn *from me* for your taking care of *for me*.

⁵⁸² *Instructions*; determination toward a desired object.

⁵⁸³ *Statutes*; solid (unmovable) determinations appointed.

⁵⁸⁴ *Law*; an ordered writing of dazzling appearance, ordered in the sense of laid out in circular rows; a brilliant monument. It has the sense of a dually reciprocal entity requiring the full participation of law giver and law observer—the word *observer* being key; a <u>charge</u> is a ward to be *kept*, which in keeping becomes a <u>statute</u>; a <u>law</u> is a living monument to be *observed*, gazed upon, and contemplated; that the desired *effect* of <u>instructions</u> becomes operative.

26:6—26:18

⁶ And he is dwelling—Isaac—in Gerar. ⁷ And they are asking—•men of the place—to his wife; and he is saying, 'She *is* my sister:' that he fears to cause to say, 'My wife'—lest they are killing me—•men of the place—over Rebecca, that, good of appearance—she.

⁸ And it is becoming, that they lengthen to him there—the days—and he is gazing⁵⁸⁵—Abimelech king of Philistines—out from in the window, and he is seeing, and behold! Isaac sporting⁵⁸⁶ *with* **Rebecca** his wife.

⁹ And he is calling—Abimelech—to Isaac, and he is saying, 'Yes! behold! she *is* your wife—and how ? you say, She *is* my sister?' and he is saying—Isaac—'That I say, Lest I am dying over her.'

¹⁰ And he is saying—Abimelech—'What ? this you do to us? Soon he lies—one of the people—*with* your **wife**, and you bring on us guilt!' ¹¹ And he is instructing—Abimelech—**all of** the people, to cause to say, 'The one touching in the ♂man, even this, and in his wife, to die he dies.'

¹² And he is sowing—Isaac—in the land, even her, and he is finding in the year, even her, hundred*fold of* barley, and he is blessing him—Jehovah. ¹³ And he is increasing—the ♂man—and he is continuing to continue⁵⁸⁷ and increasing, until that increasing exceedingly. ¹⁴ And it is to him possession of flock, and possession of herd, and laborer many; and they are envying **him**—Philistines. ¹⁵ And all of the wells which they dig⁵⁸⁸—his father's servants—in Abraham his father's days, they stop them up—Philistines—and they fill them *with* dust.

¹⁶ And he is saying—Abimelech—to Isaac, 'Go you! from with us; that you are buttressed⁵⁸⁹ from us exceedingly.' ¹⁷ And he is going from there—Isaac—and he camps in the watercourse of Gerar, and he is dwelling there. ¹⁸ And he is returning—Isaac—and he is digging **wells** of the waters which they dig in his father Abraham's days, and they are stopping them up—Philistines—

---

⁵⁸⁵ *Gazing*; leaning out; to peep.

⁵⁸⁶ *Sporting*; word similar to *Isaac* and *laughter*; see also note 21:9.

⁵⁸⁷ *Continue*; to walk; to go.

⁵⁸⁸ *Dig*; also meaning *to search out* as Joshua 2:2 to *search out* the land.

⁵⁸⁹ *Buttressed*; staunch; strengthened in the bones. The idea is that Isaac was independently strong and had no need of them.

after death of Abraham. And he is calling to them names as the names which he calls to them—his father.

¹⁹ And they are digging—Isaac's servants—in the watercourse, and they are finding there well of waters, living ones. ²⁰ And they are contending—ones shepherding of Gerar—with ones shepherding of Isaac, to cause to say 'To us the waters!' And he is calling name of the well 'Extortion,' that they themselves violate with him. ²¹ And they are digging another well, and they are contending also over her, and he is calling her name 'Accusation.'⁵⁹⁰'

²² And he is removing from there, and he is digging another well, and they contend not over her. And he is calling her name name Broadways⁵⁹¹, and he is saying, 'That now he broadens—Jehovah—for us, and we *are* fruitful in the land.'

²³ And he is ascending from there... Beer-Sheba. ²⁴ And he is appearing to him—Jehovah—in the night, even he; and he is saying 'I—God of Abraham your father; nothing you are fearing; that, *with* **you**—I. And I bless you, and I increase your **seed**, in cause *of* Abraham My servant.' ²⁵ And he is building there, altar, and he is declaring in name of Jehovah, and he is stretching out there his tent, and they are digging there—Isaac's servants—well.

²⁶ And Abimelech—he goes to him from Gerar, and Ahuzzath⁵⁹² his associate, and Phichol head of his host. ²⁷ And he is saying to them—Isaac—'? What reason? you come to me; and you—you hate **me** !—?, and you are sending me from you.'

²⁸ And they are saying, 'To see, we see: that he becomes—Jehovah—with you, and we are saying, 'She shall become, please! oath between us: between us and between you; and we cut covenant with you, ²⁹ if you are doing with us evil; as which we touch you not, and as which we do but good with you, and we send you in peace, you now being blessed of Jehovah.'

---

⁵⁹⁰ *Accusation*; 'Sitnah'; as Ezra 4:6.
⁵⁹¹ *Broadways*; 'Rehoboth'; also a city built by Asshur in 10:11.
⁵⁹² *Ahuzzath*; possession; this heritage. It is probably a title, as the meaning connotes a close associate who mitigates real estate litigation. With Phichol and Abimelech, Isaac is being confronted with legal, military, and royal issues (legislative, executive, and judicial respectively), reflected in the next three things Isaac brings up.

26:30—27:7

³⁰ And he is making for them, feast, and they are eating, and they are drinking, ³¹ and they are rising early in the morning, and they are swearing, ♂man to his brother, and he is sending them—Isaac—and they are going from him in peace.

³² And it is becoming in the day, the same, and they are coming—Isaac's servants—and they are declaring to him over circumstances of the well which they dig, and they are saying to him, 'We find water.' ³³ And he is calling **her** Shebah[593], on this name of the city, Beer-Sheba, unto the day, even this.

³⁴ And he is—Esau—son of forty Year, and he is taking wife, **Judith**[594], daughter of Beeri[595] the Hittite, and **Bashemath**[596], daughter of Elon[597] the Hittite; ³⁵ and they are becoming bitterness of spirit to Isaac and to Rebecca.

27 And it is becoming that he *is* old—Isaac—and they are dimming—his eyes—from seeing, and he is calling **Esau** his son, the great one[598]; and he is saying to him, 'My son!' And he is saying to him, 'Behold me!'

² And he is saying, 'Behold! please! I *am* old, I know not day of my death. ³ And now, lift you! please! your implements, your quiver and your bow, and *go* forth you! field, and hunt you! for me game, ⁴ and make you! for me delicacies, as which I love, and bring you! to me, and I eat, so that she blesses you—my soul—before I am dying.'

⁵ And Rebecca is hearing in causing to speak—Isaac—to Esau his son. And he is going—Esau—the field to cause to hunt of game—to cause to bring. ⁶ And Rebecca, she speaks to Jacob her son, to cause to say, 'Behold, I hear your **father** speaking to Esau your brother to cause to say, ⁷ Bring you! to me game, and make you! for me delicacies, and I eat, and I bless you to face of Jehovah, to face of my death.

---

[593] *Sheba*; seven; root word for *oath* from the tradition of repeating something seven time to swear. See 21, verses 14, 31.

[594] *Judith*; God-given; later meaning *Jewish*.

[595] *Beeri*; my well; stream of fragrance.

[596] *Bashemath*; spice; corrupted to death; encountering a delay; transforming into heat.

[597] *Elon*; might; plain; region of night-watchings.

[598] *The great one*; same word as *elder* in verse 15.

⁸ 'And now, my son, listen you! in my voice, to which I *am* instructing **you**. ⁹ Go you! please! to the flock, and take you! for me from there two of kids of goats, good ones, and I do **them** delicacies for your father, as which he loves. ¹⁰ And you bring to your father, and he eats, across which he blesses you to face of his death.'

¹¹ And he is saying—Jacob—to Rebecca his mother, 'Behold! Esau my brother: hairy ♂man, and I: smooth⁵⁹⁹ ♂man. ¹² Perhaps he feels me—my father—and I become in his eyes as one deceiving, and I bring on me contempt, and not blessing.' ¹³ And she is saying to him—his mother—'On me your contempt⁶⁰⁰, my son; yes, listen you! in my voice, and go you!, take you! for me.'

¹⁴ And he is going, and he is taking, and he is bringing to his mother; and she is doing—his mother—delicacies, as which he loves—his father. ¹⁵ And she is taking—Rebecca—**garments** of Esau her son, the elder one—the desirable ones which *with* **her** in the house, and she is putting on **Jacob** her son, the younger one. ¹⁶ And **skins** of kids of the goats she wraps on his hands, and on the the smoothness of his neck. ¹⁷ And she is giving the **delicacies**, and the **bread** which she does in Jacob her son's hand.

¹⁸ And he is coming to his father, and he is saying, 'My father!' and he is saying, 'Behold me! who ? you, my son?' ¹⁹ And he is saying—Jacob—to his father, 'I, Esau your first-born; I do as which you speak to me. Rise you! please! sit you!, and eat you! from my game, so that she blesses me, your soul.'

²⁰ And he is saying—Isaac—to his son, 'What ? this—you hurried to cause to find, my son?' And he is saying, 'That he brought about⁶⁰¹—Jehovah your God—to my face.'

²¹ And he is saying—Isaac—to Jacob, 'Approach you! please! and I feel you, my son, ? whether you, this my son, Esau or not.'

²² And he is approaching—Jacob—to Isaac his father, and he is feeling him, and he is saying, 'The voice, voice of Jacob, but the

---

⁵⁹⁹ *Smooth*; as in English, this has the additional meaning of a *smooth talker*.

⁶⁰⁰ *On me your contempt*; there is a hint of irony here that she felt a touch of the contempt already by not being consulted.

⁶⁰¹ *That he brought about*; the analogous English phrase is *Things just fell into line*. The Hebrew expression is from the timber trade in which everything goes smoothly when things are aligned properly.

hands, hands of Esau.' ²³ And discerns him not, that they are—his hands—as the hands of Esau his brother, hairy ones; and he is blessing him. ²⁴ And he is saying, 'You ? this my son Esau?' and he is saying, 'I.'

²⁵ And he is saying, 'Approach you! to me, and I eat from my son's game, so that she blesses you, my soul;' and he is approaching to him, and he is eating; and he is bringing to him wine, and he is drinking.

²⁶ And he is saying to him—Isaac his father—'Approach you! please! and kiss you! to me, my son.' ²⁷ And he is approaching, and he is kissing to him, and he is smelling **fragrance** of his garments, and he is blessing him, and he is saying,

'See you! fragrance of my son as the fragrance of field which, he blesses him—Jehovah,

²⁸   And he gives to you—God—from night-mist of the heavens,

    And from fatness of the earth,

    And abundance of grain and new wine;

²⁹   They serve you—peoples

    And they bow themselves down to you—tribes[602];

    Be you! master to your brothers,

    And they bow themselves down to you—sons of your mother;

    Ones cursing of you are cursed,

    And ones blessing of you are blessed.'[603]

³⁰ And it is becoming, as which he finishes—Isaac—to cause to bless Jacob, and he is, yes; to *go* forth, he *goes* forth—Jacob—from face of Isaac his father, and Esau his brother, he comes from his hunt. ³¹ And he is doing—also he, delicacies; and he is bringing to his father, and he is saying to his father, 'He rises! my

---

[602] *Tribes*; same as *peoples* in 25:23.

[603] Note that Rebecca and Jacob had largely misunderstood the purposes of Isaac here. Nothing is mentioned in this blessing regarding being the inheritor of the promises to Abraham, as later in 28:4 when the issue has been forced. Rebecca, in an effort to secure the bloodline promises for Jacob, missed the fact that her pleasure-loving husband merely wished to bestow upon his pleasure-serving son Esau a lavish blessing to show his appreciation. The only element of favoritism in terms of the promises was that he was to have mastery over his brothers.

father, and he eats from his son's game, so that she blesses me—your soul.'

³² And he is saying to him—Isaac his father—'Who ? you?' And he is saying, 'I, your son, your first-born, Esau.' ³³ And he is trembling—Isaac—great trembling, until exceedingly, and he is saying, 'Who, now ? he, the one hunting game and he is bringing to me, and I am eating from all before you are coming, and I am blessing him? —also, being blessed he is.'

³⁴ And to hear of—Esau—his father's **words**, and he is crying cry great and bitter, until exceedingly; and he is saying to his father, 'Bless you me! also me! my father.' ³⁵ And he is saying, 'He comes—your brother—in deceit[604], and he is taking your blessing.'

³⁶ And he is saying, '? That one calls his name Jacob, and he is supplanting[605] me these *two* times? My **birthright** he takes; and behold! now he takes my blessing.' And he is saying, '? You reserve not for me, blessing?'

³⁷ And he is answering—Isaac—and he is saying to Esau, 'Behold, >Man[606] I set him to you, and **all of** his brothers I give to him for servants, and grain and new wine I uphold him; and for you indeed, what ? I do, my son?'

³⁸ And he is saying—Esau—to his father, '? One blessing, she to you[607] my father? Bless you me! Also I my father!' And he is lifting up—Esau—his voice and he is weeping.

³⁹ And he is answering—Isaac his father—and he is saying to him,

> 'Behold! from[608] fatness of the earth,
> He is becoming your dwelling,
> And from night-mist of the heavens, from over;
40   And over your sword do you live,
> And your **brother** you serve;
> And it becomes when you wander,

---

[604] *Deceit*; the word has the sense of usurping.
[605] *Supplant*; see note 25:26.
[606] *>Man*; mighty one; *gibbor*; see 6:4.
[607] *She to you*; referring to the *soul* of Isaac which does the blessing, and which is feminine.
[608] *From*; apart from, and so next throughout.

And you break off his yoke from on your neck.'
⁴¹ And he is hating⁶⁰⁹—Esau—**Jacob**, over the blessing which he blesses him—his father. And he is saying—Esau—in his heart, 'They approach, days of mourning of my father, and I kill **Jacob** my brother.'
⁴² And it is being told to Rebecca—**words** of Esau her son, the elder one—and she is sending and she is calling for Jacob her son, the younger one, and she is saying to him, 'Behold! Esau your brother—self-comforting to you—to cause to kill you. ⁴³ And now, my son, listen you! in my voice, and rise you! flee you! for you to Laban my brother, toward Haran. ⁴⁴ And you dwell with him days, ones until which she is turning back—fury⁶¹⁰ of your brother. ⁴⁵ Until he turns back—your brother's ire⁶¹¹—from you, and he forgets **what** you do to him, and I send and I take you from there. To what? I am bereaved: also two of you, one day?'
⁴⁶ And she is saying—Rebecca—to Isaac, 'I despair⁶¹² in my life from faces of daughters of Heth; if taking—Jacob—wife of the daughters of Heth as these from the daughters of the land, To what? for me, life?'

28 And he is calling—Isaac—to Jacob, and he is blessing **him**, and he is instructing him, and he is saying to him, 'You take not wife from daughters of Canaan. ² Rise you! go you! toward Padan-Aram, houseward Bethuel, your mother's father, and take you! for you from there wife from daughters of Laban, your mother's brother. ³ And God Providence⁶¹³, he blesses **you**, and he *makes* fruitful you, and he increases you, and you become to assembly of peoples⁶¹⁴. ⁴ And he gives to you **blessing** of Abraham, to you and to your seed—**you**, to cause you to possess **land** of your sojournings, which he gives—God—to Abraham.'⁶¹⁵

---

⁶⁰⁹ *Hating*; not the regular word for hating, it has the idea of *begrudging* and *anathemizing*; i.e., separating from as vile.
⁶¹⁰ *Fury*; heat of anger.
⁶¹¹ *Ire*; literally *nostrils*; here used to picture the rapid breathing of anger.
⁶¹² *Despair*; literally *to cut loose*. It is the same word without accent marks as *thorns* (which get cut away) and *awaken* (cutting from the dreaming).
⁶¹³ *God Providence*; El-Shaddai; often translated *God Almighty*; see 17:1 for the first occurrence.
⁶¹⁴ *Peoples*; congregated peoples; *tribes*.

28:5—28:14

⁵ And he is sending—Isaac—**Jacob**, and he is going toward Padan-Aram, to Laban, son of Bethuel the Aramaean[616], brother of Rebecca, mother of Jacob and Esau.

⁶ And he is seeing—Esau—that he blesses—Isaac—**Jacob**, and sends **him** toward Padan-Aram to cause to take for him from there, wife; to cause him to bless **him**, and he is instructing over him to cause to say, 'You take not wife from daughters of Canaan,⁷ and he is listening—Jacob—to his father and to his mother, and he is going toward Padan-Aram...⁸· And he is seeing —Esau—that evil ones, daughters of Canaan in the eyes of Isaac his father. ⁹ And he is going—Esau—to Ishmael, and he is taking **Mahalath**[617], daughter of Ishmael, Abraham's son, sister of Nebaioth[618], over[619] his wives, to him for wife.

¹⁰ And he is *going* forth—Jacob—from Beer-Sheba, and he is going toward Haran, ¹¹ and he is coming on in the place, and he is lodging there; that, he set—the sun. And he is taking from stones of the place, and he is placing his pillows, and he is lying in the place, the same.

¹² And he is dreaming, and behold! a stairway[620] being stationed toward the earth, and its head touching toward the heavens. And behold! angels of God—ascending ones and descending ones—in it. ¹³ And behold! Jehovah being stationed over it, and he is saying, 'I—Jehovah, God of Abraham your father, and God of Isaac. The land which—you lie on her, to you I give her, and to your seed; ¹⁴ and he becomes—your seed—as the dust of the land, and you break forth seaward, and eastward, and northward, and

---

[615] *Him... you*; the emphasis on Jacob is him as opposed to Esau being given the promises of Abraham.
[616] *Aramaean*; Syrian.
[617] *Mahalath*; sickness; appeasing; self-humiliation.
[618] *Nebaioth*; prophecies; increasings; heights. First son of Ishmael; see 25:13.
[619] *Over his wives*; this insinuates that his Canaanite wives were relegated to a lower status.
[620] *Stairway*; or *ladder*; only time used in scripture. The word has both the sense of a leap of joy and the collective esteem of the heavens for the earth.

28:14—29:2

rimward[621], and they are blessed in you—all families of the ground, and in your seed.

[15] 'And behold! I *am* with you, and I keep you in all which you are going, and I bring you back to the ground, even this; that I forsake you not until which when I do **what**[622] I speak to you.'

[16] And he is awaking—Jacob—from his sleep, and he is saying, 'Surely Jehovah is in the place, even this, and I know not.' [17] And he is fearing, and he is saying, 'What ! one being feared, the place, even this! *There* is no 'this' but rather 'house of God', and this—gate of the heavens.'

[18] And he is rising early—Jacob—in the morning, and he is taking the **stone** which he places, his pillows, and he is placing **her**, pillar, and he is pouring oil on her top. [19] And he is calling **name** of the place, the same, Bethel[623], and yet Luz[624], name of the city to the first.

[20] And he is vowing—Jacob—vow, to cause to say, 'If he is becoming—God—with me, and he keeps me in the way, even this, which I *am* going, and he gives to me bread to cause to eat, and garment to cause to put on, [21] and I return in peace to house of my father, and he becomes—Jehovah—to me, to God. [22] And this stone, even this, which I place pillar, he becomes house of God, and all which you give to me—to tithe, I tithe him to you.'[625]

29 And he is lifting—Jacob—his feet, and he is going towards land—sons of east. [2] And he is seeing, and behold! well in the

---

[621] *Rim-ward*: a Hebraism meaning *the south*, referring to the lower rim of Judah that borders the desert. Directions of this kind are centric to the land of Israel, see 12:9.

[622] *What*; same word as *which*.

[623] *Bethel*; house of God.

[624] *Luz*; acquiescence.

[625] Jacob''s vow here gives a picture of what characterizes his entire life. God had just promised to unequivocally care for him, and he turns it into a 'deal' in an effort to equalize with God. We will see this over and over, as when he tells Leah and Rachel his dream of God causing the spotted rams to progenerate, yet he is nonetheless busy putting carved rods out. This back-and-forth with God will culminate in his wrestling with the angel and demanding a blessing. It would be difficult to imagine a more opposite personality from Isaac, who was happy to sit back and let God bless him. Yet God takes Jacob up on this ground, and even refers to the vow in 31:13 when telling Jacob to return.

field, and behold! there, three droves of flock, ones crouching on her; that from the well, even her, they are watering the droves, and the great stone on the mouth of the well. ³ And they are gathered toward there, all the droves, and they roll the **stone** from on mouth of the well, and they water the flock, and they return the **stone** on mouth of the well to her place.

⁴ And he is saying to them—Jacob—'My brothers, from where ? you?' And they are saying, 'From Haran, we.' ⁵ And he is saying to them, '? You know **Laban**, son of Nahor?' And they are saying, 'We know.' ⁶ And he is saying to them, '? Peace to him?' And they are saying, 'Peace. And behold! Rachel[626] his daughter coming with the flock.'

⁷ And he is saying, 'Behold! the day *is* still great; not time of the cattle to be gathered; water you! the flock, and go you!, make it happen![627]' ⁸ And they are saying, 'We are not *be*ing able, until when they are being gathered, all of the droves, and they roll the **stone** from on mouth of the well, and we water the flock.'

⁹ Still him speaking with them, and Rachel—she comes with the flock, which, to her father; that being shepherdess, she. ¹⁰ And it is becoming, as which he sees—Jacob—Rachel, daughter of Laban his mother's brother, and **flock** of Laban his mother's brother, and he is approaching—Jacob—and he is rolling the **stone** from on mouth of the well, and he is watering **flock** of Laban his mother's brother.

¹¹ And he is kissing—Jacob—to Rachel, and he is lifting his **voice**, and he is weeping. ¹² And he is declaring—Jacob—to Rachel that her father's brother—he—and that Rebecca's son—he —and she is running and she is declaring to her father.

¹³ And it is becoming, as to hear of—Laban—report of Jacob his sister's son, and he is running to cause to meet him, and he is embracing to him, and he is kissing to him, and he is bringing him to his house. And he is recounting to Laban **all of** the things, even

---

[626] *Rachel*; an ewe; acting on hope; lifted high by the wind. The connotations are multiple and ethereal.

[627] *Make it happen*; literally, *act physically*. There are varying ways to translate this, including *you disorderly!*

these. ¹⁴ And he is saying to him—Laban—'Yes; my bone and my flesh—you.'⁶²⁸ And he is living with him, month of days.

¹⁵ And he is saying—Laban—to Jacob, '? That my brother—you—and you serve me gratuitously? Declare you! to me what ? your hire.' ¹⁶ And to Laban, two of daughters; name of the elder—Leah⁶²⁹, and name of the younger—Rachel; ¹⁷ and eyes of Leah, tender⁶³⁰ ones, but Rachel—she is lovely of shape and lovely of appearance.

¹⁸ And he is loving—Jacob—Rachel, and he is saying, 'I serve you seven years in Rachel your daughter, the young one.' ¹⁹ And he is saying—Laban—'Good to give of me **her** to you from to give of me **her** to another man; dwell you! with me.' ²⁰ And he is serving—Jacob—in Rachel seven years; and they are becoming in his eyes as days, ones, in his loving **her**.

²¹ And he is saying—Jacob—to Laban, 'Give you! my **wife**, that they *are* fulfilled, my days, and I come to her.' ²² And he is gathering—Laban—**all of** •men of the place, and he is doing feast. ²³ And it is in the evening, and he is taking **Leah** his daughter, and he is bringing **her** to him, and he is coming to her. ²⁴ And he is giving—Laban—to her **Zilpah**⁶³¹, his maid, to Leah his daughter—maid.

²⁵ And it is in the morning, and behold!, she *is* Leah. And he is saying to Laban, 'What ? this you do to me? Not in Rachel I serve with you? And to what ? you deceive me?'

²⁶ And he is saying—Laban—'It is not being done so in our place, to cause to give the younger one to face of the first-born; ²⁷ fulfill you! week of this one; and we give to you also **this one**, in service which you serve with me yet seven years, other ones.'

²⁸ And he is doing—Jacob—so, and he is fulfilling week of this one, and he is giving to him **Rachel** his daughter, to him for wife. ²⁹ And he is giving—Laban—to Rachel his daughter **Bilhah**⁶³² his maid to her to maid. ³⁰ And he is coming also to Rachel, and he is

---

⁶²⁸ There is quite a bit of irony here; Jacob told Laban **all of** the events that led to his visit. Laban could fully identify and appreciate the ways in which Esau had been usurped.

⁶²⁹ *Leah*; weary; action without end.

⁶³⁰ *Tender*; this can mean either gentle or weak, as in half-blind.

⁶³¹ *Zilpah*; flippant-mouth; to trickle.

⁶³² *Bilhah*; frantic soul; abundance of busy-work.

loving also **Rachel** from Leah. And he is serving with him still seven years, other ones.

³¹ And he is seeing—Jehovah—that being hated, Leah; and he is opening her **womb**, but Rachel, barren. ³² And she is *becom*ing pregnant—Leah—and she is birthing son, and she is calling name of him Reuben⁶³³, that she says, 'That he sees—Jehovah—in my misery, that now he loves me, my husband⁶³⁴.'

³³ And she is *becom*ing pregnant further, and she is birthing son, and she is saying, 'That he hears—Jehovah—that being hated—I—and he is giving to me also **this one**;' and she is calling his name Simeon⁶³⁵.

³⁴ And she is *becom*ing pregnant further, and she is birthing son, and she is saying, 'Finally! the step; he is joined—my husband—to me, that I birth for him three sons.' On so he calls his name Levi⁶³⁶.

³⁵ And she is *becom*ing pregnant further, and she is birthing son, and she is saying, 'This time⁶³⁷, I worship⁶³⁸ Jehovah;' on so she calls his name Judah⁶³⁹. And she is staying from causing to birth⁶⁴⁰.

30 And she is seeing—Rachel—that she births not for Jacob, and she is envying—Rachel—in her sister, and she is saying to Jacob, 'Give you! to me sons, and if without, dying—I.' ² And it is heating—Jacob's anger—in Rachel, and he is saying, '? In stead of God—I—who withholds from you fruit of womb?'

³ And she is saying, 'Behold! my maid Bilhah, come you! to her, and she births on my knees, and I am built, even I, from her.' ⁴ And she is giving to him **Bilhah** her maid for wife, and he is

---

⁶³³ *Reuben*; see you a son.
⁶³⁴ *Husband*; ♂*man*; see note in Introduction.
⁶³⁵ *Simeon*; listening; sign of corruption; darkening the name.
⁶³⁶ *Levi*; joined; addition; supplement; entwined.
⁶³⁷ *This time*; same expression translated in the previous verse as *Finally! the step*.
⁶³⁸ *Worship*; with extended hands; the word is taken from doing something with the hands.
⁶³⁹ *Judah*; he is praised; God-given life.
⁶⁴⁰ *She is staying from causing to birth*; the expression indicates that she left Jacob to Rachel at this point, perhaps not by choice. Compare verses 9 and 13. The causal interweavings in the text are thick.

coming to her—Jacob. ⁵ And she is *becom*ing pregnant—Bilhah—and she births for Jacob son. ⁶ And she is saying—Rachel—'He adjudicates me—God—and also he hears in my voice, and he is giving to me son;' on this she calls his name Dan⁶⁴¹.

⁷ And she is *becom*ing pregnant further—Bilhah—and she is birthing—Bilhah, maid of Rachel—second son for Jacob. ⁸ And she is saying—Rachel—'Wrestlings of God I wrestle with my sister, also I prevail;' and she is calling his name Naphtali⁶⁴².

⁹ And she is seeing—Leah—that she stays from causing to give birth, and she is taking **Zilpah** her maid, and she is giving **her** to Jacob for wife. ¹⁰ And she is birthing—Zilpah, Leah's maid—for Jacob son; ¹¹ and she is saying—Leah—'He comes—troop;' and she calls his **name** Gad⁶⁴³.

¹² And she is birthing—Zilpah, Leah's maid—second son for Jacob; ¹³ and she is saying—Leah—'In my happiness, that they *call* me happy—daughters;' and she is calling his **name** Asher⁶⁴⁴.

¹⁴ And he is going—Reuben—in days of wheat-harvest, and he is finding mandrakes⁶⁴⁵ in the field, and he is bringing **them** to Leah his mother. And she is saying—Rachel—to Leah, 'Give you! please! to me from mandrakes of your son.'

¹⁵ And she is saying to her, '? Little, to your taking of my husband, and to cause to take also **mandrakes** of my son?' And she is saying—Rachel—'Therefore he lies with you tonight, instead of your son's mandrakes.'

¹⁶ And he is coming—Jacob—from the field in the evening; and she is *go*ing forth—Leah—to cause to meet him, and she is saying, 'To me you are coming, that to hire I hire you in my son's mandrakes;' and he is lying with her in the night—he.

¹⁷ And he is listening—God—to Leah, and she is *becom*ing pregnant, and she is birthing for Jacob son, fifth. ¹⁸ And she is

---

⁶⁴¹ *Dan*; judgment, especially contradictory.
⁶⁴² *Naphtali*; my wrestling; perpetuating argument.
⁶⁴³ *Gad*; agitating or invading troop; an incision.
⁶⁴⁴ *Asher*; happy; burning flame; motive.
⁶⁴⁵ *Mandrakes*; whatever plant this is—most likely the *mandragora*—the word give the sense of *powerful mutual satisfaction,* a *lover,* and *a chosen vessel.* As such, without the accent marks it is also used for a cooking pot used for special mixtures, thus the sense of an aphrodisiac is often assumed.

saying—Leah—'He gives—God—my hire, which, I give my maid to my husband;' and she is calling his name Issachar[646].

19 And she is *becom*ing pregnant—Leah—and she births sixth son for Jacob. 20 And she is saying—Leah—'He apportions me—God—**me**—good portion; this time he night-loves[647] me—my husband—that I birth for him six sons;' and she is calling his **name** Zebulun[648]. 21 And after she births daughter, and she is calling her **name** Dinah[649].

22 And he is remembering—God—**Rachel**, and he is listening to her—God—and he is opening her womb. 23 And she is *becom*ing pregnant, and she is birthing son, and she is saying, 'He gathers—God—my reproach;' 24 and she is calling his **name** Joseph[650], to cause to say 'He adds—Jehovah—to me, son—another.'

25 And it becomes, as which she births—Rachel—**Joseph**, and he is saying—Jacob—to Laban, 'Send you me! and I go to my place, and to my land; 26 give you! my **wives** and my **children**, whom I serve **you** in them, and I go; that you—you know my **service** which I serve you.'

27 And he is saying—Laban—to him, 'If please! I find grace in your eyes—I divine: and he is blessing me—Jehovah—for your sake.' 28 And he is saying, 'Strike[651] your hire on me, and I give.'

---

[646] *Issachar*; he is payed; shown and proved; engraved in reality.
[647] *Night-loves me*; or *passes the night writhing with me*. The word is similar to *portion* in the sentence; Leah is transferring the idea of a *portion* from Jehovah to *sexual preference* from Jacob with a slight twist of the word. Additionally, the thought of making love for pleasure rather than purpose was believed to produce a daughter rather than a son, which is what in fact happened with Dinah.
[648] *Zebulun*; *swarming toward unity*. There are several ideas playing here, as Leah adds a single letter to *passes the night writhing with me* to create something more appropriate for a son. There is the hint that *unity* means between her and Jacob. *Swarming* has the sense of boiling and constant activity. This is possibly a bit much for Zebulun, for the letter Vav (u) is switched in its place when we get to his name again in 46:14.
[649] *Dinah*; abundant youth; vigorous satisfaction.
[650] *Joseph*; he adds; day of achievement; summit of meaningfulness.
[651] *Strike*; to violently perforate. Laban was saying, *Go ahead and hurt me; I'll agree to give.*

30:29—30:40

²⁹ And he is saying to him, 'You—you know *that* **which** I serve you, and *that* **which** it becomes, your substance *with* **me**; ³⁰ that—little which it is to you to my face, and it breaks forth to the multitude; and he is blessing—Jehovah—you to my foot; and now, when ? do I—also I—for my house?'

³¹ And he is saying, 'What ? I give to you?' And he is saying—Jacob—'You give not to me anything; if you are doing for me the thing, even this, I return; I shepherd; your flock I guard: ³² I pass in all of your flock today to take away from there every flockling spotted and variegated, and all of brown flockling among the lambs, and variegated and spotted in the goats—and it becomes my hire. ³³ And she testifies in me—my righteousness—in day hereafter, that she comes over my hire to your face: any which, he is not spotted and variegated in the goats, and brown in the lambs —being stolen—he—*with* **me**.' ³⁴ And he is saying—Laban —'Behold! O that it becomes as your word!'

³⁵ And he is taking away in the day, even that, the bucks: the striped ones and the variegated ones, and **all of** the she-goats, the spotted and the variegated ones, all of which, white in him, and all of brown in the lambs, and he is giving in hand of his sons. ³⁶ And he is placing way of three of days between him and between Jacob. And Jacob *is* shepherding **flock of** Laban, the ones being left.

³⁷ And he is taking to him—Jacob—rod of white sapling, and hazel⁶⁵² and plane⁶⁵³, and he is peeling in them peelings, white ones, stripping to the white which, on the rods; ³⁸ and he is stationing the **rods** which he peels in channels; in troughs of the waters which, they are coming—the flock—to cause to drink before the flock, and they are conceiving in causing them to come to cause to drink.   ³⁹ And they are conceiving—the flock—to the rods, and they are birthing—the flock—striped ones, spotted ones, and variegated ones.

⁴⁰ And the lambs he parted—Jacob—and he is giving face of the flock to striped ones and all of brown ones in Laban's flock; and he is setting for him droves to his, separate, and he sets them not

---

⁶⁵² *Hazel*; the word connotes a tree which spreads out rapidly in the in-between spaces, as of fields and woods.

⁶⁵³ *Plane*; the word connotes a lowland shade tree used to delineate borders.

30:40—31:10

on Laban's flock. ⁴¹ And it becomes in all of conceiving of the flock, the ones being tight, that he places—Jacob—the **rods** to eyes of the flock in the channels, to cause them to conceive in the rods; ⁴² and in drooping of the flock he is not placing; and it becomes, the drooping ones to Laban, and the tight ones to Jacob.

⁴³ And he is breaking forth—the ♂*man*—exceedingly, exceedingly! And it is becoming to him flocks many, and maids, and servants, and camels, and donkeys.

31 And he is hearing **words** of Laban's sons to cause to say, 'He takes—Jacob—**all of** which to our father, and from which to our father, he does **all of** the weight.' ² And he is seeing—Jacob—Laban's face, and behold! *There* is no 'him' with him as before previously[654].

³ And he is saying—Jehovah—to Jacob, 'Return you! to land of your fathers, and to your kindred, and I am with you.'

⁴ And he is sending—Jacob—and he is calling for Rachel and for Leah—the field to his flock. ⁵ And he is saying to them, 'Seeing —I—your father's face that *there* is no 'him' to me as before previously; but my father's God is with me. ⁶ And you—you know that in all of my vigor I serve your **father**, ⁷ and your father, he schemes[655] in me, and he slides[656] my **hire** ten of accountings; but he allows him not—God—to cause to spoil with me. ⁸ 'If thus he is saying, 'Spotted ones, he becomes your hire,' then they birth —all of the flock—spotted ones; and if thus he is saying, 'Striped ones, he becomes your hire,' and they birth—all of the flock—striped ones; ⁹ and he is excising—God—**substance** of your father, and he is giving to me.

¹⁰ 'And it is becoming in the time to conceive of the flock: that I am lifting my eyes, and I am seeing in the dream, and behold! the he-goats, the ones *going* up on the flock: striped ones, spotted

---

[654] *Before previously*; literally *before yesterday three days before.* The extended description of time difference accentuates the fact that more than Jacob's increasing was at play. Laban now has sons, and Jacob's position of primary heir—one of the excuses for giving Leah before Rachel—is no longer viable. Laban's treatment of him is less of family and more of a cash cow... and even that is not materializing the way Laban hoped.

[655] *Schemes*; plots to divide.

[656] *Slides*; resets the equilibrium.

31:10—31:21

ones, and virile ones. ¹¹ And he is saying to me—angel of God—in the dream, Jacob! and I am saying, Behold me!.

¹² 'And he is saying, Lift you! please! your eyes, and see you! all of the he-goats, the ones *going* up on the flock: striped ones, spotted ones, and virile ones; that I see **all of** which Laban does to you. ¹³ I—the God of Bethel⁶⁵⁷ which you anoint there pillar, which you vow to me there vow; now, rise you! *go* forth you! from the land, even this; and return you! to land of your kindred.'

¹⁴ And they are answering—Rachel and Leah—and they are saying to him, '? Still to us portion and inheritance in house of our father? ¹⁵ ? Not strangers we are reckoned to him? that he sells us, and he is devouring also to devour our **silver**. ¹⁶ That all of the wealth which he excises—God—from our father, to us—it—and to our sons. And now, all which he says—God—to you, do you!'

¹⁷ And he is rising—Jacob—and he is lifting his **sons** and his **wives** on the camels, ¹⁸ and he is driving **all of** his substance⁶⁵⁸, and **all of** his acquisitions which he acquires: substance of his acquisitions which he acquires in Padan-Aram, to cause to come to Isaac his father, toward land—Canaan.

¹⁹ And Laban, he goes to cause to shear of his **flock**⁶⁵⁹, and she is stealing, Rachel the teraphim⁶⁶⁰ which, to her father. ²⁰ And he is stealing—Jacob—the heart of Laban the Aramaean over he declares not to him that fleeing—he. ²¹ And he is fleeing, he and

---

⁶⁵⁷ *God of Bethel*; El-Beth-El.

⁶⁵⁸ *Substance*; in terms of livestock, and so throughout.

⁶⁵⁹ Rachel, as well as Jacob, knew that traditionally there was a feast after the a shearing, and that Laban would be out of it for a few days, as Nabal in First Samuel 25.

⁶⁶⁰ *Teraphim*; family gods in the sense of a family crest or coat of arms. The possessor had the rights to final arbitration of any family dispute or litigation; this was Jacob's potential position by marrying Laban's eldest daughter that was being taken from Jacob for Laban's sons. We might say that Rachel stole Laban's right to be the family *godfather* and kept it for Jacob. The word *teraphim* has the dual sense of *healing* (of family disputes) and all *modifications* (of traditions, permissions for marriages, inheritances, etc.).

all of which to him; and he is rising, and he is crossing the River[661], and he is setting his face—mountain of the Gilead[662].

²² And it is being told to Laban in the third day that he flees—Jacob. ²³ And he is taking his brothers with him, and he is pursuing after him, way of seven of days, and he is overtaking **him** in mountain of the Gilead.

²⁴ And he is coming—God—to Laban the Aramaean in the dream of the night, and he is saying to him, 'Guard you! to you, lest you are speaking with Jacob from good to evil.' ²⁵ And he is overtaking—Laban—**Jacob**; and Jacob, he pitches his **tent** in the mountain; and Laban, he pitches *with* his **brothers** in mountain of the Gilead.

²⁶ And he is saying—Laban—to Jacob, 'What ? do you? and you are stealing my **heart**, and you are driving forth my **daughters** as being captives of sword! ²⁷ To what ? you hide to cause to flee? and you are stealing **me**, and you tell not to me, and I am sending you in rejoicing and in songs, in tambourine and in harp, ²⁸ and you include me not to cause to kiss to my sons and to my daughters!—now you are foolish to do. ²⁹ There is power of my hand to cause to do with you evil, but God of your father last night, he speaks to me, to cause to say, Guard you! to you from one speaking with Jacob from good to evil.

³⁰ 'And now, to go you go, that to long you long for your father's house: to what ? you steal my **gods**?'

³¹ And he is answering—Jacob—and he is saying to Laban, 'That I fear; that I say, Lest you are snatching your **daughters** from with me. ³² With whom you are finding your **gods**—he lives not; before our brothers scrutinize you! for yourself what ? *is* with me, and take you! for yourself.' And he knows not—Jacob—that Rachel, she steals them.

---

[661] *The River*; the Euphrates.

[662] *Gilead*; heap of witness; rolling forever; dance of sensuality. It is on the eastern border of the land of Canaan, east of the Jordan, about a 500 mile journey across the desert, or 900 miles along the northern fertile crescent. Jacob wanted to get to a place in which the 'sons of the east' had no political jurisdiction. In order to make the journey in ten days, he would have been driving the livestock as fast as they could withstand.

31:33—31:44

³³ And he is coming—Laban—in Jacob's tent, and in Leah's tent, and in two of the maid's tents, and he finds not. And he is *com*ing forth from Leah's tent, and he is coming in Rachel's tent.

³⁴ And Rachel—she takes the **teraphim**, and she is putting them in the camel's saddle, and and she is sitting on them. And he is feeling—Laban—**all of** the tent, and he finds not. ³⁵ And she is saying to her father, 'As not so it is angering in eyes of my lord that I am not *be*ing able to cause to rise from your face, that way of women to me.' And he is searching, and he finds not the **teraphim**.

³⁶ And he is angering—Jacob—and he is contending with Laban. And he is answering—Jacob—and he is saying to Laban, 'What ? my trespass? What ? my sin, that you burn[663] after me? ³⁷ that you feel **all of** my furnishings: What ? find you from **all of** the furnishings of your house? place you! thus before my brothers and your brothers, and they judge between both of us.

³⁸ 'This twenty Year, I with you; your ewes and your she-goats miscarry not, and the rams of your flock I eat not; ³⁹ one torn I bring not to you; I—I bear her; from my hand you seek her. One being stolen of day and one being stolen of night I become; ⁴⁰ in the day he consumes me—drought, and frost in the night, and she is wandering[664]—my sleep—from my eyes.

⁴¹ 'This—to me—twenty Year in your house: I serve you four ten[665] Year in your two daughters, and six of years in your flock; and you slide my hire ten of times; ⁴² unless the God of my father, God of Abraham, and the Fear of Isaac[666], is to me, that now empty you send me away; my **humiliation** and **toil** of my hands he sees—God—and he is judging last night.'

⁴³ And he is answering—Laban—and he is saying to Jacob, 'The daughters, my daughters; and the sons, my sons, and the flock, my flock, and all which, you seeing, to me him. And to my daughters, what ? do I to these today, or to their sons whom they birth? ⁴⁴ And now, come you! We cut covenant, I and you, and he becomes to witness between me and between you.'

---

[663] *Burn*; the word has the sense of *attack to enfeeble*.
[664] *Wandering*; flitting around.
[665] *Four Ten*; fourteen.
[666] *Fear of Isaac*; this is used as a name of God; see verse 53.

31:45—31:53

⁴⁵ And he is taking—Jacob—stone, and he is raising her, pillar. ⁴⁶ And he is saying—Jacob—to his brothers, 'Pick you up! stones,' and they are taking stones, and are doing heap; and they are eating there on the heap; ⁴⁷ and he is calling to him—Laban—Jegar-Sahadutha[667]; and Jacob, he calls to him Galeed[668].

⁴⁸ And he is saying—Laban—'The heap, even this, witness between me and between you today;' on so he calls its name Galeed ⁴⁹ and the Mizpah[669], which he says, 'He watches—Jehovah—between me and between you, that we are concealed, ♂man from his fellow; ⁵⁰ if you are humiliating[670] my **daughters**, and if you are taking wives over my daughters[671]—*there* is no ♂man with us—see you! God witness between me and between you.'

⁵¹ And he is saying—Laban—to Jacob, 'Behold! the heap, even this; and behold! the pillar which I consecrate between me and between you; ⁵² Witness! the heap, even this; and witness! the pillar; if I pass not to you the **heap**, even this; and if you pass not to me the **heap**, even this; and the **pillar**, even this, for evil[672]. ⁵³ God of Abraham and God of Nahor, they judge between us—God of their father.' And he is swearing—Jacob—in Fear of his father Isaac.[673]

---

[667] *Jegar-Sahadutha*; *Jegar* means fatigue from continued action, *Sahadutha* means *wistfulness* in the sense of coveting property that cannot be obtained or can only be obtained through exhausting difficulty. Laban has in effect named the place, *I am sick and tired of trying to get my stuff back.*

[668] *Galeed*; same word as *Gilead* in verse 21 with the sense of *occasion of certitude.*

[669] *Mizpah*; lookout; watch tower.

[670] *Humiliating*; the word means to treat their long term security fraudulently; i.e., degrade their inheritance. Ironically, this is what he himself had just done.

[671] *Over my daughters*; Laban's fear is that his daughters could be relegated to concubine status, thus eliminating the inheritance rights of his grandsons.

[672] *For evil*; Laban, stripped of the articles of his position as godfather of his clan, wishes to insure that if Jacob *does* have the teraphim, that he will not use it to interfere with Laban's affairs. Likewise he is admitting that his right to interfere with Jacob's affairs is gone.

[673] Laban is distinguishing between the God that Abraham worshipped and the God that Nahor worshipped; in essence appealing to Jacob's identity as of the clan of Eber. Jacob responds by swearing simply by the God of his father Isaac, using the name for God "Fear of Isaac" from verse 42.

31:54—32:10

⁵⁴ And he is sacrificing—Jacob—sacrifice in the mountain, and he is calling to his brothers to cause to eat bread; and they are eating bread, and they are lodging in the mountain. ⁵⁵ And he is rising early—Laban—in the morning, and he is kissing to his sons and to his daughters, and he is blessing **them**[674]; and Laban he is going. And he is returning—Laban—to his place.

32 And Jacob—he goes to his way, and they are impinging on—in him—angels of God. ² And he is saying—Jacob—as when he sees them, 'Camp of God, this;' and he is calling name of the place Mahanaim[675].

³ And he is sending—Jacob—messengers[676] to his face to Esau his brother, towards land of Seir[677], field of Edom. ⁴ And he is instructing **them** to cause to say, 'Thus you say to my lord, to Esau: Thus he says, your servant Jacob: With Laban I sojourn, and I am tarrying until now; ⁵ and it is becoming to me ox and donkey, flock and man-servant, and maids; and I am sending to cause to declare to my lord, to cause to find grace in your eyes.'

⁶ And they are returning—the messengers—to Jacob to cause to say, 'We came in to your brother, to Esau, and also coming to cause to meet you, and four of hundreds ♂man with him.' ⁷ And he is fearing—Jacob—exceedingly, and his is distressing to him, and he is dividing the **people** which with him, and the **flock**, and the **herd**, and the camels, to two of camps. ⁸ And he is saying, 'If he is coming—Esau—to the camp, the one, and he strikes it—and it becomes the camp, the one remaining, to escape.'

⁹ And he is saying—Jacob—'God of my father Abraham, and God of my father Isaac, Jehovah the one saying to me Return you! to your land, and to your kindred, and I *do* good with you, ¹⁰ I *am* unworthy from all of the kindnesses, and from all of the faithfulness which you do with your servant; that, in my staff I

---

[674] *Them* is emphasized to point out that Laban is not blessing Jacob. This is a lead-in to the blessing Jacob obtains from wrestling with the Angel.

[675] *Mahanaim*; camps, or *two camps*. Song of Solomon 6:13 uses this occasion to describe the beauty of one who can operate competently in two realms.

[676] *Messengers*; same word as *angels* in the previous verse, and so throughout.

[677] *Seir*; safeguard of reverence; shaggy; hairy; goat-like; it is used for both hairy goats and devils and satyrs as in Isaiah 13:21 and 34:14, the root meaning *a shudder of horror* or *an opening*.

32:10—32:22

cross the **Jordan**[678], even this, and now I become to two of camps. [11] 'Deliver you me! please! from hand of my brother, from hand of Esau; that fearing I **him**, lest he is coming and he smites me—mother on sons. [12] And you—you say, to do good, I do good with you, and I set your **seed** as sand of the sea, which, he is not numbered from multitude.'

[13] And he is lodging there in the night, even him. And he is taking from the one coming in his hand, present for Esau his brother: [14] she-goats *two* hundreds, and bucks twenty; ewes *two* hundreds, and rams twenty; [15] camels, ones suckling, and their sons thirty, young cows forty, and young bulls ten; she-donkeys twenty, and foals ten. [16] And he is giving in hand of his servants, drove, drove to himself; and he is saying to his servants, 'Pass you! to my face; and spirit you put between drove and between drove.'

[17] [679]And he is instructing the **first**, to cause to say, 'That he is encountering you—Esau my brother—and he asks you, to cause to say, To whom ? and to where ? you are going? and to whom ? these to your face? [18] and you say, to your servant, to Jacob; she *is* present being sent to my lord, to Esau; and behold! he also behind us.'

[19] And he is instructing also the **second**, also the **third**, also **all of** the ones going after the droves, to cause to say, 'As the word, even this, you speak to Esau in your causing to meet **him**, [20] and you say also, Behold! your servant Jacob behind us;' that he says, 'I shelter his face in the present, the one going to my face, and after so, I see his face; perhaps he lifts up my face.' [21] And she is passing—the present—on his face; and he lodges in the night, even he, in the camp.

[22] And he is rising in the night, the same, and he is taking **two of** his wives, and **two of** his maids, and **one of** ten[680], his children,

---

[678] *Jordan*; bowing to judgment; to descend.
[679] In this paragraph a burst of Hebrew verb tenses rarely used since the first chapter are employed.
[680] *One of ten*; eleven; though in the expression, only *one of* is emphasized. It is also peculiar that Dinah, who would bring the number of children to twelve, is not counted even though it says 'children' instead of 'sons'.

32:22—32:28

and he is crossing **crossing of** Jabbok[681]. 23 And he is taking them, and he is causing them to cross the **brook**, and he is causing to cross . . .**which to** him[682].

24 And he is being left[683]—Jacob—to his aloneness, and he is wrestling—♂man—with him until ascending of the dawn. 25 And he is seeing that he is not able—to him; and he is touching[684] in hollow of his thigh, and she is straining, hollow of Jacob's thigh, in his causing to wrestle with him. 26 And he is saying, 'Send you me *away*! that he ascends—the dawn.' And he is saying, 'I send you not, except if—you bless me.'

27 And he is saying to him, 'What ? your name?' And he is saying, 'Jacob.' 28 And he is saying, 'Jacob he says not any more, but Israel[685]; that you measure the age[686] with God and with •men, and

---

[681] *Jabbok*; he will empty out; forever evacuating. This stream runs through a deep and wild ravine on the east of the land of Canaan halfway between the Dead Sea and the Sea of Galilee. It was the northern border of the Ammonites, and later the border between Reuben and the half tribe of Manasseh.

[682] ...***Which to*** *him*; normally the text would read ***all of*** *which to him*; a hiatus in the text is introduced to emphasize that the issue is in doubt of what that may end up being with Esau coming. Yet the text maintains the emphasis.

[683] *Left*; a strong word implying both what is left over and what abounds as extra. There is a strong element of this idea in the name *Israel*, though constructed with differing letters.

[684] *Touching*; also meaning to strike.

[685] *Israel*: he is prince of God; he will rule as God. These first two are given as the standard division into the three roots *he*, *to prevail* (as a prince or ruler), and *strength* or *El*, which fit the context. Underlying these is the two root meaning composed of *substantiality* or *being*, and *to fix the gaze upon for effect* in the sense of Proverbs 20:8, *A king sitting on the throne of judgment scatters away all evil with his eyes.* This latter root could also be stated *whatever he looks upon he takes*. The combination of these gives the meaning for Israel as *the chosen overcomer* or *♂man of the kingdom*; i.e. the Messiah. Also hidden in the name are the ideas of *that which liberates*, *that which is left over and abounds as extra* (see note on *left* verse 24), and *leaping like a deer* (with joy) as the last verse of Song of Solomon. Throughout all of these there is a sense of being a lone individual.

[686] *Measure the age*; the common translation as *prince* denotes but half of the richness of this word. It is *to stand as a bulwark forever, liberating captives from their life sentences*, and *the fortress to which all times return*. Thus *measure the age* connotes both the action and the strength from which that action is taken.

you return the spoil[687].' ²⁹ And he is asking—Jacob—and he is saying, 'Declare! please! your name.' And he is saying, 'To what ? this; you are asking to name of <u>me</u>?' And he is blessing **him** there.

³⁰ And he is calling—Jacob—name of the place Peniel[688]: that 'I see God face to face, and she is being rescued—my soul.' ³¹ And he is rising to him—the sun—as when he passes over **Penuel**[689], and he is limping on his thigh; ³² on this they eat not—the sons of Israel—**tendon** of the one wounded[690], which *is* on hollow of the thigh to this day, even this; that he touches in hollow of Jacob's thigh, in tendon of the one wounded.

33 And he is lifting—Jacob—his eyes, and he is seeing and behold! Esau coming, and with him four of hundreds ♂man. And he is dividing the **children** on Leah, and on Rachel, and on two of the maids. ² And he is placing the **maids** and their **children** first, and **Leah** and her children following, and **Rachel** and **Joseph** following.

³ And he, he passes to their face, and he is bowing himself down earthwards seven times, until to his nearing to his brother. ⁴ And he is running—Esau—to cause to meet him, and he is embracing him, and he is falling on his neck, and he is kissing him, and they are weeping. ⁵ And he is lifting his **eyes**, and he is seeing the **women** and the **children**, and he is saying, 'Who ? these to you?' And he is saying, 'The children whom he graces—God—your **servant**.'

---

[687] *Return the spoil*; the idea of spoil is from the context here; the word means to prevail and return in an opposing scenario; to bring things back to where your strength or plans reside.

[688] *Peniel*; face of God. There is the sense here that God's face is turned and inclined toward him.

[689] *Penuel*; face of God. The switch from *Peniel* to *Penuel* connotes that more than just meets they eye has occurred. The first has the sense that Jacob has seen God face to face, and is continuing on. The second has the sense that a profound mystery has been unfolded, and that there is no passing from it. It is remarkable how the text points out that an inconceivable mystery is to be found in the account with the change of only one letter, and emphasis on that change.

[690] *Wounded*; the Hebrew word is stronger, connoting that there was a wounding of the life force itself.

33:6—33:17

⁶ And they are nearing—the maids—they and their children, and they are bowing themselves down. ⁷ And she is nearing also—Leah and her children—and they are bowing themselves down; and afterward he nears—Joseph and Rachel—and they are bowing themselves down.

⁸ And he is saying, 'Who ? to you, all of the camp, even this, which I encounter?' And he is saying, 'To cause to find grace in my lord's eyes.' ⁹ And he is saying—Esau—'Much is to me, my brother: to you which is to you.'

¹⁰ And he is saying—Jacob—'Not so! please! if please—I find grace in your eyes and you accept my present from my hand, that on this I see your face, as to see of face of God, and you are satisfied⁶⁹¹ *with* me. ¹¹ Take you! please! my **blessing**, which, she is brought to you; that he graces me—God—and that all is to me.' And he is urging in him, and he is accepting. ¹² And he is saying, 'We journey and we go; and I go to your front.'

¹³ And he is saying to him, 'My lord, knowing that the children—tender ones—and the flock and the herd—ones unweaned—on me, and they overdrive them; day one, and they die—all of the flock. ¹⁴ He passes, please!—my lord—to his servant's face, and I—I meander⁶⁹² to my whisperings⁶⁹³, to the task's pace which *is* to my face, and to the children's pace, until which—I am coming to my lord, toward Seir⁶⁹⁴.'

¹⁵ And he is saying—Esau—'I place, please! with you from the people whom—me.' And he is saying, 'To what ? this? I am finding grace in my lord's eyes.'

¹⁶ And he is turning back in the day, even he—Esau—to his way toward Seir. ¹⁷ And Jacob—he journeys toward Succoth⁶⁹⁵, and he

---

⁶⁹¹ *Satisfied*; the word connotes also satisfaction of the payment of a debt.

⁶⁹² *Meander*; to move along piece by piece; the image is from a stream meandering over its rocks. Jacob is not just being reticent to accompany Esau here; he had just pushed his flock to the limit making record time across the desert getting away from Laban.

⁶⁹³ *To my whisperings*; while the word can mean simply *gently*, it is properly the murmurings and whisperings of divination.

⁶⁹⁴ *Seir*; safeguard of reverence; shaggy; hairy; goat-like; it is used for both hairy goats and devils and satyrs as in Isaiah 13:21 and 34:14, the root meaning *a shudder of horror* or *an opening*.

is building for himself, house[696], and for his cattle he does booths, on this has he calls name of the place Succoth.

[18] And he is coming—Jacob— . . . peaceful city of Shechem[697], which *is* in land of Canaan, in his causing to come from Padan-Aram, and he is camping *with* **face** of the city, [19] and he is procuring **allotment** of the field where he stretches there his tent, from hand of sons of Hamor[698], father of Shechem, in hundred kesitah[699]. [20] And he is placing there, altar, and he is calling to him —God, God of Israel[700].

34 And she is *going* forth—Dinah daughter of Leah whom she has borne to Jacob—to cause to appear among daughters of the land.[701] [2] And he is seeing **her**—Shechem son of Hamor the Hivite, prince of the land—and he is taking **her**, and he is lying *with* **her**, and he is humbling her. [3] And she is clinging—his soul —in Dinah, daughter of Jacob, and he is loving the maiden, and he is speaking on the the maiden's heart.

[4] And he is saying—Shechem—to Hamor his father, to cause to say 'Take you! for me the **girl**, even this, for wife.' [5] And Jacob— he hears that he defiles **Dinah** his daughter; and his sons, they are

---

[695] *Succoth*; booths; a round structure more permanent than a tent; we might say a *yurt*. It is the same word as *booths* later in the verse.

[696] *House*; the sense is establishing the beginnings of a permanent center. The next chapter become relevant to this sense, as Jacob had to abandon his place.

[697] *Shechem*: back, shoulder blade, mountain slope; same word as Japheth and Shem putting the cloak on their *backs* to cover Noah's nakedness. This was the first stop of Abram when he entered the land, and where God appeared to him. Contrasted in the verse with Padan-Aram where Laban lived, it would indicate that this was Jacob's first full stop.

[698] *Hamor*; an ass (donkey); obtuse and vain.

[699] *Kesitah*; bullion. As Jacob had just made his fortunes in a foreign land, he did not yet have Canaanite currency to use in his transactions, in which case the word *shekel* would have been used. So he had to weigh out bars of bullion for his purchase; and as a foreigner he is paying about twice the land worth. This word is also used at the end of the book of Job when each of his friends gave him a *kesitah*, indicating that they were from far and wide.

[700] *God, God of Israel*; El-Eloahe-Israel, a new name for God.

[701] The sense is that Dinah wished to put herself on display with the daughters of the land who displayed themselves.

34:5—34:19

with his **cattle** in the field; and he broods⁷⁰²—Jacob until their coming.

⁶ And he is *going* forth—Hamor, father of Shechem—to Jacob to cause to speak with him. ⁷ And sons of Jacob—they come from the field as their hearing. And they are grieving⁷⁰³—the •men—and it is heating to them exceedingly, that decadence he does in Israel, to cause to lie *with* **daughter** of Jacob—and so it is not done.

⁸ And he is speaking—Hamor—with them to cause to say, 'Shechem my son, she attaches—his soul—in your daughter; give you! please! **her** to him for a wife, ⁹ and intermarry you! with us; your daughters you give to us, and our **daughters** you take for you, ¹⁰ and with us you dwell. And the land—she is to your face; dwell you! and merchandise her! and possess in her!'

¹¹ And he is saying—Shechem—to her father, and unto her brothers, 'I find grace in your eyes, and what you say to me, I give; ¹² increase you! on me exceedingly dowry and gift, and I give as what you say to me; and give you! to me the **maiden** for wife.'

¹³ And they are responding—sons of Jacob—**Shechem** and **Hamor** his father in deceit, and they are responding, which he defiles **Dinah** their sister, ¹⁴ and they are saying to them, 'We are not able to cause to do the word, even this, to cause to give our **sister** to ♂man who, for him, foreskin; that disgrace—she—to us.

¹⁵ 'Yes, in this we consent to you; if you become as us, to cause to circumcise to you all of male. ¹⁶ And we give our **daughters** to you, and your **daughters** we take for us, and we dwell with **you**, and we become to one people. ¹⁷ And if you are not listening to us to cause to be circumcised, and we take our **daughter**, and we go.'

¹⁸ And they are pleasing—their words—in eyes of Hamor, and in eyes of Shechem Hamor's son. ¹⁹ And he delays not—the boy—to cause to do the matter, that he delights in Jacob's daughter, and he being great from all of house of his father.

---

⁷⁰² *Broods*; the idea is being silent while making plans. The word is translated *artificer* twice in the prophets.

⁷⁰³ *Grieving*; this word also means 'formulating plans' just as 'brooding' also means 'keeping silent'.

34:20—34:29

²⁰ And he is coming—Hamor and his son Shechem—to gate of their city; and they are speaking to •men of their city, to cause to say, ²¹ 'The •men, even these, peaceful⁷⁰⁴ ones, they with us. And they dwell in the land, and they merchandise **her**; and the land, behold! broad of hands to their face; their **daughters** we take for us for wives, and our **daughters** we give to them.

²² 'Yes, in this they consent to us—the •men—to cause to dwell with us, to cause to become to one people, in causing to be circumcised to us all of male, as which they—circumcised ones. ²³ Their cattle, and their substance, and all of their beasts ? —*are* they not ours? Yes, we consent to them, and they dwell with us.'

²⁴ And they are listening to Hamor and to Shechem his son, all of those *go*ing forth of gate of his city, and they are being circumcised—every male—all those *go*ing forth of gate of his city.

²⁵ And it becomes, in the day, the third, in their becoming ones suffering, that they are taking—two of Jacob's sons—Simeon and Levi, Dinah's brothers—♂man his sword, and they are coming on the city—trusting one—and they are killing all of male. ²⁶ And **Hamor**, and his son **Shechem** they kill to sword's mouth; and they are taking **Dinah** from Shechem's house, and they are *go*ing forth.

²⁷ Jacob's sons!—they come on the slain ones, and they plunder the city which, they defile their sister; ²⁸ their **flock** and their **herd**, and their **donkeys**, and **what** *is* in the city, and **what** *is* in the field, they take. ²⁹ And **all of** their estate⁷⁰⁵, and **all of** their infants⁷⁰⁶, and their **wives** they take captive, and they are plundering! —and **all of**. which, in the house.⁷⁰⁷

---

⁷⁰⁴ *Peaceful*; same word as 33:18.

⁷⁰⁵ *Estate*; the word has the sense of both that which has been gathered over a long period and that in which one hopes, as in an inheritance. Properly, *the full vigor of one"s substance*. It carries with it the idea of the extreme effort by which one gathers and maintains the substance.

⁷⁰⁶ *Infants*; the word has the sense of families of infants.

⁷⁰⁷ *What. . . what . . all of*; The character of the plundering is dramatically given by the text leaving out *all of* before the *what* (*which*) twice, then emphasizing *all of* three times. It is as if the scribe is throwing up his hands in an effort to describe the vehemence with which they plunder ...in contrast to the normal manner in which the killing of Hamor and Shechem is

34:30—35:8

³⁰ And he is saying—Jacob—to Simeon and to Levi, 'You trouble **me**, to cause me to stink in inhabitant of the land, in the Canaanite, and in the Perizzite: and I—numbered as dead; and they are gathered on me, and they smite me, and I am destroyed—I—and my house.' ³¹ And they are saying, '? As the prostitute he makes our sister?'

35 And he is saying—God—to Jacob, 'Rise you! go up you!—Bethel—and dwell you! there; and make you! there, altar to God[708], the one appearing to you in your fleeing from Esau your brother's face.'

² And he is saying—Jacob—to his house, and to all of, which with him, 'Turn aside you! **gods** of the foreigner which, in middle of you, and clean yourselves! and change you! your garments; ³ and we rise, and we go up—Bethel, and I make there altar to God—the one answering **me** in day of my distress, and he is with me in the way I go.'

⁴ And they are giving to Jacob **all of** gods of the foreigner which, in their hand, and the **rings** which, in their ears. And he is burying **them**[709]—Jacob—under the oak which, with Shechem. ⁵ And they are journeying, and he is becoming, terror[710] of God on the cities which *are* round about them, and they pursue not after Jacob's sons.

⁶ And he is coming—Jacob—toward Luz which *is* in the land of Canaan—she *is* Bethel—he and all of the people who, with him. ⁷ And he is building there, altar, and he is calling to the place, God of Bethel[711]: that there they are exposed to him—the gods—in his fleeing from his brother's face.

⁸ And she is dying—Deborah, one suckling of Rebecca—and she is being buried from beneath to Bethel under the oak, and he is calling his name 'Oak of Lamenting.'

---

    described. The implication is that the attraction to plunder was more important to Jacob''s sons than the retrieval of their sister. In the following verse Jacob emphasizes *you trouble* **me**, in contrast with the city that they have troubled, to show them what they have done.

[708] *God*; El. Same with verse 3.

[709] *Burying* **them**; this would likely include the teraphim. Jacob buries them in the event that he needs to retrieve them in the future; see verse 7.

[710] *Terror*; an extreme expression; shock and terror; complete dismay.

[711] *God of Bethel*; El Bethel.

⁹ And he is appearing—God—to Jacob further, in his coming from Padan-Aram, and he is blessing **him**. ¹⁰ And he is saying to him—God—'Your name—Jacob—it is not called your name still —Jacob—but rather Israel, he is becoming your name;' and he is calling his **name** Israel.

¹¹ And he is saying to him—God—'I ! God Providence⁷¹²; Fruitful you! and increase you! Nation and assembly of nations it becomes from you, and kings from your loins, they *go* forth; ¹² and the **land** which I give to Abraham and to Isaac, to you I am giving her and to your seed after you: I am giving the **land**.' ¹³ And he is ascending from on him—God—in the place where he speaks with him.

¹⁴ And he is setting up—Jacob—pillar in the place where he speaks with him, pillar of stone; and he is anointing on her libation, and he is pouring on her oil⁷¹³. ¹⁵ And he is calling— Jacob—**name** of the place where he speaks with him there—God —Bethel.

¹⁶ And they are journeying from Bethel, and he is becoming yet pausing⁷¹⁴ of the land to cause to come *to* Ephrath⁷¹⁵, and she is birthing—Rachel—and is paining⁷¹⁶ in her birthing. ¹⁷ And it is becoming, in her depths of life-pangs in her birthing, and she is saying to her—the one midwifing—'As nothing you are fearing; that also this, to you, son.'

¹⁸ And it is becoming, in her soul's *going* forth, that she dies. And she is calling his name Ben-Oni⁷¹⁷; but his father, he calls to him

---

⁷¹² *God Providence*; El Shaddai.

⁷¹³ *Anointing... libation, pouring... oil*; see 28:18 where Jacob does the latter; the anointing with a libation is new.

⁷¹⁴ *Pausing*; a place near either a destination or place one is leaving where one gathers one's affairs for the journey or arrival. The nearest English would be a *rest stop*.

⁷¹⁵ *Ephrath*; interruption; the idea is of almost reaching a life-goal, and suddenly being arrested. It has also the sense of falling silent in the middle of a sentence.

⁷¹⁶ *Paining*; stiffening up with pain; the word connotes difficulty in moving and the groaning that accompanies.

⁷¹⁷ *Ben-Oni*; son of my vanishing desire. The root means both *virility* and the loss thereof depending on context.

35:18—35:29

Benjamin[718]. ¹⁹ and she is dying—Rachel—and she is being buried in road of Ephrath; she—Bethlehem[719]. ²⁰ And he is setting up—Jacob—pillar over her tomb; she—pillar of Rachel's tomb to this day.

²¹ And he is journeying—Israel—and he is stretching his tent some distance[720] to Migdal-Eder[721]. ²² And it is becoming in causing to tabernacle—Israel—in the land, even her, and he is going—Reuben—and he is lying *with* **Bilhah** his father's concubine; and he is hearing—Israel.

²³ And they are—sons of Jacob—two ten[722]. Sons of Leah, Jacob's first-born Reuben; and Simeon, and Levi, and Judah, and Issachar, and Zebulun. ²⁴ Sons of Rachel: Joseph and Benjamin. ²⁵ And sons of Bilhah, Rachel's maid: Dan and Naphtali. ²⁶ And sons of Zilpah, Leah's maid: Gad and Asher. These, sons of Jacob, whom, he is born to him in Padan-Aram[723].

²⁷ And he is coming—Jacob—to Isaac his father; Mamre, Kirjath-Arba[724]; she—Hebron[725] where he sojourns there—Abraham and Isaac. ²⁸ And they are becoming—days of Isaac—hundred of Year and eighty Year. ²⁹ And he is expiring—Isaac—and he is dying, and he is being gathered to his people, aged and satisfied of days; and they are entombing **him**—Esau and Jacob his sons.

---

[718] *Benjamin*; son of the right hand; center of propagation; the idea is strong individuality that becomes a multitude, hence used for the *right hand*.

[719] *Bethlehem*; house of bread.

[720] *Some distance*; this preposition occurs but three times in scripture; literally it means *far from, but as close as one is willing.*

[721] *Migdal-Eder*; Tower of flocks.

[722] *Two ten*; twelve.

[723] *Born to him in Padan-Aram*; this is a curious expression as it is put in the singular; also Benjamin was born in the land of Canaan.

[724] *Kirjath-Arba*; or 'city' of Arba where Sarah died; see 23:2. *Kirjath-Arba* means city of four; the sign of self-knowing (*Kirjath*) with a vigorous exclamation or effort (*Arba*), i.e., satisfaction that you have gone as far as you can go. Joshua 15:13 tells us that Arba was the father of the Anakim, the giants. Caleb drove out the three families of giants from there, leaving the question of who was the fourth.

[725] *Hebron*; seat of association; communion; a deep hidden love against the background of the murmur of all the elements of life.

36 And these, genealogies of Esau; he—Edom.

² Esau!—he takes his **wives** from daughters of Canaan: **Adah**[726] daughter of Elon[727] the Hittite, and **Oholibamah**[728] daughter of Anah[729], daughter of Zibeon[730] the Hivite[731], ³ and **Basmath**[732] daughter of Ishmael, sister of Nebaioth[733]. ⁴ And she is birthing—Adah—for Esau, **Eliphaz**[734]; and Basmath, she births **Reuel**[735]; ⁵ and Oholibamah, she births **Jeush**[736], and **Jaalam**[737], and **Korah**[738]. These, sons of Esau, who, they are born to him in land of Canaan.

⁶ And he is taking—Esau—his **wives**, and his **sons**, and his **daughters**, and **all of** his house's souls, and his **cattle**, and **all of** his beasts, and **all of** his substance which he acquires in land of Canaan, and he is going to the land from face of Jacob his brother; ⁷ that he becomes, their substance, vast from causing to

---

[726] *Adah*; ornament; periodic order; voluptuousness.
[727] *Elon*; might; plain; region of night-watchings.
[728] *Oholibamah*; tent of the high place; tabernacle of God; the word connotes a sacred dwelling that is mobile.
[729] *Anah*; afflicted; answered; properly, *a new beginning and the sorrow that comes of it*; resultant gloom.
[730] *Zibeon*; regulated by temporality. This word comes the closest to the the New Testament concept of the *flesh*; that which collectively stands as a barrier to create a law of crushing limitation.
[731] *Hivite*; natural living, animalistic lives. The Hivites were from the 6th son of Canaan, see 10:16.
[732] *Basmath*; spice; reflection on death. The idea is pausing to introspect on the transition to universal sameness. As such, it could be the name given her upon marrying Esau; the return from Ishmael to Isaac's line carries the same idea.
[733] *Nebaioth*; prophecies; increasings; heights. Nebaioth was the firstborn of Ishmael, as such his daughter Basmath likely held a royal position.
[734] *Eliphaz*; God of fine gold; power of continuous joy; strength of purity.
[735] *Reuel*; 'associate with God'' is the commonly given meaning, yet properly it is *the power to disrupt* or *strong infraction*.
[736] *Jeush*; continual building; overwhelming circumstances. It is working with difficulty amid a crowd of indistinguishable noise or influence.
[737] *Jaalam*; secretive; gathering profit; receptive to a mutual bond. The latter is the idea of someone who unites a family.
[738] *Korah*; ice; bald; the effort to record the memory of things and proclaim them.

36:7—36:14

dwell together; and she is not able—the land of their sojournings—to cause to bear **them** from face of their cattle. ⁸ And he is dwelling—Esau—in mountains of Seir. Esau—he, Edom.

⁹ <u>And these; the genealogies of Esau, father of Edom, in mountains of Seir.</u>[739]

¹⁰ These: names of Esau's sons: Eliphaz son of Adah, wife of Esau; Reuel son of Bashemath, wife of Esau.

¹¹ And they are becoming—sons of Eliphaz—Teman[740], Omar[741], Zepho[742], and Gatam[743], and Kenaz[744]. ¹² And Timna[745]—she becomes concubine to Eliphaz Esau's son, and she is giving birth for Eliphaz, **Amalek**[746]. These: sons of Adah wife of Esau.

¹³ And these; sons of Reuel: Nahath[747] and Zerah[748], Shammah[749] and Mizzah[750]; these, they become sons of Basmath wife of Esau.

¹⁴ And these, they become sons of Oholibamah, daughter of Anah, daughter of Zibeon, wife of Esau; and she is birthing for Esau **Jeush** and **Jaalam** and **Korah**.

---

[739] This strange chapter has a few peculiarities that need pointed out. Verse 31 points out the list included kings who reigned before Israel had a king; thus we conclude that parts of this were written long after the initial record had been put down by Moses. One constant aim of this careful list of both Esau''s chiefs and the sons of Seir the Horite is to show that Esau kept his lineage separate. The one exception is with Timna in verse 12, which results in the Amalekites, a people who were a constant thorn in the side of Israel.

[740] *Teman*; southward; measure of influence; the extension of balance.

[741] *Omar*; saying; desire and consent to rule.

[742] *Zepho*; overflowing; the idea has the sense of waters bursting from the mouth that flood, as Revelation 12:15.

[743] *Gatam*; bursting with virtue; shout of truth.

[744] *Kenaz*; central force dispersing.

[745] *Timna*; agreeable in virtue; the word connotes uncertainty or weakness that produces an amiable character.

[746] *Amalek*; people of licking up; bond of instruction.

[747] *Nahath*; a portion of rest; also *descent into rest* connoting *dismay*.

[748] *Zerah*; dispersion of effort; working as a stranger.

[749] *Shammah*; ambition of life; becoming a name.

[750] *Mizzah*; dazzling radiance. The sense is a strong presence that manifests itself through reflecting the light.

36:15—36:22

¹⁵ These: chieftains of the sons of Esau: sons of Eliphaz, first-born of Esau: chieftain Teman, chieftain Omar, chieftain Zepho, chieftain Kenaz, ¹⁶ chieftain Korah, chieftain Gatam, chieftain Amalek; these: chieftains of Eliphaz, in land of Edom; these: sons of Adah.

¹⁷ And these: sons of Reuel son of Esau: chieftain Nahath, chieftain Zerah, chieftain Shammah, chieftain Mizzah; these: chieftains of Reuel, in land of Edom; these: sons of Basmath Esau's wife.

¹⁸ And these: sons of Oholibamah Esau's wife: chieftain Jeush, chieftain Jaalam, chieftain Korah; these: chieftains of Oholibamah daughter of Anah, Esau's wife.

¹⁹ These: Esau's sons and these their chieftains—he, Edom.

²⁰ These: sons of Seir the Horite[751], inhabitants of the land:

Lotan[752], and Shobal[753], and Zibeon, and Anah[754], ²¹ and Dishon[755], and Ezer[756], and Dishan[757]; these: chieftains of the Horite, sons of Seir, in land of Edom.

²² And they are becoming—sons of Lotan—Hori[758] and Heman[759]; and sister of Lotan: Timna[760].

---

[751] *Horites*; barren or burnt caverns; cave dwellers. See 14:6.

[752] *Lotan*; to hide in a tent or behind a veil. As an interjection is connotes *Oh that things were consistent!*

[753] *Shobal*; flowing; abundance in proportion; spiritual equality.

[754] *Zibeon and Anah*; see verse 2. Anah was Zibeon's daughter and the mother of Esau's wife Oholibamah.

[755] *Dishon*; indolent threshing; delicate propagation; years of abundance.

[756] *Ezer*; treasure; pushing to the limit.

[757] *Dishan*; same as *Dishon* without the vowel points; carefree threshing; pleasurable propagation; creating abundance.

[758] *Hori*; my cave; continual burning to consumption.

[759] *Heman*; to put into commotion; properly, it is the instigation of collective action that has yet to be manifested as what it is; as Acts 19:32, "...for the assembly (mob) was tumultuous, and the most did not know for what cause they had come together."

[760] *Timna*; agreeable in virtue; the word connotes uncertainty or weakness that produces an amiable character; see verse 11.

36:23—36:28

²³ And these: sons of Shobal: Alvan⁷⁶¹ and Manahath⁷⁶², and Ebal⁷⁶³, Shepho⁷⁶⁴ and Onam⁷⁶⁵.

²⁴ And these: sons of Zibeon and Ajah⁷⁶⁶ and Anah⁷⁶⁷: even Anah who, he finds the **fountains**⁷⁶⁸ in the wilderness, in his grazing the **donkeys** to his father Zibeon.

²⁵ And these: sons of Anah; Dishon, and Oholibamah daughter of Anah.

²⁶ And these: sons of Dishon; Hemdan⁷⁶⁹, and Eshban⁷⁷⁰, and Ithran⁷⁷¹, and Cheran⁷⁷².

²⁷ These: sons of Ezer: Bilhan⁷⁷³, and Zaavan⁷⁷⁴, and Akan⁷⁷⁵.

²⁸ These: sons of Dishan; Uz⁷⁷⁶ and Aran⁷⁷⁷.

---

⁷⁶¹ *Alvan*; aggrandizement; self-interest manifested in the gathering of material or superficial elements.

⁷⁶² *Manahath*; measure of terror; determined consternation.

⁷⁶³ *Ebal*; accumulation of abundance; the idea is the continual development of expansion. Intensified, it can reverse to mean heaps of nothing.

⁷⁶⁴ *Shepho*; prominence; the apparent aspect of anything, particularly the *crux* of the matter or the *message* it delivers.

⁷⁶⁵ *Onam*; desire for sleep; a collective losing of motivation and fading into emptiness.

⁷⁶⁶ *Ajah*; the place of desire; manifestation of the will.

⁷⁶⁷ *Anah*; afflicted; answered; properly, *a new beginning and the sorrow that comes of it*; resultant gloom; see verse 2. Anah and his wife shared the same name, quite possibly as a result of his discovery of the fountains.

⁷⁶⁸ *Fountains*; the word has the sense of underground reservoirs that emerge. Such a discovery would confer a great deal of status on Zibeon's household, possibly how a Hivite rose to prominence among the Horites.

⁷⁶⁹ *Hemdan*; life of contradictions; to find fault with everything, as in playing the 'devil''s advocate''.

⁷⁷⁰ *Eshban*; power and foundation of production, as one who constructs or emanates the unassailable.

⁷⁷¹ *Ithran*; continual murmuring in the sense of answering back; nonstop commentary.

⁷⁷² *Cheran*; shouting of a captain; the signal to act (or remember).

⁷⁷³ *Bilhan*; obvious profusion; the abundance that is here in plain sight.

⁷⁷⁴ *Zaavan*; fearful indolence; the idea is living delicately while cringing in fear of what may happen.

⁷⁷⁵ *Akan*; oppression; tortured by selfishness; anguish of enviousness.

⁷⁷⁶ *Uz*; counsel; consolidating and strengthening; persistence.

⁷⁷⁷ *Aran*; productive individual; the sense is a continual vigorous producing that flows out as from a river.

²⁹ These: chieftains of the Horite; chieftain Lotan, chieftain Shobal, chieftain Zibeon, chieftain Anah, ³⁰ chieftain Dishon, chieftain Ezer, chieftain Dishan; these: chieftains of the Horite to their chieftains in land of Seir.

³¹ And these: the kings whom, they reign in land of Edom to face of reigning of king for sons of Israel. ³² And he is reigning in Edom—Bela[778] son of Beor[779]—and name of his city: Dinhabah[780]. ³³ And he is dying—Bela—and he is reigning in his stead—Jobab[781] son of Zerah[782] from Bozrah[783]. ³⁴ And he is dying—Jobab—and he is reigning in his stead—Husham[784] from land of the Temanite[785]. ³⁵ And he is dying—Husham—and he is reigning in his stead—Hadad[786] son of Bedad[787]—the one smiting **Midian** in field of Moab; and name of his city: Avith[788]. ³⁶ And he is dying—Hadad—and he is reigning in his stead—Samlah[789] from Masrekah[790]. ³⁷ And he is dying—Samlah—and he is reigning in his stead—Saul[791] from Rehoboth[792]—the River. ³⁸ and he is dying—Saul—and he is reigning in his stead—Baal-hanan[793]

---

[778] *Bela*; abundance of material goods; extended, it can mean *want of possessions*.

[779] *Beor*; a burning to annihilation; vain and brutish.

[780] *Dinhabah*; initiating judgment; the sense is the call to order when the judge enters the courtroom.

[781] *Jobab*; unveiling; to open up a room or other void to be shown.

[782] *Zerah*; dispersion of effort; working as a stranger.; see verse 13.

[783] *Bozrah*; sheepfold; literally a fascinating sight in a swamp.

[784] *Husham*; collective greedy haste; the word connotes disorder.

[785] *Temanite*; people of the south; measure of influence; the extension of balance; see *Teman* verse 11.

[786] *Hadad*; apportioned majesty; dividing up and spreading.

[787] *Bedad*; solitary; empathetic sharing.

[788] *Avith*; overturning; continually perverting.

[789] *Samlah*; distinguished movement; the sign (as one's clothing) of where one is heading in life.

[790] *Masrekah*; fading to the touch; tenuous harvest.

[791] *Saul*; asking; the idea is a somewhat plaintive cry between the opposing circumstance of calm and chaos.

[792] *Rehoboth*; infrastructure; public establishments. It was one of the defense-cities that Asshur built to withstand Nimrod in 10:11. This would mean that Saul was likely a Shemite.

[793] *Baal-hanan*; lord of grace; lord of the new fortress.

36:38—37:1

son of Achbor[794]; ³⁹ And he is dying—Baal-hanan son of Achbor—and he is reigning in his stead—Hadar[795]—and name of his city: Pau[796], and his wife's name: Mehetabel[797] daughter of Matred[798], daughter of Mezahab[799].

⁴⁰ And these: names of chieftains of Esau to their families, to their places, in their names: chieftain Timnah[800], chieftain Alvah, chieftain Jetheth[801], ⁴¹ chieftain Oholibamah, chieftain Elah[802], chieftain Pinon[803], ⁴² chieftain Kenaz, chieftain Teman, chieftain Mibzar[804], ⁴³ chieftain Magdiel[805], chieftain Iram[806]. These: chieftains of Edom, to their dwellings, in land of their possession. He—Esau—father of Edom.

37 And he is dwelling—Jacob—in land of his father's sojournings in the land of Canaan.

---

[794] *Achbor*; integrity; practical life distinguished by purity.
[795] *Hadar*; honor in its season.
[796] *Pau*; howling.
[797] *Mehetabel*; activity stirring up to industry.
[798] *Matred*; causing pursuit; continuing; stirring up to take possession.
[799] *Mezahab*; waters of gold.
[800] *Timnah*; similar to verses 11 and 34; agreeable in virtue; the word connotes uncertainty or weakness that produces an amiable character.
[801] *Jetheth*; self-assured success; final return.
[802] *Elah*; an oak; also *Eloah*, the singular name of God.
[803] *Pinon*; turning to the new abundance.
[804] *Mibzar*; a fortress;
[805] *Magdiel*; continual massive and powerful assault.
[806] *Iram*; growth (in an irresistible impulse) to ascend; a central fortress or city.

37:2—37:10

² These: genealogies of Jacob:

Joseph, son of seven of ten Year—he becomes concerned *with* his **brothers** in the flock, and he—boy—*with* **sons** of Bilhah and *with* **sons** of Zilpah his father's wives. And he is bringing—Joseph—**reiteration**[807], concerns, to their father.
³ And Israel—he loves **Joseph** from all of his sons, that, son of possessed years he to him; and makes for him robe of distinctions[808]. ⁴ And they are seeing—his brothers—that **him** he loves—their father—from all of his brothers, and they are hating[809] **him**, and they are not able to speak of him to peace.
⁵ And he is dreaming—Joseph—dream, and he is declaring to his brothers, and they are adding further to hate of **him**. ⁶ And he is saying to them, 'Hear you! please! the dream, even this, which I dream: ⁷ and behold! we—binding bundles in midst of the field, and behold! she rises—my bundle—and also she is set up, and behold! they are surrounding—your bundles—and they are bowing themselves down to my bundle.'
⁸ And they are saying to him—his brothers—'? To reign, you reign over us? or to rule, you rule in us?' And they are adding further to hate of **him**, over his dreams, and over his words.
⁹ And he is dreaming yet another dream, and he is recounting—him—to his brothers, and he is saying, 'Behold! I dream dream further, and behold! the sun and the moon and one of ten[810] stars —ones bowing themselves down to me.'
¹⁰ And he is recounting to his father and to his brothers; and he is hushing[811] in him—his father—and he is saying to him, 'What ? this dream, even this, which you dream? To come, we come[812]—I,

---
[807] *Reiteration*; also could read *their dividing of the household*.
[808] *Distinctions*; many parts of a whole. The idea of a robe of many colors fits, as the distinct colors of the rainbow.
[809] *Hating*; using as the object of their impetuousness. The word connotes immaturity and devisiveness.
[810] *One of ten*; eleven.
[811] *Hushing*; or *rebuking*. The word has the sense of drying something up and a long sadness.
[812] *The dream, even this, which you dream*; if the letters are divided differently, this phrase reads "What? the dream, this very idea? Rachel is dead and gone. ? We come, I and your mother and your brothers..."

and your mother and your brothers—to cause to bow down to you earthward?' ¹¹ And they are envying—his brothers; but his father —he keeps the **word**.

¹² And they are going—his brothers—to cause to feed their father's **flock** in Shechem⁸¹³, ¹³ and he is saying—Israel—to Joseph, '? *Are* not your brothers, ones shepherding⁸¹⁴ in Shechem? Go you! and I send you to them.' And he is saying to him, 'Behold me!;' ¹⁴ And he is saying to him, 'Go you! please! see you! **peace** of your brothers, and **peace** of the flock, and return you me! word.' And he is sending him from vale of Hebron, and he is coming toward Shechem.

¹⁵ And he is finding him—♂man—and behold! deceived⁸¹⁵ in the field. And he is asking him—the ♂man—to cause to say, 'What ? you are seeking?' ¹⁶ And he is saying, 'My **brothers** I *am* seeking; declare you! please! to me at what place they shepherd.' ¹⁷ And he is saying—the ♂man—'They journey from here, that I hear ones saying, We go toward Dothan⁸¹⁶.' And he is going—Joseph—after his brothers, and he is finding them in Dothan⁸¹⁷.

¹⁸ And they are seeing **him** from afar, and in yet he is approaching to them, and they are conspiring *against* **him** to cause to kill him.

¹⁹ And they are saying, ♂man to his brother, 'Behold! Master of the dreams, even this, he comes! ²⁰ And now, carry it out! and we kill him, and we fling him into one of the pits, and we say, Animal—evil⁸¹⁸—she devours him; and we see what ? they become, his dreams.'

---

⁸¹³ *Shechem*; Jacob is looking for the *peace* of his sons and his flock as they were daringly shepherding in the very area that they had left after destroying the city. Normally the cities around would have gathered to retaliate; see 35:5. In verse 15 here we find that Jacob's sons had been being monitored by the residents.

⁸¹⁴ *Shepherding*; without the accent marks, it reads *evil ones*.

⁸¹⁵ *Deceived*; the word connotes that Joseph had deliberately been given misinformation by his brothers regarding their whereabouts.

⁸¹⁶ *Dothan*; dividing the largess.

⁸¹⁷ *Dothan*; Dothan was further north than Shechem. While Shechem was on a three-way trade route, merchants wishing to travel directly to Egypt rather than trade with the Canaanite people of the hill-country would take the Dothan Pass and travel along the flatter western lands. In addition to the lush pasture there, it is implied that Jacob`s sons were attracted to the trading potential of the area.

37:21—37:32

²¹ And he is hearing—Reuben—and he is rescuing him from their hand, and he is saying, 'We smite not soul.' ²² And he is saying to them—Reuben—'Not so—you are shedding blood; fling you! **him** into the pit, even this, which *is* in the wilderness, and hand you are not stretching in him,'—in order to rescue **him** from their hand, to cause to return of him to his father.

²³ And it it is becoming, when he comes—Joseph—to his brothers, and they are stripping **Joseph** of his **robe**, **robe** of the distinctions which *is* on him. ²⁴ And they are taking him, and they are flinging **him** toward the pit, and the pit—empty; there is no water in it.

²⁵ And they are sitting to cause to eat bread, and they are lifting their eyes, and they are seeing, and behold! a caravan of Ishmaelites coming from Gilead, and their camels, ones bearing spices[819] and essential oils[820], and decoctions[821], ones going to cause to descend toward Egypt.

²⁶ And he is saying—**Judah**—to his brothers, 'What ? gain that we kill our **brother**, and we cover his **blood**? ²⁷ Go you! and we sell him to the Ishmaelites, and our hand, she happens not in him; that our brother, our flesh—he *is*.' And they are listening—his brothers.

²⁸ And they are passing—•men, Midianites, ones merchandising—and they are drawing out, and they are raising **Joseph** from the pit, and they are selling **Joseph** to the Ishmaelites in twenty silver, and they are bringing **Joseph** toward Egypt.

²⁹ And he is returning—Reuben—to the pit, and behold! Joseph is not in the pit; and he is tearing his garments, ³⁰ and he is returning to his brothers, and he is saying, 'The boy—he is not, and I—where ? *am* I going?'

³¹ And they are taking the **robe** of Joseph, and they are killing one shaggy of goats, and they are dipping the **robe** in the blood. ³² And they are sending the **robe** of distinctions, and they are

---

[818] *Evil*; there is some irony being employed by the text here, the word *shepherding* from the previous verses being the same.

[819] *Spices*; material extracted by crushing or bruising.

[820] *Essential oils*; concentrated strong mixtures made to last.

[821] *Decoctions*; a mixture concentrated by the perfumers' art used for medicine or ceremonies. The word connotes secrets and mystery.

37:32—38:5

bringing to their father, and they are saying, 'This we find; recognize you! please! the robe of your son—she—or not.' ³³ And he is recognizing her, and he is saying, 'My son's robe. Animal—evil—she devours him: prey! prey!—Joseph!'

³⁴ And he is tearing—Jacob—his clothes, and he is putting sackcloth in his loins, and he is mourning over his son days, many ones. ³⁵ And they are rising—all of his sons and all of his daughters—to cause to comfort him; and he is refusing to allow to be comforted; and he is saying, 'That—I descend to my son mourning toward Sheol,' and he is lamenting **him**—his father.

³⁶ And the Midianites[822]—they sell **him** to Egypt, to Potiphar[823], a eunuch of Pharaoh, head of the executioners.

38 And it is becoming in this period[824], even her, and he is descending—Judah—from his brothers, and he is turning aside unto ♂man, Adullamite[825], and his name, Hirah[826]. ² And he is seeing there—Judah—daughter of ♂man, Canaanite, and his name, Shuah[827], and he is taking her, and he is coming to her.

³ And she is becoming pregnant, and she is birthing son, and he is calling his **name**[828] Er[829]. ⁴ And she is becoming pregnant further, and she is birthing son, and she is calling his **name** Onan[830]. ⁵ And she is adding further, and she is birthing son, and she is calling his

---

[822] *Midianites*; this spelling is slightly different from verse 28. There it is *people of contention; to fully accomplish one's own desires*. here it is *people of custom; to do a transaction in the proper manner*.

[823] *Potiphar*; producing effects from what is spoken; "What I say goes!"

[824] *In this period*; perhaps better expressed *as the result of these things happening*. The word implies that Judah is no longer comfortable continuing in his brothers' company.

[825] *Adullamite*; people of sensual pleasure; transitory friends.

[826] *Hirah*; paleness; troubled by the splendors of life.

[827] *Shuah*; an outcry, as for help.

[828] *Name*; the text's emphasis of the word "name" rather than the name itself is peculiar. It has occurred so far with Seth (twice), Enosh, Adam (in 5), Noah, Abram to Abraham, Sarai to Sarah, Isaac (twice), Bethel (twice), Gad and Asher of Zilpah, Zebulun and Dinah of Leah, Joseph, and Jacob to Israel.

[829] *Er*; passion as an irresistible impulse, as jealousy, rage, or covetousness; vehemence.

[830] *Onan*; propagation of the sense of lost hope; continued nothingness.

name Shelah[831]. And he is in Chezib[832] in her causing to birth **him**.

⁶ And he is taking—Judah—wife for Er his first-born, and her name: Tamar[833]. ⁷ And he is becoming—Er, Judah's first-born—evil in Jehovah's eyes, and he is killing him—Jehovah.

⁸ And he is saying—Judah—to Onan, 'Go you! to your brother's wife, and marry[834] **her**, and raise you! seed to your brother.' ⁹ And he is knowing—Onan—that not to him it becomes—the seed—and it becomes, whenever he comes to his brother's wife, and he ruins toward earth, to cause not to give of seed to his brother. ¹⁰ And it is being evil in Jehovah's eyes—that which he does—and he is killing also **him**.

¹¹ And he is saying—Judah—to Tamar his daughter-in-law, 'Dwell you! widow *of* your father's house, until he grows—Shelah my son.' That he says, 'Lest he is dying, he also, as his brothers.' And she is going—Tamar—and she is dwelling *at* her father's house.

¹² And they are increasing—the days—and she is dying—daughter of Shuah, Judah's wife. And he is being comforted—Judah—and he is ascending on ones shearing of his flock—he and Hirah his friend the Adullamite, toward Timnah[835].

¹³ And it is being declared to Tamar to cause to say, 'Behold! your husband's father ascends toward Timnah to cause to shear his flock.' ¹⁴ And she is turning aside her widowhood clothes from on her, and she is covering in the veil, and she is wrapping herself, and she is sitting in gate of Enaim[836], which, on way of Timnah; that she sees that he is grown—Shelah—and him, she is not given to him for wife.

¹⁵ And he is seeing her—Judah—and he is figuring her to prostituting, that she covers her face. ¹⁶ And he is reaching aside

---

[831] *Shelah*; tranquil life proceeding in order.

[832] *Chezib*; falsify; a lie; enduring within the unification of life and vanity.

[833] *Tamar*; palm tree; pushing virtue to the limit or past the limit.

[834] *Marry*; this word is used only thrice in the text, and always in the context of a brother raising up seed to a dead brother. Literally it is *permanent translation from outside to inside relationship*. There is also a connotation of disgust or spitting, as well as taking part of an enduring mystery.

[835] *Timnah*; apportioning justice.

[836] *Enaim*; people of the fountain; eye of the sea.

38:16—38:29

to her by the way, and he is saying, 'Grant you! please! I come to you;' that he knows not that his daughter-in-law—she. And she is saying, 'What ? you give to me, that you come to me?' ¹⁷ And he is saying, 'I—I send kid of goats from the flock.'
And she is saying, 'Only, you give collateral until you you cause to send.' ¹⁸ And he is saying, 'What ? the collateral which I give to you?' And she is saying, 'Your seal, and your cord, and your staff which, in your hand.' And he is giving to her, and he is coming to her, and she is becoming pregnant to him, ¹⁹ and she is rising, and she is going, and she is turning aside her veil from on her, and she is putting on garments of her widowhood.
²⁰ And he is sending—Judah—**kid** of the goats in hand of his friend the Adullamite, to cause to get the collateral from the woman's hand, and he finds her not. ²¹ And he is asking the •**men** of her place to cause to say, 'Where ? the devoted—she in the Enaim, on the way?' And they are saying, 'She becomes not in this, devoted.'
²² And he is returning to Judah, and he is saying, 'I find her not, and also •men of the place, they say, She becomes not, in this, devoted.' ²³ And he is saying—Judah—'She takes to herself, lest we are becoming to shame; behold! I send the kid, even this, and you, you find her not.'
²⁴ And it is becoming, as from three of months, and it is being declared to Judah to cause to say, 'She prostitutes—Tamar your daughter-in-law—and also, behold! pregnant to prostitution.' And he is saying—Judah—'Bring you her! and she is burned.' ²⁵ She being brought, and she—she sends to her husband's father to cause to say, 'To ♂man who, these to him, I *am* pregnant.' And she is saying, 'Recognize you! please! to whom ? the seal, and the cord, and the staff, even these!'
²⁶ And he is recognizing—Judah—and he is saying, 'She is righteous from me, that on this I give her not to Shelah my son.' And he adds not again to cause to know her.
²⁷ And it is becoming in season of her giving birth, and behold! twins in her womb. ²⁸ And it is becoming in her birthing, and he is giving out hand, and she is taking—the one midwifing—and she is tying on his hand twine, to cause to say, 'This one! he *comes* forth first.' ²⁹ And it is becoming, as to return his hand, and

38:29—39:9

behold! he *comes* forth—his brother—and she is saying, 'What ! you break out; on you the breach[837];' and he is calling his name Pherez[838]; ³⁰ And afterward he *comes* forth—his brother—on his hand the twine, and he is calling his name Zerah[839].

39 And Joseph—he descends toward Egypt. And he is buying him —Potiphar, eunuch of Pharaoh, head of the executioners, Egyptian ♂man—from hand of the Ishmaelites who, they take him down toward there.

² And he is becoming—Jehovah—with Joseph, and he is becoming ♂man accomplishing[840], and he is becoming[841] in his lord's house—the Egyptian, ³ And he is seeing—his lord—that Jehovah *is* with him, and all which he does Jehovah accomplishes in his hand. ⁴ And he is finding—Joseph—favor in his eyes. And he is serving **him**, and he is appointing him over his house, and all of what is to him he gives into his hand.

⁵ And it is becoming from then—he appoints **him** in his house and over all of what is to him—and he is blessing—Jehovah—the Egyptian's house on Joseph's account. And it is becoming—blessing of Jehovah—in all of what is to him in the house and in the field. ⁶ And he is leaving all of which, to him, in Joseph's hand, and he knows not with him anything except only the food which he is eating. And he is—Joseph—lovely of shape and lovely of appearance[842].

⁷ And it is becoming, after these things, that she is lifting—his lord's wife—her **eyes** to Joseph. And she is saying, 'Lie you! with me.' ⁸ And he is refusing, and he is saying to his lord's wife, 'Behold! my lord—he knows not with me, what ? in the house, and all which is to him he gives into my hand. ⁹ No one is greater in the house, even this, from me, and he withholds not from me

---

[837] *Breach*; same word as *break out* in the verse.
[838] *Pherez*; breaking out; a breach.
[839] *Zerah*; dispersing into the air, as radiating. Previously in 36:13 (Esau's grandson by Reuel) the meaning is given as *dispersion of effort; working as a stranger.*
[840] *Accomplishing*; the word means young vigor setting goals and reaching them.
[841] *He is becoming*; in both uses in this verse, it is emphatic, not in the passive sense.
[842] The same expression is used of his mother Rachel in 29:17.

39:9—39:20

anything, except only **you**, in which you—his wife. And how ? do I the evil—the great—even this; and I sin to God.'

¹⁰ And it is becoming, as her arranging⁸⁴³ to Joseph day, day⁸⁴⁴, and he listens not to her, to cause to lie beside her, to cause to be with her. ¹¹ And it becomes as the day, even this, and he is going toward the house to cause to do his work, and there is no ♂man from •men of the house there in the house. ¹² And she is grasping him in his garment to cause to say, 'Lie you! with me.' And he is leaving his garment in her hand, and he is fleeing, and he is *going* forth toward the outside.

¹³ And it is becoming as she sees that he leaves his garment in her hand and he is fleeing toward the outside, ¹⁴ and she is calling to •men of her house, and she is saying to them, to cause to say, 'See you! he brings to us Hebrew ♂man, to cause to sport⁸⁴⁵ in us; he comes to me, to cause to lie with me, and I am calling in loud voice, ¹⁵ and it becomes, as his hearing that I lift up my voice and I am calling, and he is leaving his garment beside me, and he is fleeing, and he is *going* forth toward outside.'

¹⁶ And she is depositing his garment beside her until causing to come—his lord—to his house. ¹⁷ And she is speaking to him according to the words, even these, to cause to say, 'He comes to me—The servant, the Hebrew—whom you bring to us, to cause to sport in me; ¹⁸ and it becomes, as to lift up my voice and I am calling, and he is leaving his garment beside me, and he is fleeing toward the outside.'

¹⁹ And it is becoming, as hearing of—his lord—**words** of his wife, which she speaks to him, to cause to say, 'According to these, he does to me—your servant,' that it is burning—his anger. ²⁰ And he is taking—Joseph's lord—**him**, and he is giving him to the house of the corrections⁸⁴⁶, place of which—prisoners of the king —ones being bound. And he is becoming there in the house of the corrections.

---

⁸⁴³ *Arranging*; the word has the sense of plotting and communicating the plot; she was constantly preparing scenarios and circumstances for them to be together.

⁸⁴⁴ *Day, day*; the Hebrew way of emphasizing *daily*.

⁸⁴⁵ *Sport*; as mocking with Ishmael in 21:9.

⁸⁴⁶ *House of the correction*; the English 'correction house'' captures this; the word also connotes the sense of a *tower* and a *place of silence*.

39:21—40:13

²¹ And he is becoming—Jehovah—with Joseph; and he is stretching out to him kindness, and he is giving his grace in eyes of chief of the house of the corrections. ²² And he is giving—chief of the house of the corrections—in Joseph's hand, **all of** the prisoners who, in the house of the corrections, and **all of** which they do there, he is doing. ²³ Nothing is chief of the house of the corrections seeing—**any of** anything—in his hand, in which Jehovah *is* with him, and what he does, Jehovah accomplishes[847].

40 And it is becoming, after the matters, even these, they sin—the cupbearer of king of Egypt and the baker— to their lord, to king of Egypt. ² And he is being angry—Pharaoh—over two of his two eunuchs, over chief of the cupbearers, and over chief of the bakers. ³ And he is giving **them** in ward of house of chief of the executioners, to house of the corrections, place of which Joseph is bound there. ⁴ And he is charging—chief of the executioners—Joseph with them, and he is serving **them**; and they are becoming days in ward.

⁵ And they are dreaming dream, two of them, ♂man his dream in one night, ♂man as interpretation of his dream, the cupbearer and the baker, whom, to the king of Egypt, whom, prisoners in the house of the corrections.

⁶ And he is coming to them—Joseph—in the morning, and he is seeing **them**, and behold them! —ones agitated. ⁷ And he is asking Pharaoh's **eunuchs** who, with him in ward of his lord's house, to cause to say, 'Why ? your faces bad to-day?' ⁸ And they are saying to him, 'Dream we dream, and interpreter—**he** is not.' And he is saying to them—Joseph—'? *Are* not interpretations to God? recount you! please! to me.'

⁹ And he is relating—chief of the cupbearers—his **dream** to Joseph, and he is saying to him, 'In my dream, and behold! vine to my face! ¹⁰ And in the vine, three tendrils, and she—as one budding; she lifts her blossoms: her clusters, they ripen grapes. ¹¹ And Pharaoh's cup *is* in my hand, and I am taking the **grapes** and I am pressing **them** to Pharaoh's cup, and I am presenting the **cup** on Pharaoh's palm.'

¹² And he is saying—Joseph—'This, his interpretation: three of the tendrils, three of days—they. ¹³ In still three of days he lifts—

---

[847] *Accomplishes*; as verse 2; *brings to fruition*.

40:13—41:4

Pharaoh—your **head**, and he restores you on your station; and you present Pharaoh's cup in his hand, according to the former verdict when you are his cupbearer.

[14] 'But only you remember me—**you**—as when he benefits to you; and do you please! with me, kindness, and you mention me to Pharaoh, and you *bring* forth me from the house, even this; [15] that, stealing I am stolen from land of the Hebrews; and also here also I do not anything that they place **me** in the pit.'

[16] And he is seeing—chief of the bakers—that he interprets well, and he is saying to Joseph, 'Indeed—I in my dream, and behold! three stacks of bread[848] on my head; [17] and in the stack, the highest, from of all of Pharaoh's food, work of a baker; and the flier eating **them** from the stack, from on my head.'

[18] And he is responding—Joseph—and he is saying, 'This, his interpretation: three of stacks—three of days, they. [19] In still three of days he lifts—Pharaoh—your head from on you; and he hangs **you** on a tree, and he eats—the flier—your **flesh** from on you.'

[20] And it is becoming in the day, the third day of **Pharaoh's** birthday, and he is doing feast for all of his servants. And he is lifting the **head of** chief of the cupbearers, and **head of** the chief of the bakers in center his servants. [21] And he is restoring **chief of** the cupbearers on his cupbearing, and he is giving the cup on Pharaoh's palm. [22] And **chief of** the bakers he hangs, as which he interprets to them—Joseph. [23] But he remembers not—chief of the cupbearers—Joseph; and he is forgetting him.

41 And it is becoming, from end of years, days, and Pharaoh—dreaming, and behold! standing on the river. [2] And behold! from the river ones ascending: seven young cows, lovely ones of appearance, and well formed of flesh, and they are pasturing in the reeds. [3] And behold! seven young cows, other ones, ones ascending after[849] them from the river; bad ones of appearance, and thin ones of flesh. And they are standing beside the young cows on the river's edge, [4] and they are eating the young cows—bad ones of the appearance and thin ones of the flesh, **seven**—the

---

[848] *Bread*; freshly baked bread; the word has reference to the aroma.

[849] *After them*; same word as *other ones* in the verse. That which is following, behind, or other.

41:4—41:18

young cows, lovely ones of appearance, and the well formed ones. And he is awaking—Pharaoh.

⁵ And he is sleeping, and he is dreaming second, and behold! seven clusters, ones rising in one stalk, well formed ones, and healthy ones. ⁶ And behold! seven clusters, thin ones and ones being ravaged of east, ones sprouting after them. ⁷ And they are devouring—the clusters, the thin ones, **seven**—the clusters, the well formed ones, and the full ones. And he is awaking—Pharaoh —and behold! ...dream.

⁸ And it is becoming in the morning, and she is being agitated— his spirit—and he is sending and he is calling **all of** the magicians[850] of Egypt, and **all of** her wise. And he is recounting— Pharaoh—to them his **dream**, and there is no one interpreting **them** for Pharaoh.

⁹ And he is speaking—the chief of the cupbearers—with Pharaoh to cause to say, 'My **sins**! I—one reminding of the day. ¹⁰ Pharaoh —he is exasperated on his servants, and he is giving **me** in ward of house of chief of the executioners; **me**—and **chief** of the bakers. ¹¹ And we are dreaming dream in one night—I and he— ♂man according to interpretation of his dream we dream.

¹² And there, with us, Hebrew boy, servant to chief of the executioners; and we are recounting to him, and he is interpreting for us our dreams—♂man according to his dream he interprets. ¹³ And it is becoming, as which he interprets to us, so it becomes: **me** he restores on my station, and **him** he hangs.'

¹⁴ And he is sending—Pharaoh—and he is calling **Joseph**, and they are running him from the pit. And he is shaving, and he is changing his garments, and he is coming to Pharaoh.

¹⁵ And he is saying—Pharaoh—to Joseph, 'Dream I dream, and one interpreting? —**him** there is not. And I—I hear over you, to cause to say: you are hearing dream, to cause to interpret **him**.' ¹⁶ And he is answering—Joseph—Pharaoh, to cause to say, 'Without me: God, he answers **peace** of Pharaoh.'

¹⁷ And he is iterating—Pharaoh—to Joseph: 'In my dream, behold me! standing on the river's edge. ¹⁸ And behold! from the river, ascending ones, seven young cows, well formed ones of flesh,

---

[850] *Magicians*; the word literally means *to separate out the impure and purify by fire*, thus those who study the essence of things.

41:18—41:28

lovely ones of figure, and they are pasturing in the reeds. ¹⁹ And behold! seven young cows, other ones, ones ascending after them —emaciated ones, and badly figured ones—exceedingly, and wasted ones of flesh; I see not as these in all of land of Egypt to badness.
²⁰ 'And they are eating—the young cows, the wasted ones and the bad ones, **seven**—the young cows, the first ones, the well formed ones. ²¹ And they are coming to their middle, and it is known not that they come to their middle, and their appearance, bad—as when in the start. And I am awaking.
²² 'And I am seeing in my dream, and behold! seven bunches, ones rising in one stalk, full ones and healthy ones. ²³ And behold! seven ears, undeveloped ones, thin ones, ones ravaged of east, ones sprouting after them. ²⁴ And they are devouring—the clusters, the thin ones, **seven**—the clusters, the healthy ones. And I am telling to the magicians, and there is no one declaring to me.'
²⁵ And he is saying—Joseph—to Pharaoh, 'Pharaoh's dream— one—the same: **what** God does he declares to Pharaoh. ²⁶ Seven young cows!—the healthy ones: seven years, they. And seven clusters!—the healthy ones: seven years they; dream—one—the same.[851] ²⁷ And seven!—the young cows, the wasted ones, and the bad ones, the ones ascending after them: seven years—the same. And seven!—the bunches, the wasted ones, ones being ravaged of the easts—they are becoming seven: . . .years of famine. ²⁸ The same! The word which I speak to Pharaoh, what the God does, he shows Pharaoh.[852]

---

[851] Joseph is using oratorical form here; virtually every statement is emphatic. To have someone emerge from a prison and deliver what normally would be a practiced and polished speech on the fly would have been quite impressive to Pharaoh and his court.

[852] *The words which I speak...*; Joseph is employing a very delicate device here, in which one never uses the personal pronoun "I" (or the second person pronoun "you") when addressing Pharaoh unless claiming authority from God to do so. Joseph is deliberately putting himself above the magicians in authority from the divine, a point which would not have been missed by any of his audience.

²⁹ 'Behold! seven years, ones coming—fullness⁸⁵³!—great in all of land of Egypt. ³⁰ And they ascend—seven years of famine after them. And it is forgotten, all of the fullness in land of Egypt; and he consumes⁸⁵⁴—the famine—the land. ³¹ And he is not known—the fullness—in the land from face of the famine, even it, after; because that severe—it—exceedingly.

³² 'And on causing to be repeated—the dream—to Pharaoh *two* times, that being established—the matter—from with the God, and hastening—the God—to cause to do it.

³³ 'And now! He sees—Pharaoh—♂man; one planning and wise⁸⁵⁵, and he sets him over land of Egypt. ³⁴ He acts!—Pharaoh—and he supervises supervisors over the land, and he fifths⁸⁵⁶ **land** of Egypt in seven years of the fullness. ³⁵ And they gather **all of** food of the years, the healthy ones, the ones coming, even these; and they heap up grain under Pharaoh's hand; food in the cities; and they protect. ³⁶ And it becomes—the food—overseen to the land for seven years of the famine which, they become in land of Egypt. And she is not cut off—the land—in the famine.'

³⁷ And it is pleasing⁸⁵⁷, the matter, in Pharaoh's eyes, and in all of his servants' eyes. ³⁸ And he is saying—Pharaoh—to his servants, '? He is found, as this ♂man, whom God's spirit, in him?' ³⁹ And he is saying—Pharaoh—to Joseph, 'After causing to know—God—**you**—**all of** this, there is no one planning and wise like you. ⁴⁰ You!—you are over my house, and on your mouth he follows⁸⁵⁸, all of my people; but the throne, I am great from you.'

⁴¹ And he is saying—Pharaoh—to Joseph, 'See you!, I give **you** over all of land of Egypt.'

⁴² And he is turning aside—Pharaoh—his seal-ring from on his hand, and he is giving **her** on Joseph's hand, and he is dressing

---

⁸⁵³ *Fullness*; this is the same word as *seven* without the accent marks. It means *filled to perfection* or *finished*.

⁸⁵⁴ *Consumes*; this is a play on concepts, contrasted with the word *fullness*. Both mean to finish; one to perfection, the other to consumption.

⁸⁵⁵ *Wise*; as able to assimilate things and inwardly discern them, as a taster might do.

⁸⁵⁶ *Fifths*; as in *tithes* but a fifth part.

⁸⁵⁷ *Pleasing*; spiritually sound; having integrity for lasting results.

⁸⁵⁸ *Follow*; to act in concert with; imitate.

41:42—41:51

him garments of harmony[859], and he is placing wreath of the gold on his neck, ⁴³ and he is causing to ride **him** in the second[860] chariot which, to him, and they are calling to his face, 'Kneel you!' . . .and to give **him** over all of land of Egypt.

⁴⁴ And he is saying—Pharaoh—to Joseph, 'I—Pharaoh; and without you he lifts not—♂man—his **hand** and his **foot** in all land of Egypt.' ⁴⁵ And he is calling—Pharaoh—Joseph's name Zaphnath-Paaneah[861], and he is giving to him **Asnath**[862] daughter of Potipherah[863], priest of On[864], for wife. And he is *go*ing forth—Joseph—over land of Egypt.

⁴⁶ And Joseph—son of thirty Year in his standing to Pharaoh's face, king of Egypt. And he is *go*ing forth—Joseph—from before Pharaoh's face, and he is passing in all of land of Egypt. ⁴⁷ And she is yielding—the land—in seven years of the fullness in handfuls.

⁴⁸ And he is gathering **all of** food of seven years when they become in land of Egypt. And he is giving food in the cities; food of the city's field which *is* round about her, he gives in her center. ⁴⁹ And he is heaping up—Joseph—grain as sand of the sea, increasing exceedingly until that he quits causing it to be numbered; there is no numbering.

⁵⁰ And to Joseph, he is borne two of sons, in not yet coming—year of the famine—whom she births for him—Asnath daughter of Potipherah, priest of On. ⁵¹ And he is calling—Joseph—**name** of the first-born Manasseh[865], that 'He withdraws *from* me—God

---

[859] *Harmony*; similar to the word for *linen* and the *color white*, it connotes purity and perfect proportion.

[860] *Second*; duplicate.

[861] *Zaphnath*; answer to that which is hidden; profusion of proper analysis. *Paaneah*; guide and diviner of omens. Thus *Zaphnath-Paaneah* would be he who both interprets omens and knows how to properly respond.

[862] *Asnath*; sound foundation of distributing; a portion of the underlying structure. In this case it would be the religious and governmental structure of Egypt.

[863] *Potipherah*; a stream of speech that produces concrete results; the lawgiver. Similar to *Potiphar* in 37:36.

[864] *On*; the "I" or sameness of self; the sphere of moral activity.

[865] *Manasseh*; a forum for tranquility; moving forward with peace, emptied of stress. The usual meaning given is *causing to forget*, which holds a bit of the idea.

41:51—42:2

—**all of** my travail, and **all of** my father's house.' ⁵² And **name** of the second he calls Ephraim⁸⁶⁶, that 'He makes me fruitful—God —in land of my humiliation.'

⁵³ And they are consummated—seven years of the fullness—when it becomes in land of Egypt. ⁵⁴ And they are cracking open⁸⁶⁷— seven years of the famine—to cause to come as when he said— Joseph. And it is becoming famine in all of the lands, and in all of the land of Egypt, it is food. ⁵⁵ And she is famishing—all of land of Egypt; and he is crying—the people—to Pharaoh for the food. And he is saying—Pharaoh—to all of Egypt, 'Go you! to Joseph; what he says to you, you do.'

⁵⁶ And the famine, he becomes over all of the earth's face. And he is opening—Joseph—**all of** which, in them, and he is °selling⁸⁶⁸ to Egyptians. And he is gripping—the famine—in land of Egypt. ⁵⁷ And all of the earth, they come toward Egypt, to cause to °procure, to Joseph; that he grips—the famine—in all of the earth.

42 And he is seeing—Jacob—that there is °food⁸⁶⁹ in Egypt, and he is saying—Jacob—to his sons, 'To what ? are you seeing yourselves?⁸⁷⁰' ² And he is saying, 'Behold! I hear that there is °food in Egypt. Go down⁸⁷¹ you! toward there, and °procure⁸⁷²

---

⁸⁶⁶ *Ephraim*; fruitfulness; consequences of the path; the idea is the power behind heading toward a goal, and the consequences of staying the course; we might say *the positive results of having integrity*.

⁸⁶⁷ *Consummated, cracking open*; there is a play on words here, the two expressions for each of the seven years differing only by one letter.

⁸⁶⁸ °*Selling*; see note following from 42:1.

⁸⁶⁹ °*Food*; the word strictly means *distinguished by overcoming* in either a positive or destructive manner. Thus it is used for *breaking* of something as overcoming it, *trade* (of grain) as having a surplus, and food itself as being extra, bought, or traded. In this verse the overcoming is also implied to Egypt itself; the whole world had a famine, but Egypt somehow *overcame* the widespread destitution and distinguished itself by having extra to *trade*. The word is clustered so heavily in these chapters that it has been rendered, in this instance °*food*, and in its other forms with the same " ° " before it.

⁸⁷⁰ *Seeing yourselves*; the contrast is with Jacob *seeing* that Egypt had food. As the 'people of promise" they were unused to looking outside of themselves for help; it was a matter both of habit and family pride.

⁸⁷¹ *Go down*; to act with resolution and determination, either ascending or descending.

⁸⁷² *Procure*; same word as *food* earlier in this verse and verse one; see note above.

you! for us from there, and we live, and we die not.' ³ And they are going down—Joseph's ten brothers—to cause to °procure grain from Egypt.   ⁴ And **Benjamin**—Joseph's brother—he sends not—Jacob—with his brothers, that he says, 'Lest he meets him—damage[873].'

⁵ And they are coming—sons of Israel—to cause to °procure among those coming, that he becomes—the famine—in land of Canaan.   ⁶ And Joseph—he—the ruler over the land—he—the one °selling to all the people of the land. And they are coming—Joseph's brothers—and they are bowing themselves to him—noses toward earth.

⁷ And he is seeing—Joseph—his **brothers**, and he is recognizing them, and he is distinguishing himself to them, and he is arranging to speak with them, interrogating; and he is saying to them, 'From where ? come you?' And they are saying, 'From land of Canaan—to °purchase food.'

⁸ And he is recognizing—Joseph—his **brothers** and they—they recognize him not. ⁹ And he is remembering—Joseph the **dreams** which he dreams of them. And he is saying to them, 'Spying ones —you! To cause to see the land's **nakedness** you come.' ¹⁰ And they are saying to him, 'No, my lord, but your servants, they come to °purchase food. ¹¹ All of us—sons of one ♂man, we; upright[874] men, we; they are not—your servants—spying ones.' ¹² And he is saying to them, '*Is it* not that the land's nakedness you come to cause to see?' ¹³ And they are saying, 'Two-ten[875], your servants—brothers, we; sons of one ♂man in   land of Canaan; and behold! the small one with our father today, and the one, he is not.'

¹⁴ And he is saying to them—Joseph—'It which I appoint to you to cause to say, spying ones—you. ¹⁵ In this you are validated: Pharaoh's life! if you are only *going* forth from here except only in coming of your brother, the small one, here. ¹⁶ Send you! from you, one; and he brings your **brother**, and you—you be bound.

---

[873] *Damage*; strictly, *any results from vulnerability that perpetuates*; as Mephibosheth was lame for life as a result of being dropped when he was an infant.

[874] *Upright*; stable and confirmed, as the expression, *he is good people*.

[875] *Two-ten*; twelve.

And they are validated—your words—the truth with you; and if not—Pharaoh's life! that spying ones—you.' ¹⁷ And he removes **them** to ward three of days.

¹⁸ And he is saying to them—Joseph—in the day, the third, 'This you do, and you live! The **God**—I—fearing one. ¹⁹ If upright ones —you—one brother of you, he is bound in your ward house, and you, go you! take you! °food of your household's famine. ²⁰ And your **brother**, the small one, you bring to me, and they are assured—your words—and you die not.'

And they are doing so, ²¹ and they are saying, ♂man to his brother, 'Truly guilty⁸⁷⁶ ones—we—on our brother, when we see his soul's distress, in his causing to supplicate to us, and we listen not: on this she comes to us—the distress, even this.' ²² And he is answering—Reuben—**them**, to cause to say, 'Said I not to you, to cause to say, Not so, you are sinning in the boy? against the lad? and you listen not, and also—his blood—behold! being required.'⁸⁷⁷

²³ And they—they know not that perceiving—Joseph—that the translator *is* between them. ²⁴ And he is turning round from them, and he is weeping, and he is turning back to them, and he is arranging to them, and he is taking from them **Simeon**, and he is binding **him** to their eyes.

²⁵ And he is instructing—Joseph—and they are filling with grain their vessels⁸⁷⁸, and to cause to return their silver to them, ♂man to his sack, and to cause to give to them provision for the road; and he is doing so to them.

²⁶ And they are lifting their °food on their donkeys, and they are going from there.²⁷ And he is opening—the one—his sack to cause to give fodder to his donkey in the lodging, and he is seeing his **silver**, and behold it! in his pack's⁸⁷⁹ mouth! ²⁸ And he is

---

⁸⁷⁶ *Guilty*; the word connotes powerfully leaving one's proper place or departing from one's proper actions.

⁸⁷⁷ Note from 37:29-30 that Reuben, who was not there when they sold him, assumed him dead.

⁸⁷⁸ *Vessels*; the word connotes *everything* that can carry grain. It is used for instruments of music, pots for cooking, furnishings of the temple, etc., and generally means *all of them*.

⁸⁷⁹ *Pack*; different word from *sack*, used 15 times in scripture, only in Genesis, and only in connection with this account. The best English equivalent

42:28—42:38

saying to his brothers, 'It is returned, my silver, and also behold! in my pack!' And it is *go*ing forth, their heart, and they are trembling, ♂man to his brother, to cause to say, 'What ? this he does—God—to us!'

²⁹ And they are coming to Jacob their father, toward land of Canaan, and they are declaring to him **all of** the things coming upon them, to cause to say, ³⁰ 'He arranged—the ♂man, lord of the land—*with* **us** interrogation! And he is presenting **us** as spying ones of the **land**.   ³¹ And we are saying to him, Upright men—we—we are not spying ones; ³² two-ten⁸⁸⁰—we—brothers, sons of our father; the one, he is not, and the small one to-day with our father in land of Canaan.

³³ 'And he is saying to us—the ♂man, lord of the land—In this I know that upright ones, you; your brother: the one—leave you! with me, and your house's **famine** take you! and go you! ³⁴ and bring you! your **brother**—the small one—to me, and I know that not spying ones, you; that upright ones, you. Your **brother** I give to you, and the **land** you merchandise.'

³⁵ And it is becoming, they—ones drawing out their sacks—and behold! ♂man's pouch of his silver in his sack. And they are seeing **pouches** of their silver, they and their father, and they are fearing.   ³⁶ And he is saying to them—Jacob their father—'Me you bereave; Joseph—he is not, and Simeon—he is not, and **Benjamin** you take. Over me they become—all of them.'

³⁷ And he is saying—Reuben—to his father, to cause to say, '**Two** of my sons you kill, if I bring him not to you; give you! **him** over my hand, and I—I bring him back to you.' ³⁸ And he is saying, 'He descends not—my son—with you; that his brother—he—to his aloneness remains. And she meets him—damage⁸⁸¹—in the way which you go in her, and you bring down my old age⁸⁸² in sorrow toward Sheol.'

---

would be *my stash* but that hardly communicates. The sense is the personal set of belongings that hold everything under the jurisdiction of the one holding it.

⁸⁸⁰ *Two-ten*; twelve.
⁸⁸¹ *Damage*; strictly, *any results from vulnerability that perpetuates*; see note 42:4.
⁸⁸² *Old age*; typically translated *grey hairs*, the word means *respected old age*; literally *honor for the merit of housing the family*.

43 And the famine *is* heavy in the land. ² And it is becoming, as when they finish to cause to eat the °**food** which they bring from Egypt, and he is saying to them—their father—'Turn you back! °purchase you! for us, bit of food.'

³ And he is saying to him—Judah—to cause to say, 'Testifying he testified in us—the ♂man—to cause to say, You do not see my face except your brother with you. If you become sending our **brother** with us, we go down, and °procure for you food; ⁵ and if you are not sending, we do not go down, that the ♂man, he says to us, you do not see my face except your brother, with you.'

⁶ And he is saying—Israel—'To what ? you spoil to me, to cause to declare to the ♂man ? yet to you—brother?' ⁷ And they are saying, 'Asking, he asked—the ♂man—to us, and to our kindred, to cause to say, ? Your father yet alive? Is there brother to you? And we *are* forthright to him over the mouth of the matters, even these; ? to know, are we knowing that he does say, Bring down you! your **brother**?'

⁸ And he is saying—Judah—to Israel his father, 'Send you! the boy with me, and we rise, and we go, and we live, and we die not, even we, even you, even our family. ⁹ I—I guarantee him; from my hand do you seek him; if I bring him not to you, and I set him to your face... and I sin to you all of the days; ¹⁰ that except we hesitate[883], that now we returned these *two* times.'

¹¹ And he is saying to them—Israel their father—'If so, now, this do you: take you! from select harvest of the land in your vessels, and take you down! to the ♂man a present, few essential oils, and some honey, spices and decoctions, pistachios and almonds; ¹² and double silver take you! in your hand, and the **silver**, the being returned in your pack's mouth, you do restore your hand; perhaps—mistake—it; ¹³ and your **brother**, take you! and rise you! return you! to the ♂man. ¹⁴ And God Providence[884], he gives to you compassion to the ♂man's face, and he releases to you your **brother**, other one, and **Benjamin**. And I—when I am bereaved, I am bereaved.'

¹⁵ And they are taking—the •men—the present, even this, and double silver they take in their hand, and **Benjamin**. And they are

---

[883] *Hesitate*; to waffle between unanswered questions.
[884] *God Providence*; El Shaddai

rising, and they are descending, Egypt, and they are standing to Joseph's face. ¹⁶ And he is seeing—Joseph—with them, **Benjamin**, and he is saying to who *is* over his house, 'Bring you! the •men toward the house, and slaughter you! Slaughter and prepare you! that *with* **me** they eat—the •men—in the noon.'

¹⁷ And he is doing—the ♂man—as which he says—Joseph—and he is bringing—the ♂man—the •men toward Joseph's house. ¹⁸ And they are fearing—the •men—that they are brought into Joseph's house, and they are saying, 'On occasion of the silver, the returned in our packs at the first—we, coming ones—to cause to roll⁸⁸⁵ himself on us, and to cause to fall on us, and to cause to take **us** for servants, and our **donkeys**.'

¹⁹ And they are approaching to the ♂man who *is* over Joseph's house, and they are speaking toward him—opening of the house —²⁰ and they are saying, 'O! my lord, to descend we descend in the first to cause to °purchase food; ²¹ and it is becoming, that we come to the lodging, and we are opening our packs, that behold! ♂man's silver in his pack's mouth; our silver in its weight, and we are returning **it** in our hand; ²² and silver—other—we bring down in our hand to cause to °purchase food; we know not ? who—he places our silver in our packs.'

²³ And he is saying, 'Peace to you, nothing you are fearing; your God and God of your father, he gives to you hidden treasure in your packs; your silver, it came to me.' And he is *bring*ing forth to them **Simeon**. ²⁴ And he is bringing—the ♂man—the •men, toward Joseph's house, and he is giving water, and they are washing their feet; and he is giving provender to their donkeys. ²⁵ And they are preparing the **present** until coming of Joseph in noon, that they hear that there they eat bread.

²⁶ And he is coming—Joseph—to the house, and they are bringing to him the **present**, which, in their hand into the house, and they are bowing themselves down to him, toward earth. ²⁷ And he is inquiring to them to peace, and he is saying, '? Peace, your father, aged one whom you mention? Is he yet living?' ²⁸ And they are saying, 'Peace to your servant our father, he is yet living.' And they are stooping, and they are bowing themselves down.

---

⁸⁸⁵ *Roll*; oppress to extinction; the word connotes piling up, in this case piling up causes to condemn.

²⁹ And he is lifting his eyes, and he is seeing **Benjamin** his brother, son of his mother, and he is saying, '? This one—your brother, the small one—whom you mention to me?' And he is saying, 'God—he favors you, my son.'

³⁰ And he is hastening—Joseph—that they are yearning—his compassions—to his brother, and he is seeking to cause to weep, and he is entering into the chamber, and he is weeping there; ³¹ and he is washing his face, and he is *going* forth, and he is controlling himself, and he is saying, 'Place you! food.'

³² And they are placing to him by himself, and to them by themselves, and to the Egyptians, the ones eating with him, by themselves: that they are not able—the Egyptians—to cause to eat with the Hebrews bread; that abomination, it, to the Egyptians.[886]

³³ And they are sitting to his face; the first-born according to his birthright, and the small one according to his smallness, and they are astonished, the •men; ♂man to his fellow. ³⁴ And he lifts up portions[887] from his face to them, and she is being increased, the portion of Benjamin from portions of all of them; five hands. And they are drinking, and they are becoming tipsy with him.

44 And he is instructing **who**, over his house, to cause to say, 'Fill you! •men's packs; food as which they are managing to carry, and put you! silver of ♂man in his pack's mouth; ² and my **cup**[888], cup

---

[886] The prohibition of eating with the Hebrews was both racial and religious. See the last three paragraphs of Appendix VIII for the background. Racially, the Egyptians considered themselves the geographical center of the world''s nations, kind of a second-place to what was attempted at Babylon. Religiously, the times were just changing from the age of Taurus to the age of Aries, just as now we''re entering the age of Aquarius from the age of Pisces. The pre-Deluvian mysteries were fading out in favor of what Noah started with his "vineyard", i.e., the searching out of divine mysteries in relation to God rather than as given by the Nephilim. Eber's line, the Hebrews, were thus diametrically opposed to Egypt. How this filtered down to the common man was that sheep, symbolic of the new age of Aries, were forbidden, and cows, symbolic of the established age of Taurus, were both the providers of meat and the icon of strength for Egypt.

[887] *Portions*; the word implies drink, which here would affect the story of Benjamin being put in the position of being tempted to steal Joseph's cup.

[888] *Cup*; the word is formed from the two roots for *concave* and *convex*; it connotes a formal and iconic vessel; used elsewhere only for the candlestick of the tabernacle and Jeremiah setting wine before the

of silver, you put in mouth of the small one's pack, and **silver** of his °food.' And he is doing according to word of Joseph which he arranges.

³ The morning, he lights, and the •men, they are sent away; they and their donkeys. ⁴They—they *go* forth; the **city** they distance not, and Joseph, he says to whom *is* over his house, 'Rise you! pursue you! after the •men; and you overtaken them, and you say to them, To what ? you repay evil in lieu of good? ⁵ ? Not this which he is drinking—my lord—in it? And he, to divine he is divining in it. You spoil when you act!'

⁶ And he is overtaking them, and he is speaking to them the **words**, even these. ⁷ And they are saying to him, 'To what ? is he speaking—my lord—according to words, even these? Far be it! to your servants from causing to do according to the word, even this. ⁸ Behold! silver which we find in our pack's mouth we restore to you from land of Canaan; and how ? should we steal from house of your lord silver or gold? ⁹ Whom it is found with him from your servants, and he dies, and moreover, we become to my lord for servants.'

¹⁰ And he is saying, 'Even now, also, according to your words, so he whom it is found with him, he is becoming to me, servant; and you—you are innocent.' ¹¹ And they are hurrying, and they are lowering ♂man his **pack** to the earth , and they are opening ♂man his pack. ¹² And he is searching—in the eldest he begins, and in the youngest he finishes—and it is being found—the cup—in Benjamin's pack. ¹³ And they are tearing their garments, and he is leading, ♂man on his donkey, and they are returning to the city.

¹⁴ And he is coming—Judah and his brothers—to Joseph's house. And he—still him—there. And they are falling to his face toward earth. ¹⁵ And he is saying to them—Joseph—'What ? the deed, even this, which you do? You know not that to divine, he is divining—♂man who *is* as me?'

¹⁶ And he is saying—Judah—'What ? say we to my lord? what ? do we speak? and what ? justify we ourselves? The God, he finds depravity[889] of your servants; Behold us!—servants to my l ord,

---

Rechabites.

[889] *Depravity*; always used for collective guilt that is manifested in one party's actions; as the matter of Peor in Judges, or the house of Eli's judgment from

even we, even whom it is found—the cup—in his hand.' ¹⁷ And he is saying, 'Far be it! to me from causing to do this; the ♂man whom it is found—the cup—in his hand, he becomes to me servant; and you—go you up! to peace to your father.'

¹⁸ And he is approaching—Judah—and he is saying, 'O! my lord, he speaks, please!—your servant—word in my lord's ears, and as not being hot, your anger in your servant; that like you—as Pharaoh. ¹⁹ My lord, he asks his **servants**, to cause to say, ? Is to you father or brother? ²⁰ And we are saying to my lord, There is to us father, aged, and boy of old ages, small one; and his brother—he—dead, and he is being left—he—to his aloneness, to his mother; and his father, he loves him.

²¹ 'And you are saying to your servants, *Bring* him down! to me, and I set my eyes on him. ²² And we are saying to my lord, He is not being able—the boy—to cause to leave his **father**, and he leaves his **father**, and he dies. ²³ And you are saying to your servants, If he is not *com*ing down—your brother, the small one—with you, you add not to cause to see my face.

²⁴ 'And it is becoming, that we ascend to your servant my father, that we are declaring to him my lord's **words**. ²⁵ And he is saying —our father—Return you! °purchase for us bit of food. ²⁶ And we are saying, We are not being able to cause to descend; if there is our young brother—the small one—with us, and we descend; that we are not able to cause to see the man's face, and our brother, the small one, there is no 'him' with us.

²⁷ 'And he is saying—your servant my father—to us, you—you know that two she births for me—my wife. ²⁸ And he is *going* forth—the one—from with me, and I am saying, Surely to tear, he is torn; and I see him not unto here. ²⁹ And you take, moreover, **this one** from with my face, and he falls on him—danger, and you *bring* down my old age in evil to Sheol.

³⁰ 'And now, as my coming to your servant my father, and the boy, there is no 'him' with us and, his soul being bound up in his soul, ³¹ and it becomes, as his seeing that the boy is not, and he dies. And they bring down—your servants—**old age** of your servant our father in sorrow to Sheol. ³² That your servant

---

Samuel's first visitation.

44:32—45:11

guarantees the boy from with my father, to cause to say, If I am bringing him not to you; and I sin to my father all of the days.
³³ 'And now, he dwells, please!—your servant—instead of the boy, servant to my lord; and the boy, he goes up with his brothers; ³⁴ that how ? do I go up to my father, and the boy, there is no 'him' with me? —lest I see the evil which, it finds my **father**.'

45 And he is not able—Joseph—to cause to control himself to all the ones being appointed on him, and he is crying out, '*Go* forth you! all of ♂man from on me!' And he stands not—♂man—*with* him in causing to reveal himself—Joseph—to his brothers. ² And he is giving his **voice** in weeping, and they are hearing—Egyptians—and he is hearing—house of Pharaoh.

³ And he is saying—Joseph—to his brothers, 'I—Joseph. ?—Yet my father living?' And they are not able—his brothers to cause to answer **him**, that they are consternated from his face.

⁴ And he is saying—Joseph—to his brothers, 'Approach you! please! to me.' And they are approaching. And he is saying, 'I—Joseph your brother whom, you sell **me** toward Egypt. ⁵ And now, not as so you are grieving, and not as so it is angering in your eyes that you sell **me** to here, that to preserve life he sends me—God—to your face.

⁶ 'That these *two* years the famine in the earth's center, and still five years which, there is no plowing and harvest. ⁷ And he is sending me—God—to your face, to cause to set for you remnant in the earth, and to cause to give life for you to great recovery. ⁸ And now, you—you send me not to here, that the God, and he sets me to father to Pharaoh, and to lord to all of his house, and one ruling in all of land of Egypt.

⁹ 'Hurry you! and *go* up to my father, and you say to him, Thus he says, your son; Joseph, He sets me—God—to lord to all of Egypt. Descend you! to me; not so you are staying. ¹⁰ And you dwell in land of Goshen[890], and you are near to me; you and your sons, and your son's sons, and your flock, and your herd, and all of, which to you. ¹¹ And I maintain **you** there; that yet five years—famine—lest you are dispossessed, you and your house, and all of, which to you.

---

[890] *Goshen*; palpable change.

45:12—45:26

¹² 'And behold! your eyes—seeing ones—and eyes of my brother Benjamin, that my mouth, the one speaking to you. ¹³ And you declare to my father **all of** my glory in Egypt, and **all of** which you see; and you hurry, and you *bring* down my **father** to here.'

¹⁴ And he is falling on Benjamin's neck, his brother, and he is weeping, and Benjamin, he weeps on his neck. ¹⁵ And he is kissing to all of his brothers, and he is weeping over them; and after this they speak—his brothers—with him.

¹⁶ And the sound, it is heard—Pharaoh's house—to cause to say, 'They come—Joseph's brothers!' And it is fortuitous in Pharaoh's eyes, and in his servants' eyes. ¹⁷ And he is saying—Pharaoh—to Joseph, 'Say you! to your brothers, This you do! load you! your **beasts**[891], and you travel! and you go! toward land, Canaan, ¹⁸ and you fetch! your **father**, and your **households**, and you come! to me. And I give to you **goodness** of Egypt's land, and you eat!—**fat** of the land.

¹⁹ 'And you—you are commanded: this do you! take you! to you from Egypt's land, wagons for your children[892], and for your wives, and you bear your **father**, and you come. ²⁰ And your eye—nothing she is reviewing over your furnishings, that goodness of all of Egypt's land, to you—it.'

²¹ And they are doing so—sons of Israel. And he is giving to them—Joseph—wagons over Pharaoh's mouth, and he is giving to them provision for the road; ²² to all of them he gives—to the ♂man—changes of garments, and to Benjamin he gives three of hundreds silver, and five changes of garments; ²³ and to his father he sends as this: ten donkeys, ones bearing from good of Egypt, and ten of she-donkeys, ones bearing grain and bread, and food for his father for the road.

²⁴ And he is sending away his brothers, and they are going, and he is saying to them, 'Must not be you are bickering in the way.'

²⁵ And they are ascending from Egypt, and they are coming—Canaan's land—to Jacob their father. ²⁶ And they are declaring to him, to cause to say, 'Joseph *is* yet alive!' and that he—one ruling

---

[891] *Beasts*; used only six times in scripture, beasts as *eaters* or *devourers*. Pharaoh may be demonstrating a touch of humor.

[892] *Children*; the word connotes running around continuously.

45:26—46:7

in all of land of Egypt. And his heart faints[893], that he gives not credence[894] to them. ²⁷ And they are presenting to him **all of** Joseph's words which he speaks to them; and he is seeing the **wagons** which he sends—Joseph—to cause to bear **him**, and she is living, spirit of Jacob their father. ²⁸ And he is saying—Israel says, 'Enough!'[895] Still Joseph my son *is* alive; I go and I see him before I am dying.'

46 And he is journeying—Israel—and all of, which to him; and he is coming to Beer-Sheba, and he is sacrificing sacrifices to God of his father Isaac. ² And he is speaking—God—to Israel in visions of the night, and he is saying, 'Jacob, Jacob!' And he is saying, 'Behold me!'

³ And he is saying, 'I—the God, God of your father[896]—nothing you are fearing from causing to descend to Egypt, that that to great nation I set you there. ⁴ I—I descend with you to Egypt, and —I—I *bring* you up also to *go* up, and Joseph—he sets his hand on your eyes.' ⁵ And he is rising—Jacob—from Beer-Sheba.

And they are bearing—sons of Israel—**Jacob** their father, and their **children**, and their **wives**, in the wagons which he sends—Pharaoh—to cause to bear **him**, ⁶ And they are taking their **livestock**, and their **substance** which they acquire in the land of Canaan, and they are coming toward Egypt—Jacob, and all of his seed with him: ⁷ his sons, and his sons' sons with him, his daughters, and his sons' daughters, and all of his seed he brings with him toward Egypt.

---

[893] *Faints*; stops in the process of believing something attractive.
[894] *Gives not credence*; accepts not the full measure for his own acceptance.
[895] *Enough!*; literally, *abundant*.
[896] *The God—God of your father*; the El—Elohim of your father.

46:8—46:11

⁸ And these: names of Israel's sons, the ones coming toward Egypt—Jacob and his sons:

Jacob's firstborn, Reuben. ⁹ And sons of Reuben[897]: Hanoch[898], and Phallu[899], and Hezron[900], and Carmi[901]. ¹⁰ And sons of Simeon[902]: Jemuel[903], and Jamin[904], and Ohad[905], and Jachin[906], and Zohar[907], and Saul[908] son of the Canaanitess. ¹¹ And sons of Levi[909]: Gershon[910], Kohath[911], and Merari[912].

---

[897] *Reuben*; see you a son. As a patriarch, the name takes on the sense of *considering* (as seeing and acting upon) *the transformation*, as when Elisha *saw* Elijah taken up and picked up his mantel, or when Joab *saw and considered* that David''s heart was again toward the exile Absalom. This watching of a transformation subsequently characterizes the tribe, as they settled on the east of Jordan, helping Israel take the land but not entering themselves.

[898] *Hanoch*; dedicated; prayer and its results. This is the same word elsewhere transliterated *Enoch*; the meaning in the context of 5:18 is additionally *to institute, to found*.

[899] *Phallu*; a great treasure with hidden power.

[900] *Hezron*; startling alarm; enclosed courtyard. Also Judah has a grandson named Hezron in verse 12.

[901] *Carmi*; my vineyard; fickle leader. The name is composed of two precisely opposite roots, the one meaning *marked out for distinction* and the other *tenuous and impassive*.

[902] *Simeon*; listening; sign of corruption; darkening the name. As a patriarch, the name takes on the sense both of *a special (or private) place of becoming* in the positive, and *humiliation from over-ambitiousness* in the negative.

[903] *Jemuel*; sea of God; toward showing everything.

[904] *Jamin*; right (both senses); to amass for one's interests.

[905] *Ohad*; to reach for something to make it one's own, as a husband puts his arm around his wife.

[906] *Jachin*; he will establish; placing one's interests aside; self-control.

[907] *Zohar*; whiteness; to compose.

[908] *Saul*; asking; the idea is a somewhat plaintive cry between the opposing circumstance of calm and chaos. Also the name of a king of Edom in 36:37.

[909] *Levi*; joined; addition; supplement; entwined. As a patriarch, the name takes on the meaning of one idea producing another attractive and lasting one. The expression might be stated, *may it be and continue.*

[910] *Gershon*; outcast; sojourner.

[911] *Kohath*; holding irresolutely to mysteries; desire for the profound.

[912] *Merari*; enduring bitterness; breathing out domination, as a stream of ethereal (or spiritual) edicts.

46:12—46:14

¹² And sons of Judah[913]: Er[914], and Onan[915], and Shelah[916], and Pherez[917], and Zerah[918]. And he is dying—Er and Onan—in land of Canaan. And they are—sons of Pherez—Hezron[919] and Hamul[920].

¹³ And sons of Issachar[921]: Tola[922], and Puah[923], and Job[924], and Shimron[925].

¹⁴ And sons of Zebulun[926]: Sered[927], and Elon[928], and Jahleel[929].

---

[913] *Judah*; he is praised; God-given life. As a patriarch, the name takes on the meaning of *God's grace* (or fellowship) *distributed in life*.

[914] *Er*; passion as an irresistible impulse, as jealousy, rage, or covetousness; vehemence.

[915] *Onan*; propagation of the sense of lost hope; continued nothingness.

[916] *Shelah*; tranquil life proceeding in order.

[917] *Pherez*; breaking out; a breach.

[918] *Zerah*; dispersing into the air, as radiating. Previously in 36:13 (Esau's grandson by Reuel) the meaning in context is *dispersion of effort; working as a stranger*.

[919] *Hezron*; startling alarm; enclosed courtyard. Also Reuben has a son named Hezron in verse 9.

[920] *Hamul*; a warm hug. Literally, the happy humming during a warm hug.

[921] *Issachar*; he is payed; shown and proved; engraved in reality. As a patriarch, his name takes on the meanings *satisfied to endure, laying aside responsibility*, and *repose in service*. There is a sense of harmony and calm, as well as the sense of being pleasantly intoxicated by the goodness of life.

[922] *Tola*; worm; that which devours a heap.

[923] *Puah*; blowing; it has also the sense of a cry of sadness.

[924] *Job*; endurance; demonstrating paternal effectiveness.

[925] *Shimron*; guardianship; babbling of the stream of splendor; name of our rejoicing. This is the same word translated *Samaria* later in scripture.

[926] *Zebulun*; seething night-watch, or *swarming into spreading*, as a pot might boil over and spread out. The spelling has been changed from Leah's original naming, and holds also the inverse ideas of *rest* and *longing*.

[927] *Sered*; fright; unsure movement in trouble.

[928] *Elon*; toward relaxation; the indolence of extensive power; passing away into softness.

[929] *Jahleel*; hope of God; powerful longsuffering.

46:15—46:17

¹⁵ These: sons of Leah⁹³⁰ whom she births for Jacob in Padan-Aram—and **Dinah**⁹³¹ his daughter. All of soul⁹³² of his sons and his daughters: thirty and three.

¹⁶ And sons of Gad⁹³³: Ziphion⁹³⁴ and Haggi⁹³⁵, Shuni⁹³⁶ and Ezbon⁹³⁷, Eri⁹³⁸ and Arodi⁹³⁹, and Areli⁹⁴⁰.

¹⁷ And sons of Asher⁹⁴¹: Jimnah⁹⁴², and Ishuah⁹⁴³, and Isui⁹⁴⁴, and Beriah⁹⁴⁵, and Serah⁹⁴⁶ their sister. And sons of Beriah: Heber⁹⁴⁷ and Malchiel⁹⁴⁸.

---

⁹³⁰ *Leah*; Make it happen; literally, *act physically*. Here it takes the meaning of *endless action* which wears one out; by implication one who henpecks.

⁹³¹ *Dinah*; abundant youth; vigorous satisfaction. Here it takes on the additional sense of a *settled and satisfying judgment*. Note that Dinah is grammatically coupled with Leah as not part of those counted in the 70; this shows that her contribution to future progeny was stopped because of the affair with Shechem, Hamor's son in chapter 34.

⁹³² *All of soul*; throughout this chapter the singular 'soul' or 'he' is used for a plurality of persons, culminating in verse 27.

⁹³³ *Gad*; agitated or invading troop; an incision. As a patriarch it takes on the additional meaning of *ambition that divides*.

⁹³⁴ *Ziphion*; intelligible constancy of self-interest; watchfulness.

⁹³⁵ *Haggi*; well organized celebration, as a feast or a dance.

⁹³⁶ *Shuni*; duration of sleep; a long and satisfying nap.

⁹³⁷ *Ezbon*; the limits of what can be produced; the last son.

⁹³⁸ *Eri*; passion for the spiritual; enduring uncontrollable impulse.

⁹³⁹ *Arodi*; powerful determination towards abundance; endurance and its fruits.

⁹⁴⁰ *Areli*; vigorous, productive, and enduring power. There is a touch of longing underlying.

⁹⁴¹ *Asher*; happy; burning flame; motive. As a patriarch his name takes on the sense of *powerful balance*.

⁹⁴² *Jimnah*; fresh and boundless, as a new colony in open land.

⁹⁴³ *Ishuah*; presentation of balance; the appearance of fitting equilibrium.

⁹⁴⁴ *Isui*; constancy; consistency of appearance.

⁹⁴⁵ *Beriah*; palisade; the showing forth of integrity in a formal and appreciable form.

⁹⁴⁶ *Serah*; open to life and activity; liberation.

⁹⁴⁷ *Heber*; strength from the mysteries. a united company. This name is different from Heber their ancestor.

⁹⁴⁸ *Malchiel*; my king is God; holding powerfully on to royalty.

46:18—46:20

¹⁸ These: sons of Zilpah⁹⁴⁹, whom he gives—Laban⁹⁵⁰—to Leah his daughter, and she is birthing **these** for Jacob; six of ten⁹⁵¹ of soul.
¹⁹ Sons of Rachel⁹⁵², Jacob's wife: Joseph⁹⁵³ and Benjamin⁹⁵⁴.
²⁰ And he is being born to Joseph in land of Egypt, whom she births for him—Asnath⁹⁵⁵ daughter of Potipherah⁹⁵⁶, priest of On⁹⁵⁷—**Manasseh**⁹⁵⁸ and **Ephraim**⁹⁵⁹.

---

⁹⁴⁹ *Zilpah*; flippant-mouth; to trickle. Endless crude talking.
⁹⁵⁰ *Laban*; passion for self, embodiment of will.
⁹⁵¹ *Six of ten*; sixteen.
⁹⁵² *Rachel*; an ewe; acting on hope; lifted high by the wind. Here the idea is an powerful but ethereal force.
⁹⁵³ *Joseph*; he adds; day of achievement; summit of meaningfulness. As a patriarch the name takes on the idea of a finishing line where many reach the end of their journey.
⁹⁵⁴ Benjamin; son of the right hand; center of propagation; the idea is strong individuality that becomes a multitude, hence used for the right hand. As a patriarch the meaning becomes *construction of lasting protection*, as an enclosure.
⁹⁵⁵ *Asnath*; sound foundation of distributing; a portion of the underlying structure. In this context it is *brightest member of the empire*.
⁹⁵⁶ *Potipherah*; a stream of speech that produces concrete results; the lawgiver.
⁹⁵⁷ *On*; the "I" or sameness of self; the sphere of moral activity.
⁹⁵⁸ *Manasseh*; a forum for tranquility; moving forward with peace, emptied of stress. As a patriarch it becomes *calm within tumult*, as in the eye of a storm.
⁹⁵⁹ *Ephraim*; fruitfulness; consequences of the path; the idea is the power behind heading toward a goal, and the consequences of staying the course; we might say *the positive results of having integrity*. As a patriarch it becomes *filling up of the circle*.

46:21—46:27

²¹ And sons of Benjamin: Belah[960] and Becher[961] and Ashbel[962], Gera[963] and Naaman[964], Ehi[965] and Rosh[966], Muppim[967] and Huppim[968] and Ard[969].

²² These: sons of Rachel, whom he was born to Jacob: all of soul, four ten[970].

²³ And sons of Dan[971]: Hushim[972].

²⁴ And sons of Naphtali[973]: Jahzeel[974], and Guni[975], and Jezer[976], and Shillem[977].

²⁵ These: sons of Bilhah[978], whom he gives—Laban—to Rachel his daughter. And she is birthing **these** for Jacob: every soul, seven.

²⁶ All of the soul, the one coming to Jacob toward Egypt, ones *com*ing forth of his thigh, from besides of Jacob's son's wives, all of soul: sixty and six. ²⁷ And Joseph's sons who, he is born to him

---

[960] *Belah*; swallowing up; devouring.
[961] *Becher*; a dromedary; marked out by weeping.
[962] *Ashbel*; growing irresistible force; a fire blazing up.
[963] *Gera*; introspection.
[964] *Naaman*; pleasantness, especially one's own enjoyment.
[965] *Ehi*; my brother; hearth of fellowship, as in a fireside discussion.
[966] *Rosh*; the head; culminating point either good or bad, used for both poison and a prince.
[967] *Muppim*; producer of songs; a bard.
[968] *Huppim*; coverings; one who makes agreements, as a moderator.
[969] *Ard*; descend; subdue; all uses of extended power.
[970] *Four ten*; fourteen.
[971] *Dan*; judgment, especially contradictory. In this context his name takes on the sense of *the forceful guiding hand of judgment*.
[972] *Hushim*; ones hurrying; raging of the sea. The image is of a mass of agitated movement which gets nowhere.
[973] *Naphtali*; my wrestling; perpetual argument. As a patriarch, his name takes on the meaning of *pulling things together through wisdom*.
[974] *Jahzeel*; a great and abiding divide, as in a bottomless pit, that separates that which is 'without', i.e., on the other side. There is the idea of *apportioning* as well, through the force of having made the divide.
[975] *Guni*; a new organization; group of youths.
[976] *Jezer*; imagination; form; purpose.
[977] *Shillem*; to make peace, usually by repaying; recompense.
[978] *Bilhah*; frantic soul; abundance of busy-work. In this context there is the additional sense of *spiritual fatigue*.

46:27—47:4

in Egypt—soul—two. All of the soul to house of Jacob, the one[979] coming toward Egypt: seventy[980].

[28] And **Judah** he sends to his face to Joseph, to cause to direct to his face toward Goshen, and they are coming toward land of Goshen. [29] And he is harnessing—Joseph—his chariot, and he is *going* up to cause to meet Israel his father toward Goshen, and he is appearing to him, and he is falling on his neck, and he is weeping on his neck a while. [30] And he is saying—Israel—to Joseph, 'I die, the stroke, after my seeing your **face**, that you—still living.'

[31] And he is saying—Joseph—to his brothers and to his father's house, 'I ascend, and I declare to Pharaoh, and I say to him, My brothers, and my father's house who, in the land of Canaan, they come to me. [32] And the •men—ones grazing of flock, that •men of livestock they are. And their flock, and their herd, and all of which, to them, they bring.'

[33] 'And it becomes that he calls for you—Pharaoh—and he says, What ? your occupations? [34] and you say, •Men of livestock they are—your servants—from our youths and until now, also we, also our fathers,—so that you may dwell in land of Goshen, that, abomination of Egyptians, all of one grazing of flock.'

47 And he is coming—Joseph—and he is declaring to Pharaoh, and he is saying, 'My father, and my brothers, and their flock, and their herd, and all of which, to them, they come from land of Canaan, and behold them! in land of Goshen.'

[2] And from accomplished of his brothers he takes five •men, and places them in face of Pharaoh. [3] And he is saying—Pharaoh—to his brothers, 'What ? your occupations?' And they are saying to Pharaoh, 'Grazing of flock, your servants, also we, also our fathers.' [4] And they are saying to Pharaoh, 'To cause to sojourn in the land we come, that *there* is no pasture for the flock which, to your servants, that heavy the famine in land of Canaan. And now, they live, please! your servants, in land of Goshen.' [981]

---

[979] *The one*; this refers, not to Jacob, but to the 'soul'' (singular) by which the text characterizes the entirety of those coming to Egypt.

[980] *Seventy*; see Appendix XI for the count of 66, 70, & 75 as given here, Exodus 1:5, Deuteronomy 10:22, and Acts 6:14.

47:5—47:9

⁵ And he is saying—Pharaoh—to Joseph, to cause to say, 'Your father and your brothers, they come to you. ⁶ Land of Egypt to your face, he; In best of the land cause you to live!—your **father** and your **brothers**—they live in land of Goshen. And if you know, and in them is •men of ability, and you set them chiefs of cattle over which, to me.'

⁷ And he is bringing—Joseph—**Jacob** his father, and he is standing[982] him to face of Pharaoh. And he is blessing—Jacob—Pharaoh. ⁸ And he is saying—Pharaoh—to Jacob, 'What![983] ? days of years of life of you?' ⁹ And he is saying—Jacob—to Pharaoh, 'Days of years of sojournings of me[984], thirty and hundred of Year. Few and evil ones they become, days of years of life of me, and they attain not *to* **days** of years of life of fathers of

---

[981] Joseph''s brothers have just committed a major faux pas on several levels. Joseph had told them specifically that shepherding sheep was an abomination to the Egyptians (see note 43:32) and that *he* would mention that aspect of their livelihood to Pharaoh, while *they* were simply to state that they were engaged in livestock. Joseph had delicately slipped in the word "flock" when introducing his brothers to Pharaoh, as even mentioning the occupation in his court was frowned upon. His brothers, conversely, blurted it out as the first words out of their mouth. Then in the shocked silence of the court they went on to speak when not spoken to and mention the fact that there was no pasture in Canaan, which Pharaoh well knew, and that they were coming to sojourn in the land. This was an appeal to their own need rather than the only thing which actually affected Pharaoh''s decisions—his favor toward Joseph. Then they put the coup de grâce on their blunderings, kept talking and asked for the land of Goshen, which would make their dwelling there the consequence of their request rather than Pharaoh''s liberality. Pharaoh, thoroughly disgusted, leaves off talking with them and addresses Joseph, reiterating the points in his own terms rather than theirs. His disgust is thinly veiled when he says "*And if you know, and in them is men of ability...*" inasmuch as to say "*...because I certainly don''t see any.*"

[982] *Standing*; a formal gesture connoting equality with Pharaoh.

[983] *What*; both a question and and exclamation.

[984] *Me*; Jacob does not use "your servant" as he is establishing himself as an equal or superior.

47:9—47:16

me, in days of their sojournings.'⁹⁸⁵ ¹⁰ And he is blessing—Jacob —**Pharaoh**, and he is *going* forth from causing to face Pharaoh.

¹¹ And he is settling—Joseph—his **father** and his **brothers**, and he is giving to them holding in land of Egypt, in best of the land, in land of Rameses⁹⁸⁶, as which he instructs—Pharaoh. ¹² And he is sustaining⁹⁸⁷—Joseph—his **father**, and his **brothers**, and **all of** his father's house, food for the children's⁹⁸⁸ mouth.

¹³ And there is no bread in all of the land, that heavy, the famine, exceedingly. And she is suspended⁹⁸⁹—land of Egypt and land of Canaan—from face of the famine. ¹⁴ And he is gleaning—Joseph —**all of** the silver, the being found in land of Egypt and in land of Canaan in the °food which they, ones °purchasing. And he is bringing—Joseph—the **silver** to Pharaoh's house.

¹⁵ And it is being finished—the silver—from land of Egypt, and from land of Canaan. And they are coming—all of Egyptians—to Joseph to cause to say, 'Give you! to us bread. And to what ? we die before you, that it disappears—silver?' ¹⁶ And he is saying— Joseph—'Give you! your livestocks and I give to you in your livestocks, if it disappears—silver.'

---

⁹⁸⁵ The threefold use of a train of prepositional phrases to Pharaoh is highly significant. Jacob, as the representative of one of the three power centers on earth, is arranging his relationship with Pharaoh, representative of another power center. Firstly, he replaces "life" with "sojournings" to let Pharaoh know that there will be no competition; Pharaoh can keep his power center, Jacob is just moving through. Secondly, it would be no contest even if there were a competition, as he was more than twice Pharaoh''s age, and had access to the coveted antediluvian secrets. Thirdly, he came from an unbroken line of even more powerful sojourners who were capable of maintaining themselves apart from the degradation of earth''s cultures being scattered. These statements serve to reverse what Joseph''s brothers had done in offending Pharaoh, and puts Pharaoh''s focus once again on Joseph as the inheritor of this long line of integrity. The blessing before his speaking establishes his superiority over Pharaoh, and the blessing after speaking establishes a fellowship between them, showing that Pharaoh has accepted his position.

⁹⁸⁶ *Rameses*; expanding to bursting; growth and expansion as the result of being full, in a very material sense.

⁹⁸⁷ *Sustaining*; strong word meaning to perfectly and totally sustain.

⁹⁸⁸ *Children*; or *infants*. The word connotes running around constantly.

⁹⁸⁹ *Suspended*; the sense is very much *hanging by a thread*.

47:17—47:27

¹⁷ And they are bringing their **livestock** to Joseph, and he is giving to them—Joseph—bread, in the horses, and in livestock of the flock, and in the livestock of the herd, and in the donkeys. And he cares for⁹⁹⁰ them in the bread, in all of their cattle in the year, even her.

¹⁸ And she is ending—the year, even her—and they are coming to him in the year, the second, and they are saying to him, 'We conceal not from my lord, that when he disappears—the silver and livestock of the beast—to my lord, it is not left to my lord's face except only our body and our ground. ¹⁹ To what ? we die to your eyes? even we, even our ground? Buy you! **us** and our **ground** in the bread, and we become—we and our ground—servants to Pharaoh. And give you! seed, and we live, and we die not, and the ground, she is not devastated.'

²⁰ And he is buying—Joseph—**all of** ground of Egypt to Pharaoh, that they sold—Egyptians—♂man his field, that he grips over them—the famine; and she is becoming—the land—to Pharaoh. ²¹ And the **people**—he transfers **him** to the cities from end of Egypt's border and unto its end.

²² But the ground of the priests he buys not, that apportioned for the priests from **Pharaoh**, and they eat their portion which he gives to them—Pharaoh; on this they sell not their **ground**.

²³ And he is saying—Joseph—to the people, 'Behold! I buy **you** today and your **ground** for Pharaoh; Here! for you seed; and you sow the **ground**. ²⁴ And it becomes in the returns, that you give fifth to Pharaoh, and four of the hands, he becomes for you, for seed of the field, and your causing to eat, and for whom, in your houses, and to cause to eat for your children.'

²⁵ And they are saying, 'You are *keep*ing us alive; we are finding favor in my lord's eyes, and we become servants to Pharaoh.' ²⁶ And he is appointing **her**—Joseph—for enactment⁹⁹¹ until the day, even this, over Egypt's ground: to Pharaoh to the fifth; but ground of the priests, to theirs alone, she becomes not to Pharaoh.

²⁷ And he is living—Israel—in land of Egypt, in land of Goshen, and they are possessing in her, and they are *be*ing fruitful, and

---

⁹⁹⁰ *Cares for*; to tend, to gently lead. The idea is of conducting someone weak on a journey.

⁹⁹¹ *Enactment*; same word as *apportion* and *portion* in verse 22.

they are increasing exceedingly. ²⁸ And he is living—Jacob—in land of Egypt seven of ten⁹⁹² of Year, and it is becoming—days of Jacob, years of his life—seven years and forty and hundred of Year.

²⁹ And they are approaching—days of Israel to cause to die—and he is calling for his son, for Joseph, and he is saying to him, 'If, please! I find grace in your eyes, put you! please! your hand under my thigh, and you do with me kindness and faithfulness. Not so! please! you are entombing me in Egypt. ³⁰ And I lie with my fathers, and you carry me from Egypt, and you entomb me in their tomb.' And he is saying, 'I—I do according to your word.' ³¹ And he is saying, 'Swear you! to me.' And he is swearing to him. And he is bowing himself down—Israel—on the head of the bed⁹⁹³.

48 And it is becoming, after the matters, even these, and he is saying to Joseph, 'Behold! your father is sick.' And he is taking **two of** his sons with him, **Manasseh** and **Ephraim**. ² And he is declaring to Jacob, and he is saying, 'Behold! your son Joseph, he comes to you.' And he is strengthening himself—Israel—and he is sitting on the bed.

³ And he is saying—Jacob—to Joseph, 'God Providence⁹⁹⁴, he appears to me in Luz⁹⁹⁵, in land of Canaan, and he is blessing **me**, ⁴ and he is saying to me, Behold me! your producing⁹⁹⁶; and I increase you, and I give you to an assemblage of peoples, and I give the **land**, even this, to your seed after you; possession of age.

⁵ 'And now, two of your sons, the ones being born to you in land of Egypt before my coming to you toward Egypt, to me, they: Ephraim and Manasseh, as Reuben and Simeon they are mine— ⁶ and your family whom you generate after them, to you they become—over their brothers' name they are called in their inheritance.⁹⁹⁷

---

⁹⁹² *Seven of ten*; seventeen.
⁹⁹³ *Bed*; or couch, also the same word as staff or rod. The root is to stir, stir up, action with resistance.
⁹⁹⁴ *God Providence*; El Shaddai.
⁹⁹⁵ *Luz*; acquiescence, see 28:19 in which he renames the place *Bethel*.
⁹⁹⁶ *Your producing*; the one who is making you fruitful.
⁹⁹⁷ Legally and according to custom, Joseph could not be given the firstborn's privilege of inheriting a double portion; Jacob is circumventing this by adopting Joseph''s two sons. It is useful to quote First Chronicles 5:1 in this

48:7—48:15

⁷ 'And I—in my coming from Padan, she dies over me—Rachel—in land of Canaan, in the way, while yet a pausing⁹⁹⁸ of land to cause to enter Ephrath⁹⁹⁹, and I am entombing her there in way of Ephrath; she—Bethlehem¹⁰⁰⁰.'

⁸ And he is seeing—Israel—Joseph's **sons**, and he is saying, 'Who ? these?' ⁹ And he is saying—Joseph—to his father, 'My sons, they, whom he gives to me—God—in this.' And he is saying, 'Fetch you them! please! to me, and I bless them.'

¹⁰ And Israel's eyes—they are heavy from age, he is not *be*ing able to cause to see. And he is drawing **them** to him, and he is kissing to them, and he is embracing to them. ¹¹ And he is saying—Israel—to Joseph, 'To see of your face I judge not, and behold! he shows **me**—God—also your **seed**.'

¹² And he is *bring*ing forth—Joseph—**them** from with his knees, and he is bowing himself down, to his nose toward the earth.

¹³ And he is taking—Joseph—**two** of them, **Ephraim** in his right from Israel's left, and **Manasseh** in his left from Israel's right, and he is approaching to him.

¹⁴ And he is stretching—Israel—his **right**, and he is placing over Ephraim's head, and he the younger one, and his **left** over Manasseh's head. He well-considers his **hands**, that Manasseh—the first-born.

¹⁵ And he is blessing **Joseph**, and he is saying,
    The God,
        Whom, they walk, my fathers to his face;
            Abraham and Isaac;

---

    respect: *And sons of Reuben Israel's firstborn, that he is the firstborn, and in his defiling his father's chambers, she is given—his birthright—to the sons of Joseph Israel"s son, and caused not to register to the birthright, that Judah, mighty one [geber] among his brothers, and to prince, from him; and the birthright, to Joseph.*

⁹⁹⁸ *Pausing*; a place near either a destination or place one is leaving where one gathers one's affairs for the journey or arrival. The nearest English would be a *rest stop*.

⁹⁹⁹ *Ephrath*; interruption; the idea is of almost reaching a life-goal, and suddenly being arrested. It has also the sense of falling silent in the middle of a sentence. See 35:16.

¹⁰⁰⁰ *Bethlehem*; house of bread.

48:15—48:22

    The God,
        The one shepherding **me**,
            Yet even me
            Unto today, even this;
16   The Angel,
        The one redeeming **me** from all of evil,
        He blesses the **lads**,
            And it is called in them
                My name
            And my fathers' name:
                Abraham and Isaac;
    And they swarm[1001] to multitude in the land's center.'

17 And he is seeing—Joseph—that he is placing—his father—his right hand over Ephraim's head, and it is being evil in his eyes, and he is holding his father's hand to cause to turn her from on Ephraim's head over Manasseh's head. 18 And he is saying—Joseph—to his father, 'Not so, my father; that this one, the firstborn; place you! your right on his head.'

19 And he is refusing—his father—and he is saying, 'I know, my son, I know; he also, he becomes to people, and he also, he is great, and yet his brother, the young one, he is great from him; and his seed, it becomes the nations' fullness.' 20 And he is blessing them in the day, even that, to cause to say, 'In you he blesses—Israel—to cause to say, He places you—God—as Ephraim and as Manasseh.' And he is placing **Ephraim** to Manasseh's face.

21 And he is saying—Israel—to Joseph, 'Behold! I—dying. And he becomes—God—with you, and he restores **you** to land of your fathers. 22 And I—I give to you Shechem, one over your brothers, which I take from the Amorite's hand, in my sword, and in my bow.'[1002]

[1001] *Swarm*; enabled into a capable organization. Without the accent marks it is the same word as *fish*; used only here.

[1002] Shechem had been destroyed by Jacob's sons led by Simeon and Levi. After going up to Bethel, the Amorites (from across the Jordan) likely moved in and took over the crippled city, as was their style. This passage indicates that Jacob retook the land from the Amorite and established ownership, something that had not been done initially in the matter of Hamor.

49:1—49:10

49 And he is calling—Jacob—to his sons and he is saying, 'Be gathered you! and I declare to you **who**, he meets **you** in the last of the days.

² 'Be assembled you! and hear you! sons of Jacob,
And listen you! to Israel your father.
³ Reuben! my first-born—you,
My vigor, and beginning of my virility,
Surplus of exaltation, and surplus of strength;
⁴ Unstable as water, not so you are overreaching[1003];
That you ascend your father's spread[1004], then you profane;
...He ascended my bed.
⁵ Simeon and Levi—brothers!
Instruments of violence—their spoilings[1005]!
⁶ Into their hidden wiles, she is entering not—my soul;
In their assemblage she is uniting not—my glory;
That in their anger they kill ♂man,
And in their alliance hewed bullock.
⁷ Being cursed, their ire, that—strong,
And their rage, that she—hardened;
I distribute them in Jacob,
And I scatter them in Israel.
⁸ Judah—you—they acclaim you, your brothers;
Your hand in nape of ones *be*ing your enemy,
They bow down to you, sons of your father.
⁹ Lion's whelp—Judah,
For prey, my son, you ascend;
He bows, he crouches as lion,
And as a mature lion, who ? he rouses him?
¹⁰ He turns not scepter aside from Judah,
And lawmaker from between his feet,
Until that he comes—Shiloh[1006];

[1003] *Overreaching*; same word as *surplus*.

[1004] *Spread*; used for both a bed and intercourse; the roots mean *the center where things are gathered for touching*.

[1005] *Spoilings*; used only here; to humiliate and fill with dread for profit; to enslave.

[1006] *Shiloh*; bond of peace; hope of salvation. Acting in cohesion with that which is right and proper.

49:10—49:22

And to him, obedience of peoples.
¹¹ One binding to the vine his colt,
And to the prize *vine* the son of his donkey,
He washes[1007] in wine his clothing,
And in blood of grapes his veil;
¹² One intense[1008] of eyes from wine,
And one white of teeth from milk.
¹³ Zebulun—to port of seas he tabernacles,
And he—to port of ships;
And his side on Zidon[1009].
¹⁴ Issachar—donkey of bone crouching between the folds;
¹⁵ And he is seeing gift, that ...good,
And the **land** that she is pleasant,
And he inclines his shoulder to cause to bear,
And he becomes to tribute of one serving.
¹⁶ Dan—he judges his people as one of Israel's tribes.
¹⁷ He becomes—Dan—serpent on road, cobra[1010] on path,
The one biting horse's heels,
And he is falling, his rider, backward.
¹⁸ For your salvation I hope, Jehovah.
¹⁹ Gad—troop, he raids him,
And he—he raids heel.
²⁰ From Asher, fresh his bread;
And he—he gives king's delicacies.
²¹ Naphtali—hind released,
The one giving sayings of distinction.
²² Son *be*ing fruitful—Joseph—
Son *be*ing fruitful over fountain;
Son—ah! striding upon empire[1011];

[1007] *Washes*; in the sense of trampling.
[1008] *Intense*; night-taste. The sense is savoring the enveloping desires of night.
[1009] *Zidon*; ensnaring foe; deceptive enemy; see 10:15.
[1010] *Cobra*; used only here, the word means something conspicuous and frightening that rises up; the closest English word for serpent that fits is the image of the cobra.
[1011] *Son... empire*; the difficulty with translating this line is somewhat alleviated by taking the word normally translated *daughters* and splitting it into *son* and *ah!*, the latter being the sound one makes when under great resistance. *Empire* is normally translated *bull*, and in three cases *barricade* or *wall*. It

²³ And they are embittering him, and they multiply
And they are persecuting him, possessors of arrows;
²⁴ And she is remaining in steadfastness—his bow,
And they are springing¹⁰¹²—arms of his hands
From hands of Jacob's Mighty One;
From there—one shepherding, Israel's Stone.
²⁵ From your father's God¹⁰¹³, and he is helping you,
And **Providence**¹⁰¹⁴, and he blesses you:
Blessings of heavens from above,
Blessings of abyss crouching beneath,
Blessings of breasts and womb;
²⁶ Blessings of your father:
—They prevail over blessings of my progenitors
Unto desire of eternal hills:
They are becoming to Joseph's head,
And to crown of one consecrated of his brothers.
²⁷ Benjamin—wolf—he is tearing;
In the morning he is devouring still,
And to the evening he is apportioning spoil.'

²⁸ All of these: tribes of Israel two ten¹⁰¹⁵. And this which he speaks to them—their father—and he is blessing **them**; ♂man which according to his blessing he blesses **them**.

²⁹ And he is instructing **them**, and he is saying to them, 'I—being gathered to my people; entomb you! **me** to my fathers, to the cave which, in field of Ephron the Hittite; ³⁰ in the cave which, in field of Machpelah, which, Mamre's face, in land of Canaan, which, he buys—Abraham—the **field** from **Ephron** the Hittite for possession of tomb. ³¹ There they entomb **Abraham** and **Sarah** his wife; there they entomb **Isaac** and **Rebecca** his wife; and there I entomb **Leah**; ³² purchase of the field and the cave which, in it from Sons of Heth.'

---

means strong, harmonious, and just; that which is directed according to laws of integrity.

¹⁰¹² *Springing*; the word has the sense of purity of movement and height of joy.
¹⁰¹³ *God*; El.
¹⁰¹⁴ *Providence*; Shaddai.
¹⁰¹⁵ *Two ten*; twelve.

49:33—50:10

³³ And he is finishing—Jacob—to cause to instruct his **sons**, and he is gathering his feet to the bed, and he is expiring, and he is being gathered to his people.

50 And he is falling—Joseph—on his father's face, and he is weeping over him, and he is kissing to him. ² And he is instructing—Joseph—his **servants**, the **physicians**[1016], to cause to embalm his **father**. And they are embalming—the physicians—**Israel**. ³ And they are fulfilling for him forty Day, that so they are fulfilling days of the embalmings. And they are mourning **him**—Egyptians—seventy Day.

⁴ And they are passing—days of his mourning. And he is speaking—Joseph—to Pharaoh's house to cause to say, 'If please! I find favor in your eyes, speak you! please! in Pharaoh's ears to cause to say, ⁵ My father, he adjured me to cause to say, Behold! I die; in my tome which I dig for myself in land of Canaan, toward there you entomb me. And now, I ascend, please! and I entomb my **father**, and I return.' ⁶ And he is saying—Pharaoh, 'Ascend you! and entomb you! your **father**, as which he adjures you.'

⁷ And he is ascending—Joseph—to cause to entomb of his **father**. And they are ascending with him—all of Pharaoh's servants, elders of his house, and all of elders of land of Egypt, ⁸ and all of Joseph's house, and his brothers, and his father's house; but their children and their flock and their herd they leave in land of Goshen. ⁹ And it is ascending with them also chariot, also horsemen, and it is—the camp—exceedingly great.

¹⁰ And they are coming unto threshing floor of the Atad[1017], which, in beyond the Jordan, and they are lamenting there, lamentation great and heavy exceedingly; and he is making for his father

---

[1016] *Physicians*; Rephaim, same word used for the race of giants in 14:5. As this is the only instance in which the word is used for physician, it suggests that these servants of Joseph may actually have been members of the race who had angelic blood mixed with human, further strengthened by the fact that both *Rephaim* and *servants* are emphasized in the text. The Rephaim themselves were so called because of their superhuman ability to heal themselves, making them formidable foes. The archetype initiated with the serpent in 3:15 through Goliath through Daniel 7:20 presents their weak spot as being in the head.

[1017] *Atad*; bramble; a low moaning of consolation.

mourning, seven of days, ¹¹ And he is seeing—one dwelling of the land, the Canaanite—the **mourning** in threshing floor of the Atad, and they are saying, 'Heavy mourning, this, for Egyptians;' on this he calls her name 'Abel Mizraim[1018],' which, in beyond the Jordan.

¹² And they are doing—his sons—for him so as which he instructs them. ¹³ And they are carrying **him**—his sons—toward the land of Canaan, and they are entombing **him** in cave of field of the Machpelah, which he buys—Abraham—the **field** for possession of tomb, from **Ephron** the Hittite, on Mamre's face.

¹⁴ And he is returning—Joseph—toward Egypt, he and his brothers and all of the ones ascending with him to cause to entomb his **father**, after his entombing his **father**.

¹⁵ And they are seeing—Josephs brothers—that he is dead—their father—and they are saying, 'If he is persecuting us—Joseph—and to turn back, he is turning back to us **all of** the evil which we treat **him**.'

¹⁶ And they are instructing to Joseph, to cause to say, 'Your father, he instructed to face of his death, to cause to say, ¹⁷ Thus you say to Joseph, Ah! bear you! please! transgression of your brothers and their sin, that evil they treat you; and now, bear you! please! to transgression of servants of God of your father.' And he is weeping—Joseph—in their speaking to him.

¹⁸ And they are going also—his brothers—and they are falling to his face, and they are saying, 'Behold us! to you for servants.'

¹⁹ And he is saying to them—Joseph—'As nothing you are fearing, that ? in God's stead—I? ²⁰ And you—you devised against me evil—God—he devised her for good, so that to doing as today, even this, to cause to *keep* alive many people. ²¹ And now, not so you are fearing; I—I sustain **you** and your **children**.' And he is comforting **them**, and he is speaking over their heart.

²² And he is dwelling—Joseph—in Egypt, he and his father's house. And he is living—Joseph—hundred and ten of years. ²³ And he is seeing—Joseph—to Ephraim, sons of thirds[1019]; also

---

[1018] *Abel Mizraim*; mourning Egyptians.
[1019] *Thirds*; third generation.

50:23—50:26

sons of Machir, son of Manasseh, they are born on Joseph's knees.

²⁴ And he is saying—Joseph—to his brothers, 'I—dying, and God—to visit, he visits **you**, and he *bring*s up **you** from the land, even this, to the land which he swears to Abraham, to Isaac, and to Jacob.'

²⁵ And he is adjuring—Joseph—**sons** of Israel, to cause to say, 'To visit he visits—God—**you**, and you *bring* up my **bones** from this.'

²⁶ And he is dying—Joseph—son of hundred and ten years, and they are embalming **him**, and he is being placed in the ark[1020] in Egypt.

[1020] *Ark*; same word as the ark of the covenant, though different from the ark of the deluge. It means a strong coffer or chest.

Index to the Appendices

Appendix I *What Genesis One Does Not Say*............................182
Before we approach the text with all our answers, it is useful to consider the questions.

Appendix II *The Changes to Adam: Original Sin that Isn't*....192
An ordinary look at Adam and Eve's bodies demystifies religious dogma; did we fall from a state of goodness, or rise to a state that we couldn't handle?

Appendix III *The Two Trees: Morality vs. Mortality*...............202
A look at what being mortal means, and what God is and has always been doing about it.

Appendix IV *Jehovah vs. Elohim*...210
Ancient warring factions or common sense that a child could understand?

Appendix V *The Woman and the Seed*......................................216
A look at the ramifications of being a woman ...to Jesus.

Appendix VI *The Stories in the Genealogical Histories*.........224
It's far more than a list of names.

Appendix VII *Time*..232
Time is not *longer* than we think, it's *broader*.

Appendix VIII *The Days of the Deluge, Peleg, and Eber*.......238
How the initial power centers that are still around were set up.

Appendix IX *Sarai, Mother of Faith*..247
How Sarah picks up where Eve left off.

Appendix X *Mother of All Living*..255
    Eve, Rebecca, and the dialogue between sister, mother, and wife.

Appendix XI *Seventy Souls to Egypt*..263
    Who went down with Jacob to Egypt, and why the record is set that way.

Appendix XII *Year/years: Hidden Cycles in the Text*..............266
    How the grammar and the numerics work together.

Appendix XIII *Themes Within Themes: the Ephesian
        Pattern*..274
    How the overarching saga of Genesis is summarized in Ephesians as a model of reality.

Appendix XIV *Where Was the Field?*......................................278
    An investigation into this strange word that begins the second account of creation suggests an entire world that we are missing.

Appendix XV *Translator's Comment*..288

Appendix I

What Genesis One Does Not Say

Reading Genesis for the first time is an amazing experience. Personally, I did not get this experience; when I sit down to read it, my mind is loaded with all the presuppositions of both my culture and beliefs as well as all the arguments for or against what it must mean. Lost in this morass is *what it says*: the Words. The simple statements unapologetically set down one right after another that defy explanation, contradiction, or even defense.

The text does not try to defend itself. The text does not try to explain itself. The text does not implore or demand belief. The text does not use symbols that exist apart from reality. Contrast this with any other writing that reaches for the same genre; there is nothing that compares.

This translation is as close as I can get to reading it for the first time. What is not needed is an explanation of what it means: what is needed is clarity regarding what it *says*. There is necessarily a great deal of overlap with what it means... hence this appendix. I do not wish to argue over interpretation; a lifetime of doing so has demonstrated the utter futility of words about words. A person will believe precisely what they wish to believe; neither more nor less. And yet there is great value in the investigation of what it says. To demonstrate this value, as much to myself as to the reader, here we will look at what it *doesn't* say.

One more point before beginning, merely another of the many elephants in the room: we have limits. Suppose with me for a moment that Genesis does not. Just suppose. We take our limits—wherever they may be set—to the text and apply them as we read. The fundamental literalist believes in seven 24-hour days. This is fine, but when he tries to make the text *prove* his belief, it becomes a limit. The text is not attempting to prove a single thing. While it may do so by the bye, that is not the purpose for which it was written. The words must be twisted out of their own context to fit the context of proof, which will always prevent the reading of *what it says*. Another example: a person believes that Genesis 1 is an amazing myth that skillfully incorporates archetypes in a manner that informs us as to our origins. Which is fine, but when insistence on the mythological character of the text is expanded through the rest of scripture, no breaking point is found. The need to mythologize the text becomes a limit. And it limits the reading of what it actually says because while the text uses myths, dreams, archetypes, parables, and visions, it always explicitly states that it is doing so. Genesis 1 does not.

It is counterproductive to reiterate what it says here, because it already says what it says, and no amount of reiteration can improve on that. It is productive, however, in light of the false confidence we derive from our limits, to test those limits by pointing out a few assumptions that may not hold true upon examination.

In the beginning
...of what?

*he creates—God—the **heavens** and the **earth**.*
That is all we're given. Not order and chaos, no great opposites, no beings or gods with issues; simply the heavens and the earth in that order. No mention of what it cost God to do it, no mention of why he did it, no hint as to his plans. If we sat down to write great literature, this is the *last* way we would choose to begin.

And the earth, she becomes chaos and vacancy,
Why are we suddenly *only* talking about the earth when the great thematic introduction mentioned the heavens first? How did this earth become chaos and vacancy? Are we supposed to guess, or is the answer coming (it isn't.)? What's with the "and"; doesn't that mean this is a continuation of the thought? How does this continue the thought of God creating something *in the beginning*?

and darkness over the face of Abyss,
What abyss? Where is it? Why is it dark?

and Spirit of God ready-hovering over face of the waters.
Who is this Spirit, and why is he never again mentioned in the account if he's so important? What's he doing over the waters? Where did these waters come from? If we assume he's "ready" for the seven days of creation, what is his role?

And he is saying—God—'it becomes light;' and it is becoming light.
What is becoming light? Where is this light coming from? If the sun isn't appearing for another three days, and it's only called a "light bearer", what is different about this light? Can we see it? Did God create this light? Is creating the same as speaking?

*And he is seeing—God—the **light**, that as good;*
How do you see the light itself? Shouldn't it say that God saw the earth, now that it's lit up? Is it lit up? And what makes it good?

and he is separating—God—between the light and between the darkness.
How exactly does one do this? Is the earth being used? Wouldn't that mean that the light is from a source like the sun? What's doing the separating? Just God?

And he is calling—God—to the light 'Day,' and to the darkness he calls 'Night;'
What does it mean that he is calling "to" the light and darkness? Is this different from simply calling them day and night? And why now?

and it is becoming evening, and it is becoming morning . . . day One.
Why is evening first? We just had light and darkness as well as day and night in the previous verse, what's up with "evening" and "morning"? Why switch the terms? And why is it "day one" instead of "the first day" like the rest of the days in the chapter?

And he is saying—God—'it becomes space in the middle of the waters, and it becomes separating between waters toward waters.'

Once again, what is this "it" that is becoming the space? If this space is in the middle of the waters, how did that happen? This would mean that there's an equal amount of water on each side of the "space". How does "it" hold them apart, "separate" them?

*And he is making—God—the **space**, and he is separating between the waters which, from-under to the space, and between the waters which, from-above to the space: and it is becoming so.*
So this is water above and below? To have the same amount both places, we'd need a lot more than just clouds involved. Where is it? 8:2 says *And they are surrendering—springs of Abyss and hidden crevices of the heavens—and he is being forbidden—the water mass from the heavens* . . .which does not sound like all the water mass was used up; you don't "forbid" something that isn't there anymore.

And he is calling—God—to the space 'Heavens;' and it is becoming evening, and it is becoming morning—day second.
So this space is "Heavens"? Weren't the heavens created "in the beginning" and already there? The earth is certainly there. What's going on? And why isn't this day declared "good"? And if there's still no sun shining, how do we get a "day second", far less another evening and morning?

And he is saying—God—'They flow together, the waters, from under the heavens toward one place, and she is seen—the dryness:' it is becoming so.
"From under the heavens" means there's no more water seen under the heavens. Where did it go? Where is this "one place"? It can't be oceans because they're still under the heavens.

And he is calling—God—to the dryness 'Earth,' and to the collection of the waters he calls 'Seas.' And he is seeing—God—that as good.
Now we actually name the collection of waters "seas". Where are they, and why is that good? And how is dry dirt called "earth"; why wasn't it "earth" when it had water on it?

And he is saying—God—'She causes to vegetate, the earth, vegetation; herbage sowing seed; fruit tree making fruit to his species whose seed of him is in him on the earth;' and it is becoming so.

How does the earth cause the vegetation? Did she already have the seeds hanging around in her, or did she poof them into existence? If she poofed them, can she still do it today? If they were already there, what were they left over from? And what about trees that *don't* produce fruit? And why tell us that it's "on the earth", isn't that obvious?

And she is yielding forth—the earth—vegetation; herbage sowing seed to his species, and fruit-making tree whose seed of him is in him to his species. And he is seeing—God—that as good. And it is becoming evening, and it is becoming morning—day third.

How are these things growing without the sun? Why the insistent repetition of "to his species"? And once again, if the earth is the agent by which this is being done—and not God directly 'poofing' things—what exactly is the process?

And he is saying—God—'He becomes light-bearers in the space of the heavens, to cause to separate between the day and between the night. And they become for signs, and for appointments, and for days and years. And they become for light-bearers in space of the heavens to cause to light on the earth;' and it is becoming so.

These "light bearers" are in the "space of the heavens"? The same space that has all that water above it? This means the sun and moon and stars have water above them, if we're to take the next section seriously. And now for the first time we have "light on the earth" mentioned. Did the previous light not shine on the earth? And what is the difference between God separating between the light and darkness on day one and the light bearers separating between the day and the night here?

*And he is making—God—**two** of the light-bearers: the great ones: the **light bearer**, the great one, to ruling of the day, and the **light bearer**, the small one, to ruling of the night—and the **stars**. And he is giving—God—**them** in the space of the heavens to cause to light on the earth, and to cause to rule in the day and in the night, and to cause to separate between the light and between the* *darkness. And he is seeing—God—that as good. And it is becoming evening, and it is becoming morning—day fourth.*

In the previous section the light bearers were to separate between the day and the night; here they are to separate between the light and the darkness, just as God did in day one. Why the difference? And why are they merely called "light bearers" if, as we suppose, all light comes from the sun? And this "ruling" day and night, what about when the moon is showing at daytime? Is it simply not "ruling"? And once again, if this is the first time there is light "on the earth", what was up with the light of day one?

*And he is saying—God—'They roam the waters; roamers of living soul and flier flies over the earth on face of space of heavens. And he is creating—God—the **monsters**, the great ones, and **all of** the living soul, the moving, they who roam the waters to their species, and **all of** flier of wing to his species.*

Why do birds and fish get their own day? What is so special about them; why can't they be made on the next day with the rest of the beasts? And what is so important about fish "roaming" that the text can't even use the word "fish"? Or for that matter, can't even use the word "birds" but says "flier" instead? And what's up with the monsters—this is the only use of the word "create" other than when God creates man. And where do these "roamers" and "fliers" come from—the beasts on the next day are brought forth from the earth like the plants. Who's making these?

*And he is seeing—God—that as good. And he is blessing **them**— God—to cause to say, 'You—fruitful! and you—increase! and you —fill the **waters** in the seas! and the flier, he increases in the earth.' And it is becoming evening, and it is becoming morning— day fifth.*

What's up with "blessing" the fish and birds (and monsters)? Nobody else gets blessed except Adam. The beasts of the next day don't get blessed; the stars, sun, and moon did not get blessed. And if these "seas" are hidden away in their "one place" which is not "under heaven", where are they? And for that matter, why does Adam later get to name the birds but not the fish? Are they too far away? And why is the flier increasing "in" the earth and not "on" it or "over" it?

*And he is saying—God—'She brings forth—the earth—living soul to her species; beast and moving ones and animal of him to her— earth's—species;' and it is becoming so. And he is making—God —**animal** of the earth to her species, and the **beast** to her species, and **all of** moving ones of the ground to his species. And he is seeing—God—that as good.*

What is the difference between an "animal", a "beast", and a "moving one"? Is this like mammals, reptiles, and insects or something? And how exactly does the earth bring them forth? We can understand leftover seeds for the plants, but 'beast seeds' is somewhat of a stretch. And they probably weren't just holding their breath when all that water was on the earth. And the text is clearly stating that these are brought forth according to "earth's" species... then it goes on to say that each is according to its own species. Which is it? Do animals' species belong to the earth somehow? Where would their DNA be hidden in the dirt, or "the dryness"? And it first says that the earth is to bring these forth, then it says that God makes them. Which is it? What is the process? Why this elaborate way of describing their origin?

And he is saying—God—'We do Adam in image of us, as likeness of us, and they descend in fish of the sea, and in flier of the heavens, and in the beast, and in all of the earth, and in all of the moving, the moving one on the earth.'

Is this the 'royal we' or who is talking? To merely assign it to an idea of the Trinity is borrowing from outside the text and seems like cheating. Likewise, how can Adam be in the image and likeness of a plurality? <u>Who is the</u> "*we*"? And why the repetition of "moving"? And for that matter, why the doubling up and use of both "in" the earth and "on" the earth?

*And he is creating—God—the **Adam** in His image; in image of God he created **him**: male and female he created **them**.*

The text is obviously making a very strong point with "him" and "them". What is it? Why the repetition of "image"? Why is God suddenly singular again, what happened to "we" and "us"? Is it saying that "male and female" is necessary for that image, or is it contrasting "he created him" with "he created them" to say that the male is the image? And what happened to the "likeness" of the previous section? And what does "the Adam" have to do with "monsters", the only other thing in the whole passage that is "created" like the original "heavens and earth"?

*And he is blessing **them**—God—and he is saying to them—God —'You—fruitful! and you—increase! and you!—fill the **earth**, and you—subdue her! and you!—descend in fish of the sea, and in flier of the heavens, and in every animal, the moving one on the earth.'*

Why does the earth need subdued? We can understand the animals somewhat, but the earth itself? Why are the "beasts" left out; we have only that they "descend in" "every animal, the moving one on the earth"? Why would God tell them to fill the earth, then stick them in a garden and tell them to guard it? Which did he want them to do? And why is Adam told to "increase" just like the fish and birds, while the beasts, animals, and moving ones are given no such instructions?

*And he is saying—God—'Behold! I give to you **all of** herb seeding seed, that on the face of all of the earth, and **all of** the tree which, in him, fruit of tree seeding seed for you; he is becoming for food, and for **all of** animal of the earth, and for **all of** flier of the heavens, and for **all of** moving ones on the earth, which in him has living soul, breath of life, **all of** green herbage for food:' and it is becoming so.*

Why are the first recorded words from God to man about food? Isn't this a rather elaborate way of telling them what they can eat? It sounds like God is saying that everything is vegetarian... except for the fish who apparently do not have the "breath of life". Does this also mean that fish do not have "living soul"? What about the monsters? Why does he list herb, seed, tree, fruit, and green herbage? And why does it say "and it is becoming so" when he hasn't actually done anything, except to give instructions? And what's with the constant emphasis on "all of" repeated six times; what is actually being said here? Does *"all of the tree, which in him, fruit of tree seeding seed for you"* include the tree of the knowledge of good and evil... eventually? Why is not the creation of Adam specifically declared good? In the next section he sees that "all of" that which he has done is very good, but Adam gets no personal accolade. Why not?

*And he is seeing—God—**all of** that which he has done, and behold! very good. And it is becoming evening, and it is becoming morning—day of the sixth.*
There's that "all of" again for an even seven times. Is his summary of everything he has done somehow connected with telling them what they can eat? Why does it say "day of the sixth" instead of "sixth day" like the other days? Day of the sixth *what*?

And they are being finished—the heavens and the earth and all of their assembly.
Is this the same "heavens and earth" that he created "in the beginning" or did he redo everything? If, as it seems, he redid everything, are we supposed to understand something about the original "heavens and earth" from this account, or are we just left hanging? And what's with the plural possessive of "their assembly"; do all the things of the six days belong equally to both the "heavens" and the "earth"? Or does a text that takes great pains to make distinctions suddenly get vague? And just what is this connection between the heavens and the earth; were we supposed to somehow get it from this account? After all, the text began its introductory statement with that theme; did the writer forget what he was doing?

*And he is finishing—God—in the seventh day his work which he does; and he is ceasing in the seventh day from all of his work which he does. And he is blessing—God—the **seventh day**, and he is making holy, **him**, that in him he ceases from all of his work which he creates—God—to cause to do.*
Why is he blessing the "day" instead of the "work which he does"? These days are already weird enough, what with being defined by "evening and morning" and occurring without the sun; now he's going to bless one of them? And the thing that makes this day "holy" is the fact that he's not doing anything on it? Why does it say that he is "finishing" on the seventh day; wouldn't it make more sense to say that he finished on the sixth day and rested on the seventh? What's up with the strange way of

summarizing in the last line; how does God "create to cause to make (or do)"? And where is the "evening and morning" for this day if it's so special?

*　　　*　　　*

We find that when we read the words, more questions come up than answers. I do not intend here to leave the reader hanging or doubting the veracity of the text; my purpose is to point out that the constructs we bring to the text are insufficient tools for understanding the text. There are some suggestions given in Appendix XIV, using the clues given to us in the rest of scripture, for beginning to crack open the story being presented. And the section following Genesis 1 provides an enormous amount of answers ...while at the same time it raises an enormous amount of new questions.

This is scripture, and this is how scripture operates. It is not composed of dogma, but composed of words. Strangely, it has been given to us to be able to read these words. There is more involved with the words of the text than can be iterated. Reading them is a good place to start.

Appendix II

The Changes to the Adam: Original Sin that Isn't

In Appendix III we will discuss the necessity of the Holy Spirit to the human body. Here we will consider the human body as mortal, how it got that way, what this has to do with 'sinning' (or not), and why men and angels alike are attracted to women.

Let us start by establishing a simple rule by which to discuss this: No mysticism. Let us stick to the actual words of the Text, and since we are talking about *physical* bodies, let us refrain from appealing to grandiose doctrines; especially ones that do not occur anywhere in the text; regardless of how much they are touted by tradition. I refer primarily to the one in the title, 'original sin', but we will uncover—and hopefully disengage ourselves from—several others.

The subsequent accounts of the formation of Adam and Eve in the Text, as given in chapter two, are *most* peculiar. He was not subject to death, but did not have eternal life. He was naked but did not know it. He and all the land animals were products of the Earth, but his wife was not. He had access to the Tree of Life but he did not avail himself of it. He and his wife were created in the image of God in chapter 1, but God takes his good old time in chapter 2 coming around to the need for her, which required sleep, always synonymous with death in scripture. In short, we have more oddities in this account than any parallel myths that *any* culture could ever hope to gather into such a succinct account.

And unlike the thousands of myths around the world, this story does not resolve. The attempts to insert moral lessons into the account, such as God 'punishing' Adam and Eve for eating of the wrong fruit, fall apart upon simple reading of the actual words. It is an account of something that happened *and is still happening*; something that began a story *that is still being told*. That is the great difficulty in approaching this, the most seminal story of Mankind ever written; we find ourselves still in the story, from which vantage point it is nearly impossible to get an objective perspective. So let's get a subjective one.

Finding ourselves in this place, it is somewhat valuable to begin by noting what the story does *not* say. The reason is that if mankind has been embroiled in this struggle for thousands of years, and all the while attempting to tame it by explaining it away, we are burdened with the weight of a thousand explanations for something that, quite simply, cannot yet be fully explained. So we must clear out the rubble before examining the structure, as Nehemiah was obliged to do.

Now. Beginning at the beginning, we have the first limit placed on the Adam: "*And he is instructing—Jehovah God—on the Adam, to cause to say, 'From any of tree of the Garden eating you eat;* [17] *but from tree of knowledge of good and evil, you eat not from him, that in Day of your eating from him—dying you die.*'"

What do we see here? That the dying was not a punishment, but an *effect* of eating of the tree. We might say, "Don't eat that mushroom, it will make you see pink elephants and give you the runs." We are not being *punished* when we sit on the porcelain throne watching the pink elephants, we are simply experiencing the results of our actions. Note that when God tells Adam that the earth is being cursed for his sake, he doesn't say, "Because you disobeyed me," but "Because you listened to your wife." And the question to be considered here is this: did God curse the ground there and then, or was the ground automatically cursed as the result of Adam's action? Big difference. Or again, was it a necessary step taken by God to *preserve* Adam from something which otherwise might take him down? Never mind its effect on Adam; of what value *to God* was the cursing of the ground? Or for that matter, of what value to God was it that the Adam should die?

Let us start with the subject of dying. We have emphasized to us by the evangelicals the verses in Romans, Corinthians, and elsewhere which unequivocally state things like *"For this, even as by one man sin entered into the world, and by sin death; and thus death passed upon all men, for that all have sinned..."* Thus our minds tend to make several conclusions that scripture does *not* make; such as the idea that there was no thought or intention of death in the mind of God until the Adam introduced it.

Really?

Jesus says, *"Verily, verily, I say unto you, Except the grain of wheat falling into the ground die, it abides alone; but if it die, it bears much fruit."* So death is involved with seeds, which are mentioned already on day three. Jesus again: *"...and after this he says to them, Lazarus, our friend, is fallen asleep, but I go that I may awake him out of sleep. The disciples therefore said to him, Lord, if he be fallen asleep, he will get well. But Jesus spoke of his death, but* they *thought that he spoke of the rest of sleep. Jesus therefore then said to them plainly, Lazarus has died."* So death is involved with sleep, which happened to Adam during the formation of the Woman. What else do we find?

Job says, *"That day—let it be darkness, let not God care for it from above, neither let light shine upon it: Let darkness and the shadow of death claim it; let clouds dwell upon it; let darkeners of the day terrify it."* And Elihu later replies, *"Desire not the night, when peoples are cut off from their place."* Now we find that *night* is used for death, and that takes us back to the first and fourth days. In fact, a careful examination of each of the days of creation will show that death is plainly a necessary part of *every one of them*. Psalms 69: *"Let not the flood of waters overflow me, neither let the deep swallow me up; and let not the pit shut its mouth upon me."* ...the second day. Jonah and Jesus: *"And Jonah prayed unto Jehovah his God out of the fish's belly... ...I went down to the bottoms of the mountains; The bars of the earth [closed] upon me for ever: But you have brought up my life from the pit, O Jehovah my God,"* "*For even as Jonas was in the belly of the great fish three days and three nights, thus shall the Son of man be in the heart of the earth three days and three nights*" ...the fifth day.

Oops.

Well with that in mind, let us look at what the entirety of scripture does *not* say about Adam's disobedience to God. It never says that it was <u>sin</u>. It gets pretty close; it's called a *transgression* in Job, Hosea, Romans, and First Timothy, because he *transgressed* the commandment of God. One would think that if it's so important to realize that Adam *sinned*, that it would say so *somewhere* in the whole of Scripture. It doesn't. Why not? Simple: a being who does not know good and evil is neither moral nor immoral; he is amoral. As such, while he can be disobedient, while he can transgress, while he can fail to make the correct choice, he cannot *sin*. Sin is what happens when we know what we are doing. Or to put it in scripture's language, "To him therefore who knows how to do good, and does it not, to him it is sin." Adam didn't *know*.

The verse quoted a few paragraphs above says "...*by one man sin <u>entered</u> into the world*"; it could hardly have entered if it were already here.

Next question: Did the curse change Adam's body after he ate the fruit so that he would die? Here's what God said to Adam: "*That you listen to voice of your wife, and you are eating from the tree which I instruct you, to cause to say, You eat not from him, the ground is being cursed for your sake; in vexation you eat her all of days of your life, ¹⁸ And thorn and thistle she sprouts for you, and you eat herbage of the field; ¹⁹ In sweat of your nostrils you eat bread until you are caused to return to the ground; that from her you are taken; that dust—you—and to dust you return."* What is the contrast with returning to the ground? Look at Isaiah: "*For as the rain comes down, and the snow from heaven, and returns not to here, but waters the earth, and makes it bring forth and bud, that it may give seed to the sower, and bread to the eater: so shall my word be that goes forth out of my mouth: it shall not return unto me void, but it shall do that which I please, and it shall accomplish that for which I send it."* And compare First Corinthians [15]: *"And what you sow, you sow not the body that will be, but a bare grain: it may be of wheat, or some one of the rest: and God gives to it a body as he has pleased, and to each of the seeds its own body."* What is the point? That when God places something on the earth, it undergoes a *change* before it returns to God. His word *accomplishes* something, and it is that accomplishment that returns to him, not his original word. The seed gets a *body* that God gives it; the reaper doesn't go out and dig up the original seeds.

But not so with Adam. "Dust you are, and to dust you return." This is one of the very definitions of death; *to fail to get the requisite change needed to produce fruit to God.* Some of these ramifications are discussed in Appendix III, so let's stick to the subject: How does that fact that *"in Adam all die"* serve God's purposes? And more importantly, What physically happened to Adam that was passed on to all his generations?

Before we address the simple answers to those questions, we must bring up one more: How is it that Jesus was born without sin if he was a man born from Adam? Or to *really* stick to our subject, How is it that Jesus was *physically* born without sin if he was a man born from Adam? This brings up the subject of the Seed of the Woman which Appendix V addresses somewhat. Here, let us draw the hands of the clock back to the Garden again, and look at, not just the days, but the minutes and seconds.

Any high school student could jump in here and tell us that Adam's DNA, if changed, would both allow death and pass on that trait to his children. While I am not terribly enamored by Biology's forays into that subject, it is the extent to which common understanding has come today, so let us take it up where it is. There are two common elements (and not very many uncommon ones) that can change DNA in such a way as it gets passed on to the progeny: alcohol and radiation. It is common knowledge—though seldom taught—that if a man has four healthy kids, becomes an alcoholic, and then has four more, that the latter four will not only be stunted and sickly, but that they will pass those traits to their children. These kinds of studies were common in the 19th century. As I mentioned, Biology today has its own agendas as to what gets emphasized and what gets buried.

There is every indication that *both* were involved; that something about the fruit of the tree of the knowledge of good and evil was very closely akin to alcohol, if not naturally fermenting on the branch. A look at the role of the Greek Dionysian legend and its parallels in all ancient cultures will show a close connection between gaining mystical insight and alcohol, but here we wish to limit ourselves to scripture. And while the Hebrew allows for many a hint of an alcoholic experience—not the least of which is the repetition of the incident with Noah—it does not explicitly state it. Yet we have many supportive scriptures to this point, such as Ephesians 5:18 which directly contrasts the effects of alcohol with what was meant to be the Adam's completion—the Spirit; *"And be not drunk with wine, in which is riot; but be filled with the Spirit."* Either way, it is apparent from the cherubim with the flashing sword that Adam was now susceptible to light, i.e., radiation, in a way that he previously was not. This is one of the ways that alcohol works *with* radiation; it breaks down the body's natural ability to use, for example, sunlight, and what was previously a healthy influence becomes a degrading influence.

The previous two paragraphs have indulged in some speculation which I have chosen to pass on for the reader's own considerations; yet the point stands on its own: Adam's DNA was irreparably damaged, whatever the process. Now let's look at the timing of this particular damage, especially in comparison with the Woman. A man's seed is constantly being produced by his body; if his body's DNA is damaged, the resultant seed will be damaged. Thus, every man born of the seed of Adam has the same limitations to growth that Adam brought upon himself.

What about the Woman? God's promise to the serpent was *"And enmity I am setting between you and between the woman, and between your seed and her seed; head—he overwhelms you; and heel—you overwhelm him."* Unlike a man, a woman is born with all the eggs that she will ever have already in her. Unlike the formation of a man in the womb, when a woman is being formed the mitochondrial DNA is made *before* any of the rest of the body —including before being mixed with the male's genes—and set aside for the eggs. Later, when the egg is fertilized, her chromosomes and the chromosomes from the man will get involved, and the resultant child has traits from both. In other words, the mitochondrial DNA gets passed from mother to daughter—never from mother to son—*unchanged* from how it was formed originally in Eve.

What is the point? Adam's seed replicates the damage from the fruit. But the woman *already* had all her seed before ever eating of the fruit; while her body was damaged by the fruit, her seed was not. Yet every time she bears a child, it has required the seed of the man which is damaged, thus producing an offspring susceptible to death and sin. There are rare cases of virgin births known, but they necessarily can only produce daughters without that Y chromosome from the male. All except one; if there were ever a virgin birth of a *male*, he could be born fully human—yet without susceptibility to death or sin. Thus the promised Seed, Jesus, had to be born of a virgin. But if we're not getting mystical we need to know how *physically* Jesus got that Y chromosome. And all we have to do is go to the Text itself: *"And the angel answering said to her, Holy Spirit will come upon you, and power of Most High overshadow you, wherefore the one being generated of you—holy—will be called Son of God."* The very element that God had been waiting to give to the Adam—the Spirit—was given to produce the Seed of the Woman.

So let us review. That something physical happened to Adam which rather than producing something evil in him, produced an inability to grow to be good—all the while knowing what good was. That this physical change was passed down to his sons and daughters by dint of the damaged DNA in his seed. That woman was the safe-house for the blueprint of a perfect and undamaged human by dint of her mitochondrial DNA duplicating itself outside of the influences of the man's seed. That man would die in this body rather than being transformed into something that would return glory to God. That God allowed this because the pattern of death was prepared for in every facet of his creation. That "original sin" is never mentioned in scripture; the very concept of a mystical force that makes us evil distracts us from the simple fact that we were formed unfinished, and that God—in setting up the creation to weather death in every single day of creating—had prepared for this contingency. That Woman, housing the untainted DNA formed by God, *and* being a new creation of the kind never seen before, had the capacity to produce an original Man as God created him, and subsequently was *quite* attractive to errant angels who wished offspring of their own

It is somewhat difficult to summarize at this point since the ramifications are just beginning to blossom, but I deem it better if the reader explores them from the scriptures. Let us answer the remaining questions initially brought up: Of what value to *God* was it that the ground would be cursed and that Adam should die and return to it? As we see from the footnote in 2:7, *Adam* and *Ground* are taken from the same word. Romans 8, when taking up this subject, says *"For I reckon that the sufferings of this present season are not worthy to be compared with the coming glory to be revealed to us. For earnest expectation of the creation awaits the revelation of the sons of the God. For the creation was subjected to vanity, not of its own will, but by reason of him who subjected it in hope, that the creation itself also will be freed from the bondage of the corruption into the freedom of the glory of the children of the God. For we know that the whole creation groans and travails in pain together until now."*

This tells us plainly that the curse was of *"him who subjected it"* in order that it would *"be freed"*. This takes a bit of the onus off of Adam; though to be sure he bears a measure of the responsibility. Yet what we are seeing is not a failure of God's plans by the Serpent's meddling nor a ruining of God's plans by Adam's failure, but *an unfolding of greater plans than had been possible before*. That is to say, if Adam alone had proceeded unhindered with his wife in their path to God, God would have gotten one thing. But Adam having been hindered, and God having foreseen and prepared for this, God gets far, far more; an entire creation by which to build a new heavens and a new earth rather than merely another pair of worshippers (Adam and Eve) for his company; this new creation taken out of the side of the Seed while 'asleep' in death.

But now we see not yet all things subjected to him. But we behold him who has been made a little lower than angels, Jesus, because of the suffering of the death crowned with glory and honor, that by God's grace he should taste of death for every one. For it became him, for whom are the All, and through whom are the All, in bringing many sons unto glory, to perfect the author of their salvation through sufferings. For both the sanctifier and sanctified—all of one: for which cause he is not ashamed to call them brethren, saying, I will declare your name to my brethren, In midst of assembly will I sing your praise. And again, I will be trusting in him. And again, Lo, I and the little children whom the God has given me.

Appendix III
The Two Trees: Morality vs. Mortality

It is somewhat peculiar that the popularization of Moses' account of the Genesis 2 so often misses the fact that there were *two* trees, and that the Tree of Life was not forbidden. And yet after eating of the fruit of the Tree of the Knowledge of Good and Evil, it was *very* forbidden; a mighty Cherubim with **flame of the sword** (emphatic in the Text); the one turning round on herself, or infolding herself, set to now prevent them from eating of it. Between these two facts, we have the key to understanding.

The Adam, which includes both male and female, was created naked, and they did not know it. Two points are to be considered here.

The first one is that in the *absolute* account, Genesis 1 through 2:3, the male and the female are clearly stated as being both what constituted the Adam, and what constituted the image of God. This is reiterated in 5:1-2. Then a separate account is kindly inserted by God from 2:4 through chapter 4, in which the details of how this happened are laid out. Now it is easily apparent that something *naked* is in fact something that is *incomplete*, as Second Corinthians says in 5:1-5,

For we know that if the earthly house of our tabernacle be dissolved, we have a building from God, house not made with hands, eternal, in the heavens. For indeed in this we groan, longing to be clothed upon with our house which is from heaven; if so be that being clothed we will not be found naked. For indeed we who are in the tabernacle groan, being burdened; not for that we would be unclothed, but that we would be clothed upon, that the mortal be swallowed up by life. Now he that has wrought us for this very thing—God, who also has given to us the earnest of the Spirit.

There are two times in the absolute account that God does not specifically declare something *good*, and both are elements which were simply *unfinished*. The first was the dividing of the waters to make a space, the heavens. Search as we might, there is no declaration of 'good' on the second day; while the gathering of those same waters into the earth to let the dryness appear *was* declared good on the third day. The reason is that the space of heavens was a continuation of a previous episode, as the text shows in 1:1. and would not be fully finished until Deluge came (note that the Text treats Deluge as a sentient being), as we see with God's promise to Noah. So we see both there, and with the serpent, that the ages overlap. The Adam is a newcomer to an ancient chessboard.

The other element not specifically declared good was the creation of the Adam. He too was naked, unfinished, and not yet 'good', as Jesus demonstrates in these two sayings of Luke 18:18 and 13:31:
"And a certain ruler asked him saying, 'Good teacher, having done what, shall I inherit eternal life?' But Jesus said to him, 'Why do you call me good? There is none good but one, God.' "
"And he said to them, 'Go, tell that fox, Behold, I cast out demons and accomplish cures today and tomorrow, and the third I am perfected; but I must needs walk today and tomorrow and the following, for it must not be that a prophet perish out of Jerusalem.' "
So we see that there is a process of being perfected, and thus no longer naked, unfinished, and not yet good, as Jesus and Paul refer to. Note that the animals of the sixth day *were* specifically declared good; that declaration for the Adam is withheld for the time being.

The second point is based on that one: What was God's original intention for the process by which the Adam would be finished? We find one answer to this in the relationship between the two trees.

With these introductory points in mind, let us continue to the subject.

The presence of two trees indicates God's intention to at some point give Adam access to the tree of the knowledge of good and evil, for it would be silly to plant a tree of such magnificence just to tempt the Adam; James tells us that God tempts no one (1:13).

James also tells us that anyone who judges his brother judges the law, and furthermore that anyone who judges the law puts himself in the position of God. Thus we see that *having* the knowledge of good and evil gives us the unfortunate ability—and extreme tendency—to *judge*... the which is not appropriate for mortals. Jude tells us that even the angels avoid it. Jesus calls it the unpardonable sin, and mentions that it is akin to blaspheming the Holy Spirit.

If judging is so inappropriate for mortals, why even put the tree of knowledge there? Here we see God's handiwork in having *another* tree there, the tree of life, which was *not* forbidden. The tree of life was part of the path out of mortality to immortality. I say 'part of' because we must go all the way to the New Testament in order to discover how this finishing process works. For four thousand years the Adam struggled along in incomplete bodies, as Moses says in Psalm 90, *You are turning back mortal man to one crushed, and you are saying, 'Return you—sons of Adam,' for thousand of years in your eyes, as day of yesterday; for it is passing, and a watch of the night.* Now Satan (called *that ancient serpent* in Revelation) knew the nature of both trees; his lie was as usual a half-truth. Yes, they would know good and evil, and in that respect be like God, but the immortality that the serpent implied in being like God was in the *other* tree. And immortality is one of the necessary requirements to be competent to handle the knowledge of good and evil.

I said 'one of' again. What else is missing on the path from becoming children of God instead of mortal children of Adam?

First of all, 'immortal life' only requires two things; the inability to die, and the ability to stand before God as who he made us to be. Thus we see even the Satan coming before God to report in Job. Yet his position began to severely erode when he made the mistake of playing into God's hands by seeing to it (or so he thought) that Jesus was crucified. *"But we speak God's wisdom in mystery, that hidden, which God had predetermined before the ages for our glory: which none of the princes of this age knew, (for had they known, they would not have crucified the Lord of glory)..."* So Revelation uses the phrase when Michael throws him from heaven down to the earth, *and neither was there place found for him in heaven.* His ability to stand before God was gone, and it says later, *Woe to the earth and to the sea, because the devil has come down to you, having great rage, knowing he has a short time.* The point is that the ability to stand before God quite often goes through a testing process. The Satan was created with a specific function; when the Christ was introduced, that function rapidly becomes redundant.

Now we know from Ephesians 3:10 and elsewhere that heavenly beings can *learn*, but humans, being mortal, *grow*. The process of growth is a very delicate one and must be done in balance; a child is not given the responsibilities of an adult. Adam as created was perfectly competent to eat of the tree of life—that's what it was there for—but *not* yet competent to eat of the tree of the knowledge of good and evil. The reason it would bring death in is simple: it would irreparably interrupt the growth process. And it did. The Adam became a judge of whether his own actions were good or evil, as Cain so aptly demonstrates in assessing his own. A person who is judging of his own righteousness cannot rise above himself to understand God's righteousness. Thus the law, and 1,486 years of bouncing back and forth between the conscience and the law, which led to great volumes of material enacted and written, but no substantial results. Imagine having eaten of the tree of life at this point, and living forever in this miserable condition of not being able to accomplish anything substantial except to vainly attempt to justify one's self.

But humans do grow, and the Adam, though spread out into billions of smaller emanations, grows as well. If it was inappropriate to judge of the good or evil of one's actions, what was one to use to figure out what to do? The good couldn't be done, because one had to *assess*, that is *judge* whether it was good or not. The evil couldn't be done because, well, it was evil. Abraham discovered the secret, and passed it on—somewhat tenuously—to his progeny: faith. Though one could not believe in one's own competency to judge, one *could* believe what God said, and do that. Not because one believed that it made one righteous as the Pharisees did, but because one believed that God was good, and that he knows what is good for us. What the Pharisees missed is that the law itself is righteous, not us; it was to be followed because God said it, not because it made us righteous. *For they, being ignorant of God's righteousness, and seeking to establish their own, have not submitted to the righteousness of God.*

So faith became the bridge between morality (the tree of knowledge) and mortality (the tree of life).

And faith is something which wants God to actually *say* something or *do* something for us to believe. Creation witnesses to the goodness of God, and that gives mankind somewhat of a start. But the prophets of old—found in every culture—were necessary to provide the Word. Then starting with Moses who compiled the histories of mankind passed down from Noah, and using his rather unique relationship to God, the Word began to be formalized into print that could be copied and passed about. As this process developed, the prophets' function also changed, until the last prophet recorded in the Old Testament ends by telling us that it's all written down—go to the Word and be faithful to it. This all took quite a chunk of human history.

So here's God waiting to introduce mankind to the Tree of Life for all these years with us barely aware of it. On the scene suddenly appears the promised Seed. "Whoa, slow down!" was the general reaction, especially of those who claimed to have been waiting for this Messiah all their lives. Starting with John the Baptist, and then with Jesus and his disciples, a strange message went out to 'repent'. Repent of what? What is so new about confessing our sins, or admitting that we were wrong? It's not about sin, it's about what causes it. You ate of the tree of the knowledge of good and evil, and it not only didn't do you any good, it got you into a helpless morass from which you can't get out. If you're going to join God in this next step, first you have to admit this.

Then what? Well the Word was again coming so fast and furious that people couldn't write it down fast enough. The entire New Testament was written in a time period shorter than David's lifespan. And not only the *words* of the Word, but the Word, the Person, HIMSELF. This was definitely scary stuff. And the word was iterated so simply and straightforward that it seemed impossible to believe and in many ways, too good to be true. What did God have to say about getting life, as the 'tree of life' did not seem to be around? *He that believes on the Son has life eternal, and he that is not subject to the Son shall not see life, but the wrath of God abides upon him.* So we might go to God and say, "Does this mean that if we believe on the Son, we're not naked anymore?" He would say, "No, we haven't gotten to that yet. One thing at a time."

Believing on the Son ends up having quite a few ramifications. We have been talking about *morality* and *mortality*, so let's go back to the question, "What else is missing on the path of becoming children of God from children of Adam?" And the answer has subtly been tugging at our sleeve throughout all these scriptures: the Spirit. As mentioned in Appendix XIV, the missing element from the Adam which would have empowered him for producing fruit to God was not his wife, as he initially supposed; nor the fruit of the tree of knowledge of good and evil, as his wife initially supposed; but the Spirit. As Jesus spoke in Luke 11:12, *"If you therefore, being evil, know how to give good gifts to your children, how much more shall the Father who is from heaven give Holy Spirit to them that ask him?"* Jesus treats the subject almost like, "Of course God has been wanting to give you the Spirit all along. Ask."

This 'asking' process is simpler than it seems; it is inherent in the process of believing. Paul simply says, *"...In whom you also, having heard the word of the truth, the gospel of your salvation, —in whom, having also <u>believed</u>, you were sealed with the Holy Spirit of the promise, which is an earnest of our inheritance..."*
'Earnest' simply means 'present proof.' Now this is all fine and well, but what does the Spirit have to do with the two trees?

Simply this: the Adam was *designed and created* to house the Spirit. We were actually made to be completed—finished and 'good'—when the Holy Spirit would be working with us as an essential partner within ourselves... exactly as he does with God.

Does this mean that once we believe and interact with the Holy Spirit, that now, finally, we're finished? Nope. We interrupted the process of growth and it damaged our bodies. Gotta get new ones. The amazing thing in this process though, is that we currently can house the Spirit *in these mortal bodies*. How God can do *that* is somewhat of an amazing process.

Appendix IV
Jehovah God: JHWH vs. Elohim

Let us be completely and utterly simple with this subject, thus eliminating 80% of theology as less than useless. I speak here of the 'higher criticism' which sprang out of Germany and infected biblical scholarly study like a gangrene, similar to what evolution did to biology.

The reader will pardon this introductory interlude to the subject; it is somewhat necessary in order to demonstrate that when we miss the very simplest and most straightforward of ideas provided in Scripture, we are capable of building massive houses of cards; indeed entire cities of cards complete with skyscrapers, the very weight of which precludes ever cleaning up the subject. The best approach is the similar to what God did with Hidden Wiles (Sodom) and Television (Gomorrah); the city of cards ought to be set on fire and walked away from. Once the smoke has settled, we can begin anew with materials that are somewhat less combustible, not to say more substantial.

I have in my library a book on ants. It is thick and very thorough; the title is simply *Ants* published in 1990. It is a wealth of information; 10" wide, 12" high, and almost two inches thick; 733 pages. Now if I were to go through and eliminate all guesses, suppositions, hypotheses, and outright unsubstantiated claims regarding evolution in this book, it would be less than a quarter that size.

What is the use of all this extra propaganda? Absolutely none. Whether one subscribes to the idea that we were all sponges once or not, the evolution material is utterly and completely irrelevant to any study of ants whatsoever. It does not help me understand the physiology, the behavior, or the environmental contexts of the ants. It is simply filler-babble. What it *does* do is make the writers feel very intelligent and eliminate, by sheer weight, creative forays into unexplored relationships that the reader might otherwise pursue.

Now take a good scholarly study of some book of the Old Testament. *Occasionally* there are some insightful and penetrating observations sketched out; yet even these are drowned in a hopelessly monotonous sea of whether that particular passage was more influenced by the Yahwist, Elohimist, Deuteronomist, Priestly, Redactor, or Deuteronomic History camp of ancient writers. If in doubt, cut it up into small pieces and label them all. The *last* thing these people wish to do is notice the uninterrupted continuity and flow of the text; that Genesis and Isaiah have more in common than do the Iliad and the Odyssey.

Take a look at the four foundations of "Historical-Critical Methodology"; this is from Soulen & Soulen's *Handbook of Biblical Criticism* last revised in 2001: "(1) that reality is uniform and universal, (2) that reality is accessible to human reason and investigation (3) that all events historical and natural are interconnected and comparable to analogy, (4) that humanity's contemporary experience of reality can provide objective criteria to what could or could not have happened in past events,"

If that did not raise any red flags in your mind, little of their methodology will. What we have is a Bible. This 'Bible' has in it events that have changed reality, has told us that we cannot understand these changes without reading this 'Bible'. Likewise it is chock full from beginning to end with events that have happened in human history that we would normally consider impossible. So to help us understand this 'Bible', we apply four standards that contradict every account in it? Accolades for whoever thought *those* up; he saved Satan a great deal of trouble.

Here is what is mistaken in their four foundations: (1) Reality is *not* uniform nor universal, which is why we have events like the Deluge so carefully recorded. (2) Reality is *not* accessible to human reason and investigation alone, which is why the Bible is full of 'revelations' and 'prophecies' that need investigated rather than appealing only to our own fleeting culture. (3) Historical and natural events are indeed interconnected and comparable to analogy; the bait-and-switch here is that Higher Critics only draw analogies *from our time period to theirs*, never, as the Text instructs us to, *from their time period to ours*. (4) Contemporary experience of reality provides objective criteria to past events? Blatant arrogant propaganda, or myopic insanity; take your pick. It is absolutely impossible in *any* discipline to project a *subjective* understanding (contemporary experience) outward to discover the merits of something *objective* (past events). Likewise, it is utterly impossible to be objective about things completely out of our range of experience. This is the very reason they were written down. The fact that we need to know some things that are outside our normal day-to-day experience is what the Bible itself *says*. Over and over.

So these wonderfully intelligent gents (and for the most part they are) have taken the reasons for which the Bible was written, and made up study rules that exclude them.

Most scholarly analysis could be reduced in the same manner as my book *Ants*. It does not help me understand the text if someone over my shoulder is telling me what piece was influenced by what kind of writer ...especially if they have made this entire construct up out of their heads with no collaborating evidence whatsoever that does not depend on their *other* presuppositions, when in fact they themselves have never read the text on its own merits in the first place without defensive presuppositions which prevent sincere and unbiased reading, far less comprehension. This is filler-babble.

To the subject then.

Elohim, 'God' as we say, is a most peculiar word. First off, it's plural. But one can hardly translate it 'Gods' because it is always used with singular verbs and adjectives. It is a plural word that breaks the rules of grammar by being treated as singular. The three forms which are translated 'God' are *Elohim*, *Eloah* (the singular of *Elohim*), and *El* (typically used for God in power rather than being).

Then we have 'Jehovah', which I have left in that form in the text, as *JHWH* and *Yahweh* confuse many, and the text as laid out is straining the limits of English readability as is. 'Jehovah' was arrived at by taking the vowels of 'Adonai' (Lord) and sticking them in between the letters of JHWH. Properly, the word is *Yahweh*, though to many it is known as the Unpronouncible Name; and variously as *Hashem* (the Name) and the Tetragrammaton (from the Greek τετραγράμματον meaning simply 'four letters'). There is also *Jah*, which like *El* to *Elohim*, expresses his power of existence more than existence itself.

Now all that is fine and nice for some introductory detail, but what does it have to do with how they are so peculiarly interchanged in the text? Well we have two choices here: either decide that the writer had an extremely good reason for doing so, or go to the Higher Critics who will cut out all the *Elohim*'s and paste them on one board, cut all the *JHWH*'s out, paste them on another board, and then write several thick textbooks on the differing influences of warring factions within the scribal community. Since that has already been done, we will here take the radical and dangerous path of deciding that whoever wrote the text knew exactly what they were doing, and wrote it in such a way that any child could figure it out for themselves.

And here it is: 'God', 'Elohim', is the God acting from eternity; imperturbable, distant, and in many ways, inaccessible. 'Jehovah' is God acting within time right by our side; going through moment-to-moment emotions, reacting to everything.

Wasn't that simple?

Here's an experiment for you to try: take a Bible search program, and type in "God anger" or "God angry" and see how many hits you get. There's a very few; one with Balaam, two misquotes of God's character in Ezra, and three Psalms. All the others include 'Jehovah' as in "Jehovah your God was angry..." Now type in "Jehovah anger" or "Jehovah angry". You won't be able to get through all the hits.

Isn't that easy?

We need both names, and the other ones given (El Shaddai, El Elyon, Adonai, etc.). God is God and there is no changing him; but we are not God, and thus we are unable to ever fully apprehend him. So God kindly presents himself in differing characters so that we have some way to get the fact that this year (2013) he allowed 100,000 innocent God-fearing people to be brutally tortured, raped, and murdered in Syria, yet he cares for the ladybug on my raspberry plant. We don't have a way to process this, so he helps us out.

But aside from the Higher Critics, there are a number of nasty attackers on God's character these days. One of the currently popular ones is to describe the 'God of the Old Testament' as being vindictive, selfish, moody, childish, and often genocidal. This is generally by people who are vindictive, selfish, moody, childish, and possible genocidal; but wish to hide it under a thin veil of self-righteousness. One does not accuse others of things one is at peace with. But let us consider for a moment this 'childishness' as it pertains to Jehovah.

Elijah is considered to be one of the greatest prophets of the Old Testament. Read his account, especially First Kings 19. He was impulsive, completely ignored God's instructions to him on the holy mountain except to replace himself with Elisha, he threw a temper tantrum when Jezebel threatened him, he asked God that he would die because he had wanted to be greater than his fathers and didn't think God let him; in short, he acted like a spoiled 4-year-old.

Look at Jonah. *He* threw a temper tantrum when God refused to destroy Nineveh, and told God that the gourd shading him was more important than the lives of 120,000 children, because, well, he *needed* that shade.

Look at Gideon trying to make God prove that he could keep a sheepskin dry. Look at David's behavior when he found out that Bathsheba was pregnant. Look at Jephthah, Sampson, Judah with Tamar, and all of the rest. We have here accounts of fully grown people acting like kids. And openly, unlike today where we act like kids and bury it under a lot of noble-sounding soap-opera excuses.

Then go to Jesus words, "Verily I say to you, Unless you are converted and become as little children, you will not at all enter into the kingdom of the heavens." That's pretty strong language.

See, a child gets angry very easily, but does not hold a grudge. A child pouts, but can be brought out of the pout in an instant. A child is self-centered, but is simultaneously fascinated by other people. A child thinks he's right but changes his mind easily. In short, a child imitates Jehovah in his own way.

The Jehovah of the Old Testament, the Living God character as contrasted with Elohim, the Eternal God character, would be very very remiss if he were to hold back any of his emotions for one moment. They all come out. "And now let me alone, that my anger may burn against them, and I may consume them; and I will make of you a great nation." Yet Moses was able to turn him away from that reaction. It would be as much a lie for Jehovah to ignore the proper emotional reaction as it is for we adults to pretend that we're not having them.

Thus when we read Genesis 1 and see God, we see how God operates: according to counsel. Then we read Genesis 2 and see both characters woven together; there it is God operating according to his counsels, but also reacting according to his moment-to-moment delight with the process of his new race, the Adam. "And he is forming—Jehovah God—from the ground all of animal of the field, and all of flier of the heavens, and he is bringing to the Adam, to cause to see what (?) he calls to him." Well if he was God, didn't he already know what Adam was going to call them? Yes, but God is capable of going through experiences *just as we are*, and delights to do so even more than we do.

This is the mystery of Jehovah/Elohim. The Living God and the Eternal God.

Appendix V

The Woman and the Seed

Let us put the earth and mankind into perspective. To do this, we need to put Jesus into perspective.

"...all things were made by him and for him..."

"...for it became him, through whom are all things, and for whom are all things..."

"...to sum up the All in the Christ; the things in heaven and the things upon the earth..."

"...Jesus Christ: the same yesterday, today, and forever..."

"...who being the effulgence of His glory and the expression of His substance, and upholding all things by the word of his power..."

"...In the beginning was the Word. And the Word was with God, and the Word was God..."

"...who is the image of the Invisible God..."

That's good for a start. Now what if, rather than seeing these quotes as nice praise subjects, we take them seriously and consider what they say? There are two things we can take at face value here, and the aim of this discussion is to see how they bear on each other.

1. The world was made for Christ, not us.

2. Christ's role is to be the image of God, not himself.

Now let's go way back and think about God's dilemma in planning creation. That this creation is for the Son is plainly stated. This brings up a major problem... it is the Son's job to glorify God, to show what he is like; not vice versa. God plans and the Son carries it out; it is the Son's job to do everything for God.

So how do you do something for someone whose job it is to do everything for you?

Imagine that you had a servant who *only* was interested in serving. A servant for whom it would be the very height of insult to give a 'day off' or to switch roles for an hour. This is what God the Father faced in the Eternal Counsels when setting up this creation. Being God, he did not throw up his hands as we might, but he actually came up with something that works.

If you have someone who is a Perfect Servant, set up a scenario in which he can serve in a manner like no other. If you have someone who is always your Image, set up a creation in which he can be your image in the most delightsome, amazing, impossible, difficult, glorious, and delicate way possible.

That is what this creation is about. The entire physical universe was planned around 33-1/2 years of the mortal life of an Eternal being given a body that was capable of experiencing pain, sorrow, and death. The whole kit and caboodle. Everything before him and after him; you, me, rattlesnakes, and Yellowstone National Park sulfur springs.

So when it says that everything is made *by* him, it is in reference to him carrying out God's plans. When it says that everything is made *for* him, it is in reference to him handing it all over to God: *"For he must reign until he put all his enemies under his feet; Enemy to be abolished last? Death. For 'He subjected all under his feet.' But when he says that the All are subjected, it is evident that he is excepted who did subject the All to him. And when the All have been subjected to him, then also the Son will himself be subjected to Him that did subject the All to him, that God be all in all."*

Now two points are to be made here; the first is that if he's handing everything over to God anyway, what does he have to show for all his effort when all is said and done? The second is, What is so important about all things being made by *him*; why not just use the angels? Let's start with the second question while we think about the first. For this we look at *Scripture's* way of looking at Time; "*...since he had then been obliged often to suffer from the foundation of the world. But now once in the* *consummation of the ages he has been manifested for putting away of sin by his sacrifice.*" Consummation of the ages? The KJV has "end of the world" which is more or less the same thought. You mean *that* was the end of the world? What's going on with time?

Come to think of it, the subject of Time is too large to squeeze into this appendix, so I think I'll address it in its own place. Appendix VII will touch on Time; you may wish to read it now (as I'm going to go write it now) before continuing this particular discussion. Moving right along then, we can see from how Scripture uses *spiritual* time on occasion rather than *physical* time, that the end of the world was when Jesus died. Well now, that brings up a very interesting question: *When was the beginning of the world*? What if our ideas of calendars and clocks have mistakenly put the beginning of the world way back before anything *chronologically* happened, instead of when it *causally* happened?

In other words, what we are looking for is when Jesus sat down and decided that the Monarch butterfly's wings would be orange, and that eels would be slimy even after you cooked them. One very big clue is something that my art classes in college often missed, which is that *aesthetics* depends entirely on *experiencing* something. In architecture, we can put all the decoration we want on the entrance of a building, but if it does not affect the experience of entering the building, it is so much wasted effort. The fact is that if we could design our homes *while* we experienced living in them, the designs would be so much more excellent. But we physically operate in chronological time, thus making a great deal of things that on afterthought we would have done better.

So when we read that "*In the beginning was the Word... all became through him, and without him nothing became that had become*", we are talking about a Being who can see Adam's life, our lives, or someone 644 years from now in the *present*; His present, which includes all things. Yet consider; if the world was made *for* him, and his incarnation was when he *physically* experienced it, would not those particular 33 years be the most ideal time from which to gather the riches of creativity that we see in this physical world?

In other words, Jesus could have been walking around as a man, creating the entire universe.

But thoughts in those directions get us grounded in the subject of where the focus of the universe is centered. Having somewhat considered the potential there, let us go back to the title of this discussion: *The Woman and the Seed*. Oddly enough, the grand promise regarding the coming Seed was not made to Adam, nor to the Woman, but to the Serpent.

Now why would God give the revelation of some of his most intimate counsels to a *snake*?

For one, it moved the conflict entirely out of the Adam's realm. Had God told Adam that a future conflict of this nature would occur, it would be incumbent on Adam to prepare for it, likely taking up most of his attention through the ages as he faced off with whatever he deemed the most snakelike. But the lesson of Cain comes in here; using Jesus' words: *But I say unto you, not to resist evil*.

It wasn't his job, and still isn't. Why? Two reasons; the first is that a being who had subjected himself to the serpent by allowing his wife to be deceived by him is deemed incompetent. He had his chance to 'guard' the Garden and used it up. If you sent a soldier out to defeat the enemy's champion, and he lost, would you send the same soldier again, or choose a stronger one? This leads to the second reason: in his craft, the serpent talked to Eve, not Adam. We know Adam was right there, for she *gave to her husband with her*. And the enmity was set between the Woman and the Serpent, not the Man and the Serpent. And this finally brings us to the subject in the title.

Nothing is said to Adam about seed or children or future battles; simply that he would have a tough time tilling the ground until he returned to it. All the plans for future developments were between the Woman and the Serpent. So while men were out doing their wars and building their cities, it was the *women* who were actually on the front line. How? By having painful childbirths and listening to their husbands.

Now that last would make for a good stand-up-comedy line, but let us examine it a bit more closely. The lifeblood of moral time is desire and the lifeblood of spiritual time is authority. Now consider the words *and unto your husband your desire, and he rules over you*. Both are there. The lifeblood of chronological time is vibration: *in pangs you birth sons*. While man is sweating over the dirt, the woman is involved in <u>all three aspects of time</u>; physical, moral, and spiritual.

Now to stay focused, let us remember that at the beginning of this discussion we observed that this entire universe is centered on one event: the incarnation of the Word. The Serpent is told that this would be the seed of the *woman*. And thus a strange unfurling of human history begins in which man—holding authority over the woman—is running a show in which the actual conflict is engaged with women. But how? The answer to that question will tell us why it took 4000 years for the Woman's Seed to appear. We can divide time up into whatever sections we wish, and the divisions are often very good ones. But unless we can identify the role of Woman in those annuls, we fall short of the full picture. Here, let us compare the inception of the problem with Eve to its fulfillment with Jesus.

These unfold in seven steps (outlined in Appendix VI) as follows:
- Answering both the desire toward her husband and the desire for the Seed.
- Breaking through the travail and pangs of childbirth.
- Planning the conflict.
- Acting on the plan.
- Producing fruit to carry out both the plans and the initial desire.
- Watching the results play out.
- Receiving the Seed after the conflict with the Serpent.

There are seven things mentioned that Eve did, and likewise seven times in the Gospels that the Seed of the Woman addresses her directly by using the expression, "Woman..." They correspond to the above pattern in the order that they are found as follows:

- *She is becoming pregnant.* (Genesis 4:1)
  - *Oh woman, great is your faith; be it to you as you desire.* (Matthew 15:28)
    - **1.** Eve becoming pregnant answers her desire to have the coming Seed who would crush the Serpent's head.
- *She is birthing Cain.* (Genesis 4:1)
  - *Woman, you are loosed from your infirmity.* (Luke 13:12)
    - **2.** The 'curse' of painful childbearing is overcome by actually bearing.
- *She is saying, 'I have acquired man... Jehovah'.* (Genesis 4:1)
  - *Woman, what have I to do with you? My hour is not yet come.* (John 2:4)
    - **3.** Like Mary, Eve is premature as to her idea of how the Serpent would be engaged and defeated. Eve thought Cain was the coming seed who would be Jehovah, and Mary thought Jesus would act apart from being directed of the Father.
- *She adds to cause to birth Abel.* (Genesis 4:2)
  - *Woman, believe me. An hour is coming.* (John 4:24)
    - **4.** The actual plan for defeating the Serpent involves death. "My hour is not yet come" from **3** is answered by "An hour is coming" here; a reference to Jesus' death as Abel likewise will die.
- *She is birthing son.* (Genesis 4:25)
  - *Woman, where are your accusers? Has no one condemned you?* (John 8:10)
    - **5.** This one is the crux. Eve bears Seth who will carry the line to the coming Seed, and Jesus tells the woman "Neither do I condemn you"; in **2** she is released from her infirmity (pain of producing the coming Seed) and here in **5** she is given permission to continue on her path without further interference from a 'curse'. With Eve, the fruit was Seth who would replace Abel, with the woman in

John the fruit was mercy (and grace) which would replace the condemnation of law.
- *She is calling his **name** Seth.* (Genesis 4:25)
  - *Woman, behold your son.* (John 19:20)
    - **6.** Here she watches the results play out. Eve names the new son Seth which means a stable foundation. Mary is told to behold her son, and the text there explains that John (the writer) adopts her as mother from there on. The establishing of the coming Seed is accomplished; woman has only to meet and recognize him now. The duality in John's writing of whether Jesus is referring to himself or John is necessary; even Eve with all her faith did not know who the Seed would be, or when he would appear. In the meantime it was necessary for her to recognize all of those involved as part of the plan.
    - The "Behold your mother" spoken to John in the account is Jesus' nod to the job she has finally completed... she has finally become a true mother, and is recognized as such. This subject is taken up in Appendix X, *Mother of All Living*.
- *'That he set for me—God—Seed after reducing of Abel, for he killed him—Cain'.* (Genesis 4:25)
  - *Woman, why do you weep? Whom do you seek?* (John 20:15)
    - **7.** This is the final meeting of the Woman and the Seed. Eve sees that death was the necessary consequences of listening to the Serpent, yet does not despair like Judas but moves on. Mary likewise is less distraught over Jesus' death than the fact that his body is missing. The plan must go on, and neither Eve nor Mary can be satisfied until what was laid on her—the presence of the Seed—is accomplished.

And likewise, there is one other address directly to woman in the gospels. This one is not by Jesus, but by Peter:
- *Woman, I do not know him.*

So the text strongly suggests that there is an account hidden in plain sight that views mankind as a woman. The texts are written by men, mostly about men, and it is men who have the overt control. But a reading of any of the prophets or the New Testament shows that God's view of man, whether Israel, the church, or all of mankind, is of a woman. With that in mind, we are ready to look at Sarai the Mother of Faith in Appendix IX.

The story of the Woman and the Seed is not cut-and-dried as I have laid it out above. The patterns are given to help us to consciously navigate through matters that are deeper than words. The text gives it in the form of stories, such as the Shunammite woman in Second Kings 4 or the account of Jephthah's daughter in Judges. This subject could be titled *The Three Gardens* or even *God and the Woman*, but properly, it is simply about a woman. A woman and her seed.

Appendix VI
The Stories in the Genealogical Histories

It might be good to sketch out a few of the stories hidden in plain sight in the lists of genealogical histories. Names and their meanings were quite as important as the numerical values recorded; indeed, must often be taken together, as the number of names in a list is as significant as the names themselves. Let us start with Japheth's seven children in 10:2. They are "² Sons of Japheth: Gomer[1021], and Magog[1022], and Madai[1023], and Javan[1024], and Tubal[1025], and Meshech[1026], and Tiras[1027]". A list of seven will always follow the pattern leading to perfection, or finishing, by the following seven steps: 1 conceiving, 2 substantiation, 3 planning, 4 making 5 producing, 6 releasing, 7 returning. Thus we have the story of the Caucasian race finding itself on an uninhabited planet and proceeding thusly:

Conceiving of a *full increase of* their *substance*, Japheth's sons substantiated this thought by means of *overstretching* and *covering* every means available (cultivation of all natural resources) so that they had the wherewithal to *abound* in a manner *commensurate* with the *measure* of their own society. By *pleasure*, the *arts*, and all *creative generation*, they *settled outward*, opening up (releasing) the ability to trade in *speculative*

[1021] *Gomer*: full increase of substance; completion.

[1022] *Magog*: overstretching; covering.

[1023] *Madai*: commensurate abounding; my measure; my garments; what is enough.

[1024] *Javan*: see *the dove* in 8:8 and note; that root (the generative process of creation) and *yahyin, to* effervesce or wine both contribute to this name which finally settled on to the Greek peoples. It is both what is beautiful and philosophical, and the tyrannizing effects of wine; but properly the relationship between the two.

[1025] *Tubal*: sympathetic flowing; to settle outward.

[1026] *Meshech*: a drawing out; to speculate and act; a purchase.

[1027] *Tiras*: reflection (as in thought) of becoming granular (by grinding); effusing.

ownership; i.e., merchandising and real estate, finally becoming a granular homogeneity of affluence; thus finishing their original conception.

We will note that the white race has always followed this pattern. Furthermore, the text gives us the necessary detail on steps 1 and 4 by giving us their children; why conceive of this path in the first place, and details as to how it this conception was enacted.

³ And sons of Gomer: Ashkenaz[1028], and Riphath[1029], and Togarmah[1030]. ⁴ And sons of Javan: Elishah[1031], and Tarshish[1032], Kittim[1033], and Dodanim[1034]. ⁵ From these they are parted—coast-lands of the nations in their lands; man[1035] to his tongue, to his families in their nations.

The three sons of Gomer show us why the white race is motivated to follow the pattern of outspreading; *Ashkenaz* is the burning heat of the Caucasoid race that wishes to make its presence felt, *Riphath* is the taking of that heat to surrounding lands to demonstrate it (often by conquering), and *Togarmah* is the bringing back of the spoils to effect solidarity at home. It takes little more than a glance at the Greek and Roman empires to see this. Japheth's progeny are *meddlers* who use outside resources. Note that great restraint has been used in this paragraph to avoid using Great Britain, France, or America as examples.

And the choice of Javan (Greece eventually), the fourth son, as the only other son of Japheth whose children are named, gives us the methodology by which they spread out. When four names are listed, they always describe influence, effect, or spreading out—

[1028] *Ashkenaz*: fire in its self and its effect; caloric.

[1029] *Riphath*: the movement of spreading from a center; the active force of the name Jephthah his father. In the negative it is seen as bruising or healing; slander or influence. Centrifugal force.

[1030] *Togarmah*: corresponding force to *Riphath* above; centripetal force, gathering from outside resources for inner stability.

[1031] *Elishah*: power used to make ductile; in society, propaganda.

[1032] *Tarshish*: successive movements for self-honor; periodic military conquest.

[1033] *Kittim*: isolationism; beaters down or cutting off of outsiders; nationalism.

[1034] *Dodanim*: mutually pleasing and self-sufficient; the *selected*, those mutually in agreement.

[1035] *Man*: *Ish*, nale; individual or intellectual man.

all action—and occur in the following order: 1 That place from which movement is initiated; 2 The action of spreading influence; 3 The action of consolidating influence; and 4 The end object for which the action is undertaken.

Thus we see in *Elisha* that a commonality of purpose, often artificially enhanced (propaganda) initiates the outward *Tarshish* movement of successive military conquests, solidified by *Kittim*, a sense of entitlement and unique identity, serving *Dodanim*, a mutually self-satisfied society united by a common agreement, such as a constitution. The acorn hasn't fallen too far from the tree in 34 centuries.

Immediately following with Ham, we have instead of four emanating from seven, seven emanating from four... with somewhat different results. Let's skip Cush (also seven from four) and go to Mizraim, as his pattern is somewhat unique among Ham's sons:

And Mizraim, he generated **Ludim**[1036], and **Anamim**[1037], and **Lehabim**[1038], and **Naphtuhim**[1039], 14 and **Pathrusim**[1040], and **Casluhim**[1041], (which they issued from there—Philistines[1042],) and **Caphtorim**[1043]. Let's lay out the seven steps to completion like a chart with questions and answers to see the pattern more easily:

> What is the original conception?
>   Ludim: Pregnancies; self building.
> By what means will this be enabled?
>   Anamim: Material heaviness; great effort.
> What are the mechanics of this plan?
>   Lehabim: Flames, flashing swords; open war.
> What actions are produced?

[1036] *Ludim*: to the firebrands; travailing, pregnancies.
[1037] *Anamim*: affliction of the waters; material heaviness.
[1038] *Lehabim*: flames; glittering blades.
[1039] *Naphtuhim*: openings; hollowed caverns.
[1040] *Pathrusim*: reduced and dispersed; broken into crowds
[1041] *Casluhim*: forgiven ones; tried for atonement.
[1042] *(Philistines*: a wallowing; slighted; dispersal.)
[1043] *Caphtorim*: the converted (as translated from one belief to another).

Naphtuhim: Hollow caverns; retreat and hide.
What is produced?
Pathrusim: Society reduced and dispersed.
Left to their own devices, what happens?
Casluhim: Forgiven ones; nomadic serving race.
How is the original conception completed?
Caphtorim: Converted ones; adopting new paradigms

So we see that the sons of Mizraim (overcoming power, complete oppression) quickly fizzle out by dint of pushing too hard without a good plan. Compare that to the *eleven* sons of Canaan, every one of which is emphatic in the Hebrew:

15 And Canaan[1044], he generated **Sidon**[1045] his first-born, and **Heth**[1046], 16 and **the Jebusite**[1047], and **the Amorite**[1048], and **the Girgashite**[1049], 17 and **the Hivite**[1050], and **the Arkite**[1051], and the **Sinite**[1052], 18 and the **Arvadite**[1053], and the **Zemarite**[1054], and **the Hamathite**[1055].

When we have an eleven-pattern, the subject is not *completion* (as seven) but *response*. Seeing that Nimrod has been stopped, Mizraim has been converted, the tower of Babel ended up in dispersion, and that his race was coming to nothing (meaning of *Canaan*), he backs himself into a corner like a rabid possum. The eleven steps to *response* are: 1 Necessary Identity, 2 Tricks of the Trade, 3 Operation, 4 Influence, 5 Results, 6 Unintended Results, 7 Character of Self, 8 Newborn Energy, 9 Full System of Intent, 10 Reaction to 5 (Results), and 11 Full Response to 1 (Necessary Identity). Let's see how it looks:

[1044] *Canaan*: humiliated; physical existence becoming nothing.

[1045] *Sidon*: ensnaring foe; deceptive enemy.

[1046] *Heth*: terror; surprised reaction; stupefaction resulting from an useless effort.

[1047] *Jebusite*: inward crushing; to crush with the foot to extract liquid.

[1048] *Amorite*: a sayer; outward wringing.

[1049] *Girgashite*: rumination; continual contractual labor; endless chewing.

[1050] *Hivite*: natural livers; animalistic lives.

[1051] *Arkite*: my gnawing; brutish appetites.

[1052] *Sinite*: thorn; bloody disposition of rage.

[1053] *Arvadite*: greed for plunder.

[1054] *Zemarite*: thirst for domination.

[1055] *Hamathite*: enclosure of wrath; covetous desire; violent cravings.

Necessary Identity:
- *Sidon*: ensnaring foe; deceptive enemy; no longer able to openly fight.

Tricks of the trade:
- *Heth*: terror; surprised reaction; stupefaction resulting from a useless effort. Get your enemy to fight a straw man.

Operation:
- *Jebusite*: inward crushing; to crush with the foot to extract liquid; squeeze every bit of life out of your own people for the cause.

Influence:
- *Amorite*: a sayer; outward wringing; use strong propaganda on your enemies (as opposed to at home like Japheth).

Results:
- *Girgashite*: rumination; continual contractual labor; endless chewing. In other words, this whole process requires continuous effort.

Unintended Results:
- *Hivite*: animalistic lives. Nothing lofty to live for.

Character of Self:
- *Arkite*: my gnawing; brutish appetites.

Newborn Energy:
- *Sinite*: thorn; bloody disposition of rage produced by constant labor to fill a brutish appetite.

Full System of Intent:
- *Arvadite*: greed for plunder.

Reaction to Results (continuous effort):
- *Zemarite*: thirst for domination. Need slaves.

Full Response to Necessary Identity:
- *Hamathite*: enclosure of wrath; covetous desire; violent cravings.

Not a pretty picture of the future of a race. Note that these characteristics are not limited to racial patterns, they also describe the patterns within our personalities. One who sets out to be a *deceptive enemy* as above will necessarily follow that path.

Also I have hit my reader with several patterns here with which he is likely not familiar. The scope of these Appendixes is probably not large enough for laying out all of the scriptural patterns by their set steps; it would add some 30 pages to give a skeleton of the subject. The intention here is to alert the reader (that's you, by the way; pardon the literary protocols) that the Text is replete with these patterns, and that it makes a *great* deal of difference whether there are six or seven names in a list; as well as the order of the names. If the reader (yes, still you) wishes to see more of the scope of the subject, he is welcome to contact me and I will oblige as thoroughly as time permits. The patterns of all sets of numbers and their successive steps have been discovered using only the texts of the Scripture without input from a outside sources—the reader thus has access to the same source material and the same process of discovery. There are always pitfalls involved in simply accepting information without the process of discovery.

Then there is the fascinating progeny of Eber's son Joktan.

*And to Eber, he generates two of sons; name of the one, Peleg[1056], that in his days she is split, the earth; and name of his brother: Joktan[1057]. 26 And Joktan, he generates **Almodad**[1058], and **Sheleph**[1059], and **Hazarmaveth**[1060], and **Jerah**[1061], 27 and **Hadoram**[1062], and **Uzal**[1063]l, and **Diklah**[1064], 28 and **Obal**[1065], and*

[1056] *Peleg*: a channel; cleft; dividing.
[1057] *Joktan*: made small; here, the lessening of evil.
[1058] *Almodad*: given to achieve full measure.
[1059] *Sheleph*: a drawing out; meditation; realization from reflection.
[1060] *Hazarmaveth*: distinguishing the elements of mortality; sanctification by death.
[1061] *Jerah*: lunar; seeing our brothers.
[1062] *Hadoram*: public honor and splendor.
[1063] *Uzal*: purified fire; desire communicated (in the sense of 'letting go' without concern).
[1064] *Diklah*: becoming a song.
[1065] *Obal*: accumulating full understanding.

Abimael[1066], *and* **Sheba**[1067], 29 *and* **Ophir**[1068], *and* **Havilah**[1069], *and* **Jobab**[1070]; *all of these, sons of Joktan.*

The number thirteen represents *accountability*, which is likely why it's often considered unlucky. The pattern that it follows explains in what way the 'missing' branch of Eber's line would address being accountable before God. The thirteen pattern is 1 Named, 2 Assessment, 3 Process, 4 Communication, 5 Offering, 6 Carefree, 7 Communication (4) of filling out the Name (1), 8 Forum, 9 Preparedness, 10 Ability to utilize the Forum (8), 11 Expected Result, 12 Pulling together all resources, 13 Fruit of being able to stand. Using the 'question' format that we did with Mizraim, we have:

1 By what Name does he stand?
- *Almodad*; He is given to achieve full measure of Accountability.

2 How does he Assess this process?
- *Sheleph*; By consideration and meditation.

3 What Process will be utilized?
- *Hazarmaveth*; The recognition of the limits of mortality.

4 How does he Communicate this?
- *Jerah*; By recognizing the brotherhood of being a 'lesser light'.

5 What Offering demonstrates good faith?
- *Hadoram*; The giving of public honor to the Name.

6 In what way can he be Carefree?
- *Uzal*; Being willing to undergo testing, and being honest regarding his true desires.

7 What Result does this produce?
- *Diklah*; Becoming a song; traditions and festivals commemorating.

8 How will he show his success?

[1066] *Abimael*: my father is God; absolute fullness.
[1067] *Sheba*: restoring rest; settling into the place previously devastated. See verse 6, *Sheba* of Ham''s lineage.
[1068] *Ophir*: in the negative, reducing to ashes; here, becoming gold; substantiation achieved.
[1069] *Havilah*: previously (in verse 7) anguish; to twist or writhe painfully; here, virtual energy through trial.
[1070] *Jobab*: triumphant shout.

- *Obal*; By having accumulated full understanding.

9 What playing field does he choose?
- *Abimael*; The same absolute fullness.

10 How does he Prepare to give an Account?
- *Sheba*; By restoring the rest inherent in mortality.

11 How is he Able to restore this rest?
- *Ophir*; by achieving substantiation of his values.

12 How are all these resources organized?
- *Havilah*; by the energy gained from (6) undergoing trial.

13 What is the Fruit of being able to Stand and be Accountable?
- *Jobab*; A triumphant shout; celebration.

When we consider this process and the way of life it represents, it is remarkable how well it describes the attitudes of the Far East cultures.

Appendix VII
Time

If you enjoy being unnecessarily confused, pick up any book on Time and read it. Or go to the bright fellows who would like to have the monopoly on physics, and see what they say about dimensions. Just as in Appendixes II & III, we are going to have to clean out some rubble here before we can address the subject appropriately.

There are three very simple distinctions that need to be understood before embarking on any path of research. Without these distinctions, we can have an I.Q. of 273 and still come up with idiotic conclusions. These three distinctions do not require smarts to understand, but rather the simple acceptance of the fact that we exist as part of our universe rather than as objective know-it-all's. The fact that one can build a house of cards a mile high is quite impressive; but it in no way implies that anyone thought to put a foundation at the bottom before starting.

And in subjects like these, the house of cards is nearly always mathematics, and the missing foundation is always context. There is too much Greek and not enough Hebrew in science.

The distinctions simply involve the numbers 1, 2, and 3. Let's start with two. The misunderstanding of two involves *the failure to distinguish between a parallel and hierarchical relationship*. If a captain has two soldiers under him, he has a hierarchical relationship with them. The two soldiers have a parallel relationship with each other. In creation, *the nature of parallel relationships depend on its number of elements.* We have five fingers on one hand. They *each* have three bending spots that we call joints. The wrist also is a joint, but it moves the whole hand. Thus the wrist has a hierarchical relationship with the fingers, and the fingers have a parallel relationship with each other. Things with sets of five always imply <u>ability</u> or <u>fruit</u>. If we cut an apple sideways, we will see a five-pointed star. The apple is the <u>fruit</u> of the tree which gives it the ability to propagate. Our hand gives us ability to accomplish things (producing the fruit of our labors).

Let's apply that to three. Three always implies the dimensions of something, and there are always three dimensions. We might ask, "Then why is it dimension if 'di' means 'two'?" Because each of the three dimensions has two opposite sides. With a box, the vertical dimension has a top and a bottom. The horizontal dimension has a right and a left. The viewer's dimension has a front and a back.

But... in comes someone bright and says, "Time is the fourth dimension!" Well check your foundation; did you ever ask, "Dimensions of *what*?" Our box example is talking about dimensions of *space*. Time is not a dimension of space just as your wrist is not a finger joint, and neither is your elbow and neither is your shoulder, and neither is the 6th, 7th, 8th, etc. 'dimension' actually a dimension. Time has its own three dimensions, just as space does, and just as energy does. And time, space, and energy are themselves three dimensions of something greater; the physical universe.

Without this simple distinction between parallel and hierarchical relationships, we can use math to perpetuate levels of confusion from which there is no escape. Now let's talk about 1.

The misunderstanding of one involves *the failure to grasp the fact that unity is composed of the perfect balance of disparate components.* A man and a woman are as disparate (different) as one can get. Thus when adding them, 1 (male) + 1 (female) = 1 (unit). This matches scripture. Now if the components are the same, we have a lot of difficulty achieving unity (one). 1 (apple) + 1 (apple) = 2 (apples). And it's not just having *different* elements, the elements have to be perfectly balanced into a unity. If we take any old items, we get 1 (apple) + 1 (orange) = 2 (fruits) + 1 (this-kind-of-fruit-that-I-don't-have-to-peel) + 1 (this-one-that-I-have-to-peel) = 4. In distinguishing without unifying, we actually multiply the effects of adding. Thus, depending on context, we see that here 1 + 1 can equal 1, 2, or 4. Welcome to the Hebrew way of thinking, where a number is not just a number, but an indicator of the qualities of its context.

Thus 1 (pinky) + 1 (ring finger) + 1 (middle finger) + 1 (index finger) + 1 (thumb) = 1 (hand). We would not say, "Would you please pinky-ring-middle-index-thumb me the salt." We would say, "Would you please *hand* me the salt." Since the fingers are in perfect balance, they can be referred to as *one*. When something is balanced into *one*, it can be *named*. This is what a name is. Note what God names in Genesis 1 and what he doesn't. The day, night, heavens, earth, and seas get named. The sun and the moon do not. The crows, trout, and soybeans do not. Adam does not... until the *third* section of Genesis starting in chapter 5. In fact the next time we find anyone naming anything back in the first or second account, it's *Adam* giving names to the animals. And lastly to his wife. *Only the being directly in charge of a unity can name it*, and God had put Adam in charge of the animals and his wife. But he was *not* in charge of the day, night, heavens, earth, seas, or himself. God is.

Now let's look at 3, having understood a hierarchy, a set (parallel), and a unity. The misunderstanding of three involves *the failure to grasp that dimensions are both fully distinct and fully interlocked.* Three, peculiarly enough, has three parts, and they are as different as as can be; in fact *no one part of the three dimensions of a Unity shares any part of its role with the other two dimensions save for the fact that they all share the full Unity.* Taking 'Time', the subject of this discussion, we have past, present, and future. Every event in eternity is/was/will be Past. Every event is/was/will be Future. Every event is/was/will be Present. And not one single event will be more than one of them at a time. It makes for a tense situation.

But there is something very different about the three dimensions; each has his own flavor, his own character shared by the three dimensions of everything that has dimensions. The first dimension is always the Source. The second dimension is always the Manifestation. The third dimension is always the Active Power. If these sound a lot like the Father, Son, and Spirit, it just might be because they are the persons responsible for this universe.

Now let's discover why Time seems so convoluted, especially in prophecy and in the quote we started with in which was clearly stated that when Jesus died, it was the end of the world... yet we're still here peeling bananas and paying taxes 1,981 years later, give or take.

The fact is that Thessalonians tells us that we have a body, a soul, and a spirit. Mankind exists in three realms simultaneously, and Time works quite differently in each of these, with differing protocols. Here they are laid out briefly, with the three dimensions given for each of the three kinds of time:

1. **Physical**, or Phenomenal time:

Dimensions: Future, Present, Past (in the order of Source, Embodiment, Active Energy, as the rest of these will be.)

The thing that ties them together (that is, what element interconnects past present and future so that they work together, and so that the past can influence, or change, the future *or* present, and the future can influence or change the present or past, etc.) is *vibration*; whether gravity, light, motion, sound; whichever form it takes is less important than the fact that *all mass* and *energy* is in perfect balance that stretches across the whole span of chronological time; so moving any one tiny part of anything affects that balance. Some effects are like a <u>trigger</u>; such as the butterfly effect, that a butterfly flapping its wings in Peru can affect the weather in Siberia; other effects are <u>building blocks</u>; each simply another of several hundreds of pieces in a large puzzle, without which the puzzle couldn't go on. (Until something e*lse,* elsewhere in time, provides it.) These ideas alone, without getting into the other two types of time, can explain puzzling phenomena observed in quantum mechanics.

Vibrations have four vectors, which when operating within the capacity of the three dimensions, make possible the fabric of Phenomenal Time. We measure this with clocks.

2. **Moral**, or Man's time:
Dimensions: Intent (or *will,*) Execution, and Willingness.
The element that ties them together is ***desire***, which is the super-connector of moral time. *True* desire; not want, need, lust, whining, power grabbing and climbing, or any of the other

substitutes for true desire. Moral Time's fabric allows for not only interrelations between the dimensions, but interrelations between the three realms of time themselves; it is the Grand Relator. We measure this with history.

3. **Spiritual** time (*Not* eternity. Eternity is its own subject.)
   Dimensions: Counsels, Glory, and Power

The thing that ties them together is ***authority***, which is the lifeblood of spiritual time. Spiritual time is that in which the angels, the demons, the heavenlies, and our own spirits operate. Authority is a *very* complex subject, the tracing out of which also traces out the patterns of the histories of the heavenly forces that rule, guide, and wait for the earthly histories. A good understanding of authority demystifies many subjects and stories. In phenomenal time measured by clocks, what is important is whether an event happened *before* another event, thus allowing it to seem more *causal*. In spiritual time, what is important is how an event was *authorized* over another event, thus allowing it *dominance*. We measure this with law.

Man is in the unique position of being able to deal with all three of these equally. His three duplicates of them in himself (spirit soul body) have four powerful devices relating to the four vectors of each realm of time by which to operate. Each one of these four, properly used, can affect all three time realms. These are **being**, **believing, loving,** (or acting in love,) and **perceiving**. Physically they can be understood in **breath, action, speech,** and **eating**, in that order. Everything we do physically has a corresponding impact in both the spiritual and moral. For example, your *home* in the spiritual world is your *actions* in the physical. Your *actions* in the spiritual world are your *words* in the physical. But between this spiritual world and its physical correspondence (or vice versa) exists a different world altogether: the **Moral**. It is this sphere in which we live, giving purpose to the s*piritual,* and shape to the *physical*.

Thus the Christ appeared "once in the end of the world" in *spiritual* time, yet *chronological* time is ticking away until the 'vibrations' by which it operates catch up to the 'authority' of the spiritual event. This is done by those who 'desire' to operate in His realm. Let us finish here by looking at the past, present, and future from each of the the three realms in which we operate, following the pattern:

Our <u>past</u> is shaped by our <u>willingness</u> to access his <u>power</u>.

Our <u>present</u> is shaped by how we <u>execute</u> our lives for his <u>glory</u>.

Our <u>future</u> is shaped by our <u>intentions</u> toward his <u>counsels</u>.

Appendix VIII
The Days of the Deluge, Peleg, and Eber

The transition from pre-Deluge to post-Deluge has some very important events bookmarked by scripture. These are meant to be understood if we are understand the Call of Abram and its significance; and consequently these provide the necessary context for understanding faith itself, for Abraham is called *the Father of Faith*.

The chronology of the flood itself is given in overlapping sections. Overall, there were 150 days of the flood increasing (which include the 40 days of the heavens dumping water), 150 days of the flood receding, and 75 days of waiting around for the earth to recover, before Noah and his family could disembark.

After the first 150 days, which started on 2/17 of Noah's 600th year, it states that the ark rested (7/17). Yet it took another 2 ½ months before the tops of the mountains were seen on 10/1. In his 601st year, 1/1, it notes that the waters were dry from the *surface* of the earth, and Noah removed the ark's covering. This would be about 18 days before the conclusion of the second 150 days. Yet it is not until 2/27 of this year—75 days after the conclusion of the second 150 days—that God allows him to disembark. It is somewhat amusing that Noah began the restoration process 2.57 weeks early, and God had him stay in the ark 2.57 extra months.

The ancients used a 360-day calendar, and inserted the extra 5 ¼ days in various places in the year depending on the cycles of the moon (and their festivals which depended on the same). Noah would have counted the months during the fury of the Deluge as straight 30-day months, as there were no festivals or phases of the moon to be had. The affair with the 'window' (actually a beacon to signal his presence and initiate celestial observation), 'raven' (reestablishing of recording the lunar cycles), and the 'dove' (reestablishing of the recording of solar cycles) were a subject of extreme effort and agitation to Noah, because as of yet there were no guarantees given by God as to how (or *if*) the earth would be restored. Everyone on the ark was, in effect, holding his or her breath.

So Noah took 54 days (40 + 7 + 7) after the 300 to reestablish the continuity of the calendar, then waited three weeks until God gave him the 'get off the boat' order (21 days + 54 = 75, and 150 + 150 + 75 = 1 year and ten days, the length of the time on the ark.) The days after the first 300 of the flood increasing and decreasing can be moved back and forth a bit depending on where Noah finally inserted the 5 ¼ extra days of the year. It is also remarkable that these 75 days of extra waiting are also seen at the end of Daniel; the 360-day year x 3.5 years = 1,260 days; yet it says *"Blessed is he that waits, and comes to the 1,335 days,"* exactly 75 days later. The other date mentioned just before in Daniel is 1,290 days; 30 days after 1,260 and 45 days before 1,335; putting it where the dove brought back the olive leaf to Noah. One of the messages here could be that it's one thing to know it's time to go forward, and quite another to wait on God's word before doing so.

So having left from the ark, was God's dealings with the earth all over? Not by a long shot. And now there would be a continual relationship between what the Adam was doing on the earth, and what God was doing *with* the earth. The bow was a necessity, as the ensuing cataclysms while the earth settled into its new condition would be quite alarming, as we see from Peleg all the way to the days of the kings Uzziah and Hezekiah: *"And to Eber, he generates two of sons; name of the one, Peleg[1071], that in his days she is split, the earth;"* This splitting of the earth appears to coincide with what God did at the tower of Babel. Physically, the process can be seen by looking at any map of the ocean floors of the world; the stretch-lines are obvious... it is a picture of the earth expanding and the oceans filling in the spaces between the continental shelves. Equally obvious are the shapes of the continents—especially the coastlines—as they attempt to accommodate a flatter surface than previously. Would we take a layer of cookie dough from the surface of a softball and push it on to the surface of a basketball, we would see the exact same phenomena we see in our coastlines and inland mountains. And as

---

[1071] *Peleg*: a channel; cleft; dividing.

ocean floor samples are tested, they read younger and younger as we move from the coastlines; and while geologists love to paste extra zeroes on all their dates, what is older and what is younger is evident.

The point of continuity to keep in mind while considering these cataclysms is that God keeps everything in exact proportion. Scripture mentions that he is the God of order and the God of measure. These two ideas add up to *proportion*; that is, if the earth in Seth's day was ¼ its current size, the planets would be proportionally closer, the air would be proportionally richer, and forces like gravity, light, and celestial cycles of movement would likewise adjust to match. With God, everything works together, and changes do not change his order because the effect is simultaneous across the board. The current myth of continuity of the *form* of the earth could, with a bit of wisdom, be seen as what it really is: the continuity of *relationship*. The fact that we have fossils of dragonflies that would be too heavy to fly, fossils of creatures with 100 foot necks that today could not lift them 20 feet without their hearts exploding from the blood pressure, and records of lifespans and human exploits that require far more atmospheric oxygen and pressure than what is available today ...gives us some clues.

So seeing that God is working with the earth and humanity at the same time, we find that in these genealogical histories are placed the very workings of the earth itself. In this respect, let us turn to Eber. He generates Peleg and Joktan, and initially we only get the children of the latter (See Appendix VI for an explanation of his 13 sons). Immediately afterwards we have the account of the city and tower of Babel, which is in direct contrast with Eber, his travels, and his progeny. The name of Shem's son Arphaxad means 'restorer of Providence', his son Shelach's name means 'inspiration', and Eber his son means 'from the other side.'

"...all of these, sons of Joktan. And he is becoming, their seat, from Mesha[1072], to your coming Sephar-ward[1073]; mountain of the east."

[1072] *Mesha*: binging deliverance; (spiritual) harvest-fruits.
[1073] *Sephar*: enumeration; census; literally book, as in this very book of Moses; thus *a spiritual record*.

In the title line for Shem's children, he is called two things: "Father of all of sons of Eber" and "Brother of Japheth the Great". In agreement with Noah's blessing, this indicates that the Japheth nations followed closely and peacefully with the Shem nations—specifically the thirteen nations from the sons of Joktan. The reason that they would be traveling *back* "from the east" (that is from Iran, India and China) would have been to meet up with the sons of Ham who had generally headed the other direction... for the purpose of building Babel. This occurred in the plains of Shinar, modern day Iraq. The text takes great pains to tell us not only the materials being used, but that they were being used *in place of* normal stone and mortar.

Let's look at the simple facts given us there. The people knew that being scattered (dashed to pieces) was an eminent danger. The also knew that the city and the tower could prevent this; God confirms that this was true. The constant theme here was to prevent a process that was already in play; to halt and solidify a condition that was in danger of changing with catastrophic social and geophysical consequences. Their common purpose was the bricks and their language was the mortar. The object was to get the top of the tower—using the same word as the tops of the mountains which were covered by the Deluge—"to the heavens". Why? Every time a rainbow appeared, it reminded folk that there would be no more flood waters on that scale, so they were not afraid of that contingency. What they actually said was "...and we make for us a Name".

We noted in Appendix VII that a name can only be given by the entity in charge of it. To make for themselves a Name, then, would be to effectively block out God and take charge of themselves. The overwhelming question here is: Was it really possible to block out God? After all, he's *God*. Strangely, God himself sees this as a real danger. By what protocols would it have been possible—or is it possible today—to take ownership of the Adam from God and implement self-ownership? Let us leave that as an open question; its scope is vast, and is best left for now as a consideration of what Nimrod and later all the world leaders to the present have attempted—and are attempting.

Now let us contrast this with Eber. The names in his family all have to do with both pulling apart from the general crowd and bringing to mankind help 'from the other side'; heaven. With Eber's son Joktan, there is an attempt to 'make small' and 'lessen evil'. There is a recognition that mortality is an ongoing process that requires growth and help from God, rather than "Give help!" from each *his fellow* at Babel to "burn to burning" bricks, that is, to solidify an uncompleted condition. The very idea of making a name for one's self is the opposite of what a name is; only the being in charge of something can name it.

What we had on the earth at the time was man going in two opposite directions. Nimrod wished to gather all of mankind together to face off with God and take control of the earth, and Eber wished to be apart from this and find God's help to deal with the earth. Both camps had their problems. Nimrod's Babel is curiously leaderless in the account, and Eber's sons could not just go off and become the mystery wielding Chaldeans that eventually sprung from their culture, but were obliged to deal with Nimrod, Babel, Canaan, and all the issues that were coming out of the Pandora's Box of humanity. Shem's son Asshur sets up Nineveh and her three partner cities to stand against Babel and her three partner cities. Peleg was named after an event that was still eminent; everyone knew that it could happen and the bulk of humanity wanted to stop it. What was so significant about the earth splitting up?

Ownership of the earth was at stake. Mankind would have to take a united stand against God and shut him out, similar to what Satan had attempted once, and was/is again attempting. While God is quite patient, and is willing to wait thousands of years until humanity is ready to grow in parallel to his providence and revelation, this leaves a great deal of room for those who are *not* patient, and wish to jump the gun and grab the goods, like taking the eggs from an incubator and putting them in the refrigerator for later consumption. And mankind at this time was quite aware of what it was capable of if fully united; hence Babel. Today this realization is once again growing.

Thus, measures had to be taken to *maintain mankind in its fledgling state* so that God could complete the Adam in his own time and way. The earth herself had to be split up, and a new place for the dead came into being, the oceans; making three places to sleep after mortality had its sway; sheol, hades, and the sea (Revelation 20:13). But the splitting apart of the surface of the earth into continental shelves was, to God, merely a side-effect of what really needed to be done; the scattering of man <u>from</u> Babylon. For the rest of the saga of mankind Babylon keeps springing back up, and the normally terse book of Revelation spends two full chapters describing her final demise.

The key to why man was to be scattered <u>from</u> Babylon can be seen in the history of merchandising. We note in the account of Jacob first attempting to establish a base in front of Shechem, that the Hamor and Shechem keep repeating that the newcomers would *merchandise* the land. This is the hope they laid before the men of their city to convince them all to get circumcised. Jacob had paid for his plot in bullion, and was familiar with the lucrative trade practices of the east that traveled up over the fertile crescent, down through Canaan, and into Egypt. Shechem and Hamor hoped that Jacob's presence would 'put them on the map' as far as these trade routes worked. Nothing could be more repugnant to Jacob, but he did not appraise his new neighbors as to this fact.

Nimrod was aware of the uniting power of merchandising, and established Babylon not to be a fortress or a palace, but what it almost became: *a world trade center.* And his sights were not just set on the world; *"and its top in the heavens."* This type of heaven/earth trade tends to involve human sacrifice and all the kinds of things that had brought on the flood in the first place. Revelation mentions that among the items traded by Great Babylon are *"the bodies and the souls of men."* So God 'overloads' their language; i.e., produced circumstances that made men retreat into the safety of their own traditions instead of participating in a communication-intense endeavor of universal trade. Mankind fell back on the old method of conquering and plundering rather than merchandising, as we see in the next account of Chedorlaomer and his cohorts, that held strong up until Solomon.

So the issue in question returns to Peleg and his progeny, which is not even listed in the regular genealogies; a new section is started in which dying is not mentioned. Some facts listed in plain sight may be surprising. First of all, there was not a general decay of lifespans; the average lifespan dropped suddenly in half with Peleg. Whatever happened to the earth severely affected longevity. Note also that Shem—remember that guy who was almost 100 (98) when he got off the ark?—died only 25 years before Abraham. And Eber—after whom the *Hebrews* are named—outlived Abraham by 3 *years*. Isaac was 80 years old, and his two sons Jacob and Esau were nearly 40 when Eber died. Poor old Peleg was the first to go in that family, one year before his great-grandson Nahor. So if Sarai was born when when Haran was 65 (see Appendix IX), then Abraham would have been ten years old when God told him to leave Ur of the Chaldeans. Now we see why Terah went with. Even if Terah fully believed God's message to Abram—and it appears that he did—one does not just send a 10-year-old off by himself to the land of the largest collection of giants in the known world.

This helps round out our view of the powerful dynasty that these Eberites—or Hebrews as they were called—had. Bear in mind that we later read that Abraham went after the King of Shinar (where Babel was) with 318 trained soldiers born in his own house. This would be aside from any *other* soldiers he had, who would compose the bulk of his personal army. Now a nomadic farmer and herdsman can afford about one professional soldier per eight to twelve servants at the maximum. They are expensive to train and expensive to keep. So the text is giving us a picture of a 3,000 + retinue of servants, each with their own family averaging five strong, meaning that Abraham was leading around a town-sized group of 15,000 persons at the very least, and up to 60,000. We sometimes imagine a lonely guy out in a tent. Not exactly; the Hebrews were a highly specialized *mobile nation*, part of the heritage handed down—and overseen by—Eber, who outlived them all until Isaac.

Back to Peleg. His fathers, going backwards, lived 464, 433, 438, and 600 years old respectively. Going forward from Peleg, they lived 239, 239 (again), 230, 148, 205, and 175 respectively, ending at Abraham. So after the flood, the lifespan was cut neatly in half, then after the earth splitting in Peleg's day it was once again cut neatly in half. Another curious fact jumps out at us. Whatever happened to shorten lifespans in the days of Peleg *did not affect those born previously*. The mean (middle) death year of everyone before Peleg was year 486 after the flood. The mean death year of everyone from Peleg on was year 206 after the flood. The pre- Peleg fathers almost all outlived their sons, and in Eber's case, his great-great-great-great-great-great-great-grandson. That's more than twice as long as America has existed.

The conclusion is remarkable. Whatever happened to Adam that affected his *seed*—the birth process rather than his body—also occurred during the flood, and *also* occurred in Peleg's time. It was not extra radiation coming in from a thinner atmosphere wearing people's bodies down so that they lived shorter lives, it was something that affected the *progeneration* process itself. As we discussed in Appendix II, something very strange is going on with the DNA, which doesn't level out until the days of Moses, and surprisingly has remained stable ever since. Moses mentions in his psalm (90) that we tend to live 70 years, or 80 given some extra strength... about ten percent of the pre-flood average; and the same then as now.

Peleg's family were the guardians of the books and records brought through the Deluge with Noah, of which the book of Enoch is one of the only ones that we have publicly available. Back in Ur, eventually they became the Chaldeans, which was not so much a nation as a class of scholars and astronomers who watched the times and guarded ancient knowledge. Note that in Daniel 2:2 they are one of the three groups called when the king Nebuchadnezzar needed his dream explained. Yet this group God rejected as the future guardians of the lineage of the coming Seed, and called Abram *out from* them. Joshua 24:15 tells us that they has already lost sight of God and were embracing a multiplicity of gods.

The fallout from Babel was that there would be three centers of higher knowledge. Nimrod's forces regrouped in Egypt, which held the 'secular' secrets of knowledge, Peleg's forces stayed in the Shinar plains and became the Chaldeans who held the religious secrets of knowledge, and Abraham wandered around getting to know God himself. As we see in the subsequent histories, Abraham's seed spoils both other centers, primarily in Moses and Ezra, to produce the uniquely expansive range of what we have today as the scriptures. While naysayers can spend their lives picking the scriptures apart, no one can deny that their depth is orders of magnitude beyond any other human literature.

So Abraham's seed are called Hebrews, which distinguished them from the other Shemites such as the Syrians, so his seed maintained that special distinction handed down by their father Eber as being 'from the other side'. They were forever to be a distinct people, or as Balaam says in Numbers, "*Behold; a people solitary he is tabernacling; and in the nations he is not reckoning himself.*" More on this when we get to Jacob's blessing at the end of Genesis.

This is both because of and the reason for their lack of participation in Babel. So as we delve into the strange histories of Abram/Abraham, we are watching someone who was separated from a group that was already separated from humanity proper; someone for whom all past ties were severed, with nothing but the future and God's promises by which to navigate his way through an increasingly hostile world.

Appendix IX
Sarai, Mother of Faith

Sarai is the first woman in Seth's line named after Eve and she gets renamed Sarah just to drive the point home. More details are given us about her life than any other female in the Bible until the two Mary's of the gospels. I have called her *mother of faith* in the title not because she had more faith than Eve, but because she *applied it in a way that worked*. Upon her introduction the text tells us is that she is barren; to her is no child. This is a common situation throughout the entirety of the scriptures, and there are two corresponding elements that accompany it. First is the presence of a situation in the wife's family that has been carried into the marriage that interferes with her relationship with her husband. The second is related; it is the refusal on the part of the wife *or* husband to fully respect each other. We see these elements in active in Sarai, Lot's wife, Rebecca, Laban's wife, Rachel, Manoah's wife, Hannah, Abigail, Michael, the Shunammite, and Elizabeth, among others. Just to give one example since the subject is its own essay, the last of the list there, Elizabeth, had a husband who lacked faith in his wife, as he demonstrated to Gabriel and got himself struck dumb in the process—something that might have been equally efficacious had it been done years earlier.

But let us see how this might have applied to such a great woman as Sarai, twice stolen for her beauty at an age when most women are busy pushing up daisies. The account tells us that Abram's brother Haran died in Ur, which would be *before* Terah piled up his family (apparently in response to God telling Abram to leave) and headed towards Canaan, getting about halfway there before settling in Haran where he eventually dies, having lived there for about 65 years. It is evident that the city 'Haran' got its name from Terah's son who had died before the trip[1074]. Terah's father Nahor, not to be confused with his son given the same name, was the shortest-lived patriarch listed... a trait apparently passed on to his grandson Haran, who died shortly after Sarai's birth when he was 65.

It's evident from the text that Terah's son Haran was born first. He had Lot, and in order to be old enough to have Milcah and Iscah (Sarai) and still have them be within a few years age of Nahor and Abram to be suitable as wives (Iscah was only nine years younger than Abram), Haran would have had to be born first. Yet he is listed last. And the last time we had three brothers (Shem, Ham, and Japheth), they are listed in order of 2nd, 3rd, and 1st as to birth order. Japheth was the oldest, Shem was the middle child, and Ham was the youngest. Scripture uses a similar pattern here; Haran was the oldest, being born in year 292 after the flood when his father was 70. Abram would have been born in year 352 after the flood when his father was 130, and Nahor would likely have been the youngest child. Nahor's granddaughter Rebecca later marries Abraham's son Isaac.

So upon Haran's death in Ur, Terah adopted Haran's three children Lot, Milcah, and Iscah and left for Canaan, getting as far as Haran, which he likely named after his deceased son, and Nahor and Abram marry their nieces, who are legally their sisters by adoption; thus Abram could truthfully tell Pharaoh and Abimelech that she was his 'sister', though he had to do a bit more explaining to Abimelech, whose sarcasm at the irony of the situation comes out when he tells Sarah "I have given to your *brother* a thousand silver pieces..." He also took over the care of Lot; as per the culture (and similarly the world over), Lot was his sister's protectorate, and Abram was *his* protectorate, having taken over the position from his father Terah. So while Lot was Abram's adopted *son* through taking over Terah's job, he was his *brother* through Sarai, as he says to Lot in 13:8. If Nahor had

---

[1074] There is another possibility here which does not change the results; if Terah had a brother named Haran, who would be the uncle of Abram, Nahor, and Haran, then Terah would have adopted Milcah and Iscah upon his brother''s death, and Abram and Nahor would be marrying their cousins. This possibility requires extra-biblical assumptions with which I am generally uncomfortable.

been older than Abram, the role of being Lot's protectorate would have fallen to him. Thus we see the 'Shem, Ham, Japheth' pattern repeated in 'Abram, Nahor, Haran'.

The birth of Sarai was a very significant event. God tells the 10-year-old boy Abram to go to Canaan. Haran dies. Terah leaves Ur. It's 21 years after the deaths of Peleg and Nahor, 8 years before the death of Reu, and 31 years before the death of Serug. Everything that has been taking centuries to happen is clustered around her birth. Plus she's gorgeous and doesn't age. Definitely worth a closer look, which we do here as pertains to faith.

Thing about faith is that we don't get to have what we want. What we want is real; it's more real than anything around us that we can see, hear, and touch. And there's a trick to faith. What it does is make real now what we hope for later. What it doesn't do is give us now what we hope for. It gives us the evidence and power of it; everything but the real thing. This is the great secret that Abraham gave to humanity. When God wanted to destroy Sodom and Gomorrah, Abraham did everything he could to prevent it. When God told him to sacrifice his child, he didn't even reply; he got up early and headed out. Previously, mankind had had both wants and hopes, but the two were indistinguishable; the present blessings of faith and life focus of future hopes were at cross-purposes and had been since Adam.

Why do I mention this? Because we often adopt an idolatrous version of hope; one in which we want it *now*. After all, doesn't it say in Proverbs that hope deferred makes the heart sick? But we forget the second half of that verse, which says *desire that comes to pass is a tree of life*. It doesn't say *hope that comes to pass*. What is needed for hope is assurance that the hope is worthwhile, not the thing hoped for magically happening. What needs to magically happen is to have enough belief in that hope that we can weather anything for something we're not going to get *now*. This brings up the mystery of the relationship between Abraham and Sarah.

As mentioned in Appendix V, it is *Woman* who is put on the stage when Man is effectively shut out from any kind of meaningful action. It is the Woman who carried the Seed. And Appendixes II and III point out that Man's only recourse was to *believe God* rather than act. He could not act except on faith because all actions proceeding from himself were tainted by the 'judging' of whether that act was good or evil. Acting in faith means he does it because God says so; there is no need to judge its merits for himself. This was the one role left to males after the Garden.

But the Woman? She had a different role that came with different issues. And time and time again these issues in scripture center on childbearing. She also has a different set of weaknesses. The weakness of the Woman is that she has a weak heart. This trait can be less than useful when the entire creation is dependent on whether you have faith or not. Thus the strange union of the two has always been necessary.

What did the Shunammite woman say to Elisha when he told her she would have a son? *No my lord, do not lie to your handmaiden.* What did she say when that son died and she made a beeline for Elisha? *Did I not say, do not lie to your handmaiden?* Jeremiah twice compares extreme hopelessness to the *heart of a woman in her pangs*. Again we go back to the Garden. God designed the male and the female in such a way that one cannot do without the other. Corinthians says *Nevertheless, neither is woman without man, nor man without woman, in Lord. For just as the woman is of the man, so is man also by the woman, but the all are of the God.* And First Timothy lays out her weakness with no beating around the bush whatsoever: *For Adam was first formed, then Eve; and Adam was not deceived, but the woman being much deceived has fallen into transgression; but she will be saved through the childbearing, if they continue in faith and love and sanctification with sanity.*

What is this saying? That woman is inferior somehow? No; that being deceived changed the Woman in way that is still affecting her. Is the danger that she will somehow keep getting deceived? No; just the opposite. She is so intent on never being 'taken' again that she has shut up her heart beyond what is possible for hope. Sarah had no problem at all playing the 'sister' role. Had she not needed to be rebuked for that the text would not have mentioned that Abimelech managed to do so. The act of fully engaging with one's spouse is akin to fully engaging with God, which is dangerous, and as scripture shows time and time again, potentially devastating. Thus we drop back to a safer distance.

The last text of the the Old Testament, Malachi, puts it this way: *And you say 'Why?' Because Jehovah—he testifies between you and between wife of your youth, which you—you are treacherous in her. And she—your companion, and wife of your covenant. And did he not make one? And the remainder of spirit—to Him. And why? the one? —seeking God's seed. And you are kept in your spirit, and in wife of your youth it must not be treacherous; that he hates putting away, says he, Jehovah, God of Israel.* The key here is *remainder of spirit—to Him*. In other words, all things that are One operate in God's own jurisdiction, for he is One. Thus the act of marrying puts the man and the woman into a relationship that is overseen by God himself in a way that something equally important—say childbearing—is not. Yet how do we operate within God's own sphere when we are not God? Herein lies the difficulty.

The last part of that quote from Timothy is often ignored because the subject is obscured by nice happy words like *faith*, *love*, *sanctification*, and *sanity*. But to what do they apply? Follow the order that is always laid out in instructions regarding relationships. The faith needed is the wife's, and that toward her husband. The love needed is the husband's, and that toward his wife. The sanctification which provides sanity is the sanctification of the relationship itself; it must be set apart as important in a different way than mere circumstances of life. The sanity is the larger picture that can carry them through the necessary storms of relationship. Do we think we are alone when these storms come? Look at Jehovah's reactions with Israel all through the histories and prophets; emotionally it is overwhelming. Has anyone considered what God is hoping for?

These things are necessary and proper. And as mentioned, they are also devastating. Both in our relationships with God and with our spouses, we are forever waiting for the other shoe to drop. We prefer apprehension and fear to faith and love.

When Sarah had tried everything including Hagar to get a son, when she was well past menopause, when there was no way possible for her to believe that it could happen, she received strength because she counted him faithful who promised. Note that she did not consider him *all powerful*, as in able to raise the dead as Abraham believed when asked to sacrifice Isaac, but she considered him *faithful*; i.e., someone who delivered on his word. This is the same faith that she had in her husband, for Peter mentions that she adorned herself—put something on that was *not* part of her—with a meek and quiet spirit, calling Abraham 'lord'. Peter says that this was because she hoped in God, and was operating without that fear of the other shoe dropping.

Sarah lived to 127 years, which number means the full measure of marriage relationship. Her death initiated the first—and very significant, the exchange takes a full chapter—purchase of any part of the promised land. She left an indelible mark on the history of mankind, and that mark left a hole in Isaac her son, who saw the hope and faith of his father and mother, but did not find the love that would make the waiting of hope and toil of faith worthwhile... until Rebecca. For Sarah kept getting in trouble when the inhabitants of the land saw her; the first thing it says of Rebecca when she saw Isaac was that she veiled herself. Isaac takes her into his mother's tent—which idea comes from the tent (or veil) of mourning raised by Adam and Eve—and was comforted after his mother. In other words, he got the 'earnest', or present proof, that what his mother and Abraham were hoping for was worth the wait. He now had someone who would wait with him and believe as he believed. And for the only time between a husband and a wife in the Old Testament text, it says that he loves her.

Lamech had named Noah "rest", and said, *This one—he consoles us from our labor and from wear of our hands from the ground which he makes her a curse—Jehovah.* This was true, yet there was something yet missing; the consolation needed was fellowship for the journey, which can only come from where God designed it to come from: a spouse who shares the hope for the end of the journey. It is when we lose sight of the end—the hope —that we also lose the sanity, the sense of proportion for the present faith and love.

The helmsman is the Spirit.

If Sarah could believe in Abraham, Abraham could believe in God, for he personally experienced a role that allowed him to empathize with God... something we humans are slow to do. This empathy comes out in his ability to intercede for Sodom and Gomorrah for Lot's sake. In exchange, God gives him a subtle gift regarding the treatment of his wife in the matter of Hagar and Ismael being kicked out of the house: *all which she is saying to you—Sarah—you listen! to her voice*. This is in contrast with what he had said to Adam when the ground was cursed, *because you listen to voice of your wife*. What had changed? Woman had.

Eve had spoken to Adam—we are not told what—while being deceived. Sarah was most definitely *not* deceived as to what would happen if she let Hagar and her son hang around. In the Garden, it was the discernment of Adam that was called for, and failed. In the land of Canaan, it was the discernment of Sarah that was called for, and got God's support. And unlike Eve, Sarah did not go ahead and kick them out herself, she went to her husband. There would be no more blaming of the woman; when there was a disagreement the matter was put at the feet of the initially unwilling Abraham, who learned his lesson well: after Sarah was gone he remarried and sent the resultant six children "away from his son Isaac" to the east with gifts. It was as important to God that the child of promise, Isaac, be a child of Sarah as it was that he be a child of Abraham.

Why did I mention that the helmsman is the Spirit? The actions of the Spirit of God and Spirit of Jehovah in the text characteristically produce initiative, strong emotion, and insight. All three are needed to operate faith. The word is often used today as 'do you believe...?' which falls miles short. James point out that believing in God is no big deal; even the demons do. The questions are What are we doing about it, and Do we know what we are doing? Strong emotion can lead to rash decisions which lack insight. Insight leads to a balanced view of life, which can erode initiative. Initiative leads to sticking our necks out, which can weaken the confidence of emotion. In all these we need fellowship with God, which is the realm of the Spirit... and fellowship with God implies friendship, as Abraham was called the *friend of God*.

Then what does that make Sarah? A wife *and* a friend to her husband. Thus she becomes the Mother of Faith.

Appendix X
Mother of All Living

Let us look at two parallel passages regarding the role of a mother, Eve and Rebecca.

And she is taking from his fruit, and she is eating, and she is giving even to her ♂man with her, and he is eating. ⁷ And they are being opened, *the* eyes of two of them, and they are knowing that they *are* naked ones, and they are raising a tent of mourning, and they are making for them*selves traveling* girdles.[1075]

¹³ And he is saying—Jehovah God—to the woman, 'What *is* this you do?' And she is saying—the woman—'The serpent, he seduced me—and I am eating.'
¹⁴ And he is saying—Jehovah God—to the serpent, 'That you do this, you *are* being cursed from all of the beast and from all of animal of the field. On your belly[1076] do you go, and dust you eat all of *the* days of your life. ¹⁵ And enmity I am setting between you and between the woman, and between your seed and her seed; head—he overwhelms you; and heel—you overwhelm him.'
¹⁶ To the woman he says, 'To increase, I am increasing your vexation and your pregnancy, in pangs you birth sons, and to your husband your impulse[1077], and he rules[1078] in you.'
¹⁷ And to Adam he says, 'That you listen to voice of your wife...

[1075] *Traveling girdles*; the sense of the word is of a belt one puts on for war, or a traveling skirt put on for a journey.

[1076] *Belly*; similar to *serpent* and *crafty* (notes verse 1), *belly* connotes an utter helpless wallowing in those qualities that previously had been operated by choice. It has the sense of a constant breaking forth in an untoward direction, as well as to *groveling*.

[1077] *Impulse* does not quite do the word justice. It is a drawn-out longing that produces desire manifested in impulsive rather than considered behavior.

[1078] *Rule*; a repetitive, almost automatic or symbolic manner of behavior. Also rendered *quote* when without accent marks.

²⁰ And he is calling—the Adam—name of his wife Eve[1079]: for she becomes mother of all of *the* living One[1080].

---

⁶¹ And she is rising—Rebecca and her maidens—and they are riding on the camels, and they are going after the ♂man; and he is taking—the servant—Rebecca and he is going.
⁶² And Isaac, has goes from to come of Beerlahairoi[1081]; and he is dwelling in land of the Negev. And he is *going* forth—Isaac—to cause to meditate in the field, toward to face of evening, and he is lifting his eyes and he is seeing, and behold! camels—ones coming.
⁶⁴ And she is lifting—Rebecca—her **eyes**, and she is seeing **Isaac**, and is alighting from on the camel. ⁶⁵ And she is saying to the servant, 'Who ? this man, even this the one coming in the field to cause to meet us?' And he is saying, the servant—the same—'He: my lord;' and she is taking the veil, and she is covering herself.
⁶⁶ And he is enumerating—the servant—to Isaac **all of** the matters which he does. ⁶⁷ And he is bringing her—Isaac—toward the tent —his mother Sarah's—and he is taking **Rebecca**, and she is becoming to him for wife, and he is loving her. And he is being comforted—Isaac—after his mother.

We saw in Appendix V that there was a waiting and suffering given to Woman in order to produce the coming Seed who would bruise the Serpent's head. We saw in Appendix IX that the faith of a Woman is somewhat distinct from the faith of a Man. Here we look at what it means to be a mother.

[1079] *Eve*; life-giver... with the additional senses of *elemental existence, to declare or show,* and by extension, *a village.* Note that this naming of his wife gives the last recorded words of Adam... Man falls silent for the duration until the promised Seed; and the Woman, though subjugated by a 'silent partner', is put on to the stage. The necessity for *faith* has been crystallized; Man can no longer proactively *do*, only reactively *believe*; all action must now proceed from God's word. But the woman, not being in the position of responsibility, has an element of freedom from this reactivity... which tragically is subjugated by her impulsive desire toward her husband. This ''tragedy'' in the Greek sense of the word sets the stage for all women from Sarah to Mary.

[1080] Equally, *all of living*.

[1081] *Beerlahairoi*; Well of the Living, Seeing; see 16:14, 25:11.

There are no instructions to mothers in the New Testament. We have clear and distinct instructions throughout to wives, husbands, fathers, children, masters, and slaves... but not a word to mothers. This phenomena alerts us to the fact that there is quite the mystery hidden in the subject. To unravel this mystery, we look at the relationship between *Mother* and *Wife*.

Adam named his wife Eve—Life Giver—as his first act (and final words) after the eye-opening. The irony in his words is somewhat puzzling; the text says that he names her this because she is the mother of all living. Yet she was formed last; does it simply mean that she would be the mother of all humans from then on? As usual, if that is what the text meant to say, that is what it would have said. It calls her quite simply the mother of all living, or mother of the Living One.

While we're finding puzzling parts to this mystery, let us consider that *Eve* can also mean *a village*, and look at Galatians 4:26: "*But the Jerusalem above is free, who is mother of all of us.*" ...another strange repetition of the same idea. To make matter more difficult, when look at Jesus' words in Matthew 12:48 to find out what he says a mother is, we get "*Who is my mother? And who are my brothers? And he stretched forth his hand over his disciples and said, Behold, my mother and my brothers. For whoever will do the will of my Father who is in the heavens, <u>he</u> is my brother, and sister, and mother.*" Note there two feminine roles and only one masculine.

Was Jesus just saying "We're all one big happy family" or was he choosing his words very carefully? Let's go back to the beginning and find out.

There are three mothers in question that must be considered. Adam's, Eve's, and Jesus'. Beginning with the first couple, it seems reasonable to consider that God took the Father role for both Adam and Eve. The mother role is left in silence, and the first mention we get of a mother after them is Abraham telling Abimelech that Sarai was the daughter of his father but not the

253

daughter of his mother. Now the writer of the text decided to toss us this particular tidbit not just to round out the story of Abraham, but to continue the mystery of motherhood, and to hint rather pointedly that Adam and Eve may have had, in effect, two different 'mother' figures. Thus the next two mothers that the Genesis text finds it expedient to mention are Hagar and Rebecca's unnamed mother, Bethuel's wife. Then the next mention of the word is in the text quoted above regarding Isaac being comforted after his mother.

Now both of the interim mothers—Hagar and Rebecca's unnamed mother—are mentioned specifically in the role of arranging a marriage; the first picking a wife for Ishmael, and the second involved in the sending of Rebecca to Isaac. The two roles are diametrically opposed, and hint at what had happened with Adam and Eve. When Abraham's servant presented his case, Rebecca's brother Laban and her mother were the deciding voices; Bethuel her father is silent. In this and most ancient cultures, the older brother had the role of protector for his younger sister, and any suitors would have to placate him first. Thus both Abimelech and Pharaoh heaped riches and honor on Abram when they were under the impression that he was Sarah's brother.

In our example here, we have Ishmael—whose mother gets him a wife from Egypt where she was from—and Isaac, who is presented with a wife after his mother is dead. But the parallel does not yet carry over to Adam and Eve. We do see that Adam did not treat Eve as a wife until he was forced out of the Garden, that is, he did not "cleave to his wife" until he had "left his father and mother". Yet right before he takes her as wife, he calls her name Eve because she is the *mother* of all living. Wife and motherhood are strangely linked. Adam—separated from his (unmentioned) mother figure by the cherubim with the flashing sword—finds in Eve the necessary continuation of that role ...not as *his* mother, but as the new mother of all, his wife.

So if Adam did not treat Eve as a 'wife' while in the Garden, how *did* he treat her? And here the text provides us with Abraham as an example; Adam treated her as a *sister*. God said to him,

"Because you have listened to the voice of your wife..." in other words, "Because you treated her in a different relationship from that in which I gave her to you..." Now we begin to approach the parallel. Adam was from the ground; we might say from 'mother earth'. Ishmael was from a fleshly, that is, earthly union with Hagar (Galatians 4:24-31) in an attempt to give some practical impetus to what was solely an undefined promise of God. Isaac was the later result of that promise, coming as Hebrews says, "of one become dead." Similarly, Eve was brought forth after creation was for all practical purposes done with and wrapped up in the naming of the animals. And she is brought out from Adam's *sleep*, which again is used synonymously with death. Eve's mother is thus presented to us as death; sleep.

This both embarrasses and alarms Adam, who justifiably is concerned that the other more powerful beings who want her—such as the Serpent—will also want him out of the way if he acts as her husband. So like Abraham, he steps aside and lets the powerful and greedy have their way with her. God, of course, does not allow this with either Sarah or Eve, and the *wifeness* of both is established *after* the husbands begin to trust in God and act like husbands. We can sketch out the parallel further as to the progeny of each in the archetype—how the text compares Cain and Abel to Esau and Jacob—but here let us focus on the transformation process from not-quite-accepted-as-wife to accepted-as-wife ...and mother.

The sleep of which we have spoken, the archetype of Eve's mother, takes a pivotal role in unraveling the host of unspoken issues. Adam did not know what had happened to him; he was *asleep*. While he could figure it out later, there remained an element of mystery, of something unfathomable about the Woman. The first thing he shares with her was a fruit forbidden by God. The second was opened eyes and the realization that they were naked. And finally the crux—they raised a tent of mutual mourning and made themselves traveling girdles... they knew that they had to go *somewhere*; what was being mourned was the *loss of the opportunity to appreciate each other when the time was perfectly ripe for them to do so*. This theme is repeated throughout scripture. Where were they going? Away from paradise. The Garden was God's paradise; it was merely the place. They were leaving the paradise of each other.

Adam and Eve would make love and live as husband and wife—but not in Eden, and not as innocent children. *That* was left for the mother to instill into the new child. And it was; and it has been... for six thousand long years. And it will be; there is a new creation in which what belongs in its place is always in its place. Abraham looked for that city, as does everyone who has tasted the sweetness and the sorrow mixed together in mortality: Jerusalem above, mother of us all.

This is what is given to us in the quote above regarding Isaac and Rebecca. All the elements are there; she veils herself in honor of *her* mother, mystery and sleep. He takes her to *his* mother's tent —as if returning to the tent of mourning that Adam and Eve raised before she was called Eve.[1082] And for the only time in the entire Old Testament—the text tells us that he loves her—a husband loves his wife. And he is comforted after his mother; the gift passed on down through the mothers is realized, given by Sarah his mother, the Mother of Faith. This takes us to Jesus' words on the cross to his disciple John: "Behold your mother." In other words, "Would you like to know what was the mystery hidden in the woman while Adam was asleep that you men have been scared of all these years, that has been passed down and protected by mothers for millennia? You're looking at it."

The loss of his mortal life did more for both us and Jesus than we yet realize. Here, let us look at its application to the loss of opportunity for spouses to appreciate each other in their ideal time. The tree of life is mentioned only in Genesis, Proverbs, and Revelation, which tells us that the subject is a universal one. Thus, in the four mentions of the tree of life in Proverbs, we find that access to the tree of life is found in the *wisdom* (3:18) of the

---

[1082] It is outside the scope of this discussion but worth mentioning that while this archetype takes us back to the veil/tent of 3:7, there is a parallel mother/wife archetype in Song of Solomon 8:5 that takes us back to 3:6 and the tree itself.

healing of the tongue (15:4 later expanded on in chapter 31, *she opens her mouth in wisdom, and the law of grace on her tongue*) that produces *fruit of righteousness* (11:30) in her husband, whose *desire* for his wife is fulfilled (13:12), giving them both access to the elusive tree of life. The entire subject of the Tree of Life is wrapped up in the subject of the husband and wife.

And the story does not stop there. Continuing the Proverbs 3:18 quote above, Wisdom later says *my delights with the sons of men*. Jesus had said to Mary before his *behold your mother* statement, *behold your son*.

And the archetype of losing—and regaining—a son is throughout the text. The unstated question that keeps springing up is *what will it cost?* Or to put it more bluntly from the woman's perspective, *how the hell can it be worth it to pour everything into a son that I am going to lose?* And here we find that Wisdom does not just mean being very clever. She is the dividing line between despair and hope. She says, *all they that hate me love death*. What hatred is spoken of here: people who don't want to be smart? No, it is the hatred of which the Song of Solomon hints at: *strong as death, the love; hard as Sheol, the jealousy*. No matter how seemingly removed, the love/hate issue returns in childbirth and in marriage for women: Do you hate, or do you love, your role? And only Wisdom can provide the nourishment to choose the love.

This is why Adam named his wife the mother of all living *after* they failed. It was in direct contrast with the tree of life, to which they no longer had access. It was his last noted act of faith, that despite the failure, the answer of life was still to be found in her; not in her love for her husband, not in her love for God, not in her love for her offspring; all these fall into place when she hits the crossroads of who she is; and whether she accepts love *itself* as the gift of Wisdom. Mary was told that a sword would pierce her own soul, and that is only one part of the price. Yet Wisdom is there to tell her that love is as strong as death, and that to be jealous of what could have been rather than hoping for what can be, leads to the grave; that in the loss and impossibility of life—of which she is mother—it will be worth it.

Appendix XI
Seventy Souls to Egypt

The count of Jacob's entry into Egypt is an excellent example for seeing how and why counts were made and kept. Bear in mind that Jacob's community now numbered somewhere between 30,000 and 100,000; a volatile and dynamic mobile community that could hold its own against the best of the Canaanite cities, as their experience with Shechem demonstrated.

Thus, when a formal count is made and recorded, it is far more than a head count. There may be family members who are simply left out and there may be family members who are not yet born who make the roster. Even dead people may make the count, as we see with Er and Onan. No doubt there were many other of Jacob's grandsons that died in this interim, but none of the them made it. So it is more of a royal registry than a calculator exercise, and to find out what each registry is counting so that we understand it, we do a very strange thing: we read what it says.

I First we have the 66: *All of the soul, the one coming to Jacob to Egypt, ones coming forth of his thigh, from besides of Jacob's son's wives, all of soul: sixty and six.* This registry is the first half of the summary of the 70 names just listed. It is specifically souls significant to the bloodline who went to Egypt. When we read the previous list of names, we note first of all that Dinah is grammatically both left out of the numbering, and emphasized; the text is giving us a heads-up there to pay attention. She is left out because she took no part in participating in progeny. One could not claim the she's excluded because of being a female, for Asher's daughter Serah is numbered. We note also that Er and Onan are dead, taking the count down to 68. The next sentence in the text tells us *And Joseph's sons who, he is born to him in Egypt —soul—two*. So since they did not come *to Egypt*, we subtract two more, yet we will see in list **IV** that they are considered in Joseph's loins in the larger summary of those who descended to

Egypt. So this roster is about sixty six blood-carriers of Jacob that made the trip from Canaan to Egypt, Joseph included.

II Next we get 70: *All of the soul to house of Jacob, the one coming to Egypt: seventy*. This is not merely bloodline contributors, but everyone in "the house of Jacob" who is called "the one coming to Egypt", so we take our 66 and add Ephraim, Manasseh, Dinah, and Jacob himself, arriving at 70. This is the household roster.

III Next in Exodus 1:5 we get *And he is becoming, all of soul of ones issuing of Jacob's thigh, seventy soul; and Joseph—he is in Egypt*. This is a different 70 than the previous roster; it includes Ephraim and Manasseh, but excludes Dinah (like the first list) and Jacob himself, as he did not beget himself. So to find the missing two persons, we simply look at the original roster, and see that Exodus is including Er and Onan from the list of persons given in Genesis 46, because they *did* participate—albeit indirectly—in the perpetuation of the bloodline due to what Judah ended up doing with Tamar. Seventy again, just slightly different names. This roster is a bloodline rather than a household roster.

IV Then in Deuteronomy 10:22 we get *In seventy soul they descend—your fathers—to Egypt; and now he places you—Jehovah your God—as stars of the heavens for multitude*. This is neither the household nor the bloodline list, it is the descent-to-Egypt roster. Thus Er and Onan are out again as they did not descend, taking us down to 68. Ephraim and Manasseh are included in Joseph's earlier descent, just as the original list in Genesis 46 has children of the patriarchs who were unlikely to have yet been born. And since this roster is not limited to those who perpetuated the bloodline, Dinah can be included for 69. Adding Jacob himself brings us to 70 again. This roster ends up being identical to roster **II**, but arrived at through different means.

V Lastly we get 75 in Acts 7:14, *And Joseph sent, called to, Jacob his father, and all the kindred, seventy five souls, and Jacob went down into Egypt*. This roster is of all those called. Thus it excludes Joseph, Ephraim, and Manasseh, taking the original list of 70 down to 67. Here we see the method by which the scribes read the scriptures, and get a clue as to how we are to read them. What the text *doesn't* include is as important as what it *does*. Thus, while we can guess (or read in First Chronicles) that there were other children and grandchildren and simply add them in to make 75, that is cheating: we can only include a name if it is mentioned in Genesis of Jacob's household. So who was of the "kindred" who were called? The 67 plus Jacob, Dinah, Leah, Zilpah, Bilhah, Tamar, Er, and Onan makes 75. That includes every single person named of Jacob's "kindred" who were "called", be they alive or dead.

So here we have five different lists with five different purposes, and we see that the key to making sense of them is—before we get out our calculators and start crunching—read what it is we are to be crunching. Scripture is exceedingly precise.

Appendix XII
Year/years: Hidden Cycles in the Text

In the footnote at 5:5 of the text, we point out that the Hebrew mixes "year" with "years" in a manner that at first blush seems arbitrary, though it is simply the convention of listing numbers from one to ten in the plural when added to an even hundred multiple... with exceptions. Here we look at a way to make sense of and use the distinction.

What we wish to discover here is:
- Is there a connection between the ages of the patriarchs and the timing of the flood?
- Is there a pattern to the ages, and do distinctions like year/years contribute to that pattern?
- Is this meaningful, or are we playing with calculators? What does it help us understand?

Let's start by laying out the information we have in a chart that shows everything.

We have ten patriarchs before the flood, and ten after. Let's set them up parallel to each other.

And when the text says, for example, "900 year and 30 year", we will list 900 separately from 30. Anytime the text says "**years**" instead of "**year**" we will put a plus sign ("+") in front of that number. Let's see what we get:

	List 1 Pre-flood	First Son	Lived After	Total Age	List 2 Post-flood	First Son	Lived After	1 & 2 Total
1	Adam	130	800	900 and 30	Shem	100	500	1,530
2	Seth	100 + 5	800 + 7	900 and 12	Arphaxad	35	400 + 3	1,350
3	Enosh	90	800 and 15	900 + 5	Shelach	30	400 + 3	1,338
4	Cainan	70	800 and 40	900 +10	Eber	34	400 and 30	1,374
5	Mahalaleel	60 + 5	800 and 30	800 and 95	Peleg	30	200 + 9	1,134
6	Jared	100 and 62	800	900 and 62	Reu	32	200 + 7	1,201
7	Enoch	65	300	300 and 65	Serug	30	200	595
8	Methuselah	100 and 87	700 and 82	900 and 69	Nahor	29	100 and 19	1,117
9	Lemech	100 and 82	500 and 95	700 and 77	Terah	70	200 + 5	1,052
10	Noah	500		900 and 50	Abraham	100 and 70 + 5		1,125[1083]
Totals using the same formats:		1,315 and 231 + 10	6,300 and 262 + 7	8,100 and 460 + 15		490	2,700 and 119 + 32	11,816

All our information from the text is there, laid out according to the **grammar** of the text.

- Where the word "and" is used, it means that "Year" was used twice. For example, number 6, Jared is "100 and 62" because the text says "*And he is living—Jared—two and sixty **Year** and hundred of **Year**.*"
- Where the "+" sign is used in the chart, the text says "years" instead of "Year", for example number 5, Mahalaleel is "60 + 5" because the text says "*And he is living—Mahalaleel—five **years** and sixty **Year**.*"
- Totals of each paired set of pre- and post-flood patriarchs are on the right, and the grand total is in the lower right.

God's day is 1000 years, and each person lived a proportion of that. The flood occurred in year 1,656, and after the flood, there were 713 years until the death of Joseph, giving us 2,369 total years in Genesis. So we have the following raw figures:

[1083] Ironically, Abraham added to Noah here equals 1,125 which is 3 times the number of days Noah was on the ark.

- The ages of the patriarchs as worded in the text, including when their first son was born,
- The 360 day 'perfect' year,
- The 1,656 years before the flood,
- The 713 years after the flood,
- The relationship between pre-flood and post-flood patriarchs.

Now let's take each person's age and see how evenly 360 divides into it[1084], and what is left over. This shows how many *cyclic* years are involved. Each 360 is of a circle, so the remainders are *degrees of a 360° circle*. Our object here is to have the ages to evenly add up to a multiple of 360.

		Age		Age	Total	/360	Remainder
1	Adam	930	Shem	600	→1,530	4	90°
2	Seth	912	Arphaxad	438	→1,350	3	270°
3	Enosh	905	Shelach	433	→1,338	3	258°
4	Cainan	910	Eber	464	→1,374	3	294°
5	Mahalaleel	895	Peleg	239	→1,134	3	54°
6	Jared	962	Reu	239	→1,201	3	121°
7	Enoch	365	Serug	230	→595	1	235°
8	Methuselah	969	Nahor	148	→1,117	3	37°
9	Lemech	777	Terah	275	→1,052	2	332°
10	Noah	950	Abraham	175	→1,125	3	45°
				Totals	11,816	28	1,736°

1,736° has four more 360°'s that can be subtracted from it, leaving us with:

| 11,816 | 32 | 296° |

[1084] Note that 460, one of the figures at the bottom of the "Total Age" column in the first chart, when multiplied by 3.6 (360/100), comes to exactly 1,656, the date of the flood. The number 460 and its multiples (230, 23 especially) keep popping up as we will see.

Here 32 is the total number of 360° cycles so far. The remainder of 296° cannot come out even until we return to our first chart and add up <u>every single "+" figure</u>, which is every time in the text that the word "**years**" instead of "**Year**" is used. They add up to + 64. We add that to 296° and get 360°, and since you are probably just looking at the charts and not reading these words, here's your visual:

11,880	33	0°

And here we have our first clue. There are 33[1085] cycles of 360° in the combined ages of the twenty patriarchs, which are not apparent until we take the nuances of grammar seriously, <u>meaning we double up the word "**years**"</u> when adding to the word "**Year**".

Using this cyclic method, let's look at the other figures at the bottom of the first chart. We have the **initial** figures (meaning the word "and" is not in front of them, nor is a "+" sign) of:

- 1,315 which is   3 x 360° with a remainder of 235°[1086]
- 6,300 which is   17.5 x 360°
- 8,100 which is   22.5 x 360°
-    490 which is   1 x 360° with a remainder of 130°
- 2,700 which is   7.5 x 360°

So we see that there are definitely clear-cut patterns emerging. The task is to find out what they mean. All we have done so far is to establish that the patriarchs' ages are correlated to the 360 day year.

[1085] The 33 cycles refer to both the 33 days of a woman''s being unclean upon bearing a male, and the 33 paired chambers in Ezekiel 41:6 (almost always translated "30" because the translators do not realize that a *circular* structure is being described). We have then the dual ideas of what it takes to establish mankind as recovering from the 'uncleanness' of eating the fruit, finally producing an Abraham who can establish faith, and God''s establishing of those who take part in that process as permanent fixtures in his temple. This theme of 33 and the dual Establish/Maintain relationship is the thematic backbone of the book of Hebrews, as seen in Apostle/High Priest.

[1086] Note that Enoch and Serug, row 7 in the chart, also have a remainder of 235°.

What we need to do next is find out how the 360° year (and thus the ages of the patriarchs) are correlated with the year of the flood (1,656) and the years after the flood (713) until Joseph's death which ends Genesis.

The first clue we get is by adding up all the ages of the patriarchs from Adam to Seth before each birthed a son. This gives us precisely the number of years to the flood: 1,656. This is a bit remarkable because it appears that Seth was the second-born after Japheth, and was 98 when he left the ark; Noah would have had him at 602. In other words, there is no obvious reason why this should come out even, but it does.

The second clue we get is by adding up all the patriarchs in Genesis to find out what kind of figures we are working with. If there were 9 patriarchs, we would expect everything to be in multiples of 9. As it is, we have 10 (pre-flood), + 10 (post-flood) + 3 (Isaac, Jacob, and Joseph) = **23**.

23 is a prime number, and if it is the 'prime' number to be used, we can expect to find it virtually every time we do a calculation. Let's look at a few of the places it appears:
- 1,656 years before the flood   = 72 x **23**
- 713 years after the flood   = 31 x **23**
- 1,656 / 3.60 (360°/100)   = 20 x **23**
- 437 (Isaac, Jacob, & Joseph's combined ages) = 19 x **23**

So we see that 23 is tying in both the 360° cyclic order of ages and the lengths of the the time periods before and after the flood. Let's look at Isaac, Jacob, and Joseph as they were not included in the original chart. Combining their ages in the same grammatical manner of the chart, 437 looks like this:

- Isaac, Jacob, and Joseph = 240 and 80 + 117   (Total 437)

Recall that in order to make the combined ages of the 20 patriarchs match with a 360° cyclic pattern, we had to <u>add back in the numbers after the "+" sign</u> in the chart, in that case + 64. Here we will do the same thing. The grammar is made of 3^3, or 27 letters. Also, the first 100 years of Abraham before Isaac was born are not to be counted, as they are not listed with everyone else in chapter 11 where the text gives the ages of how old each person was when they had their first son. So we have:

- 437 (Isaac, Jacob, Joseph) x 27 = 11,799
- 11,799 minus 100 unlisted years of Abraham =11,699
- 11,699 + 117 (all the "+" use of the word "years" as we did before) = **11,816**

This is the **same figure** we got when we added up the 20 Patriarchs. Once again, using the same method, we have correlated the three last patriarchs with the first 20.

Let's summarize what we have so far.

- The ages of first 10 patriarchs before the flood and the 10 after the flood are set up parallel.
- When taken together, their ages are related to thirty-three 360 day years.
- The ages also correspond exactly to the time periods before and after the flood.
- Isaac, Jacob, and Joseph likewise correspond exactly to everyone that came before.

So while we have found some nice numerical phenomena, we don't fully know what it means yet. Let us keep going.

There is a scriptural parallel between Isaac-Jacob-Joseph and Abraham-Noah-Adam, set up by the phrase, "These are the generations of. . ." Using the same grammatical format as the first chart, their ages are:

- 240 and 80 + 117 (Isaac, Jacob, and Joseph: total 437)
- 1,900 and 150 + 5 (Abraham, Noah, Adam: total 2,055)
- **2,140** and **230** + 122 (All six together, total: 2,492)

We notice that **2,140** and **230** in the last line add up to the total number of years in Genesis, **2,370**. So these six summarize the entire book. Is there a way that their respective ages tell us why the flood occurred when it did?

Let's look at these six patriarchs according to the grammar:

```
Abraham & Isaac   200     and 150 +   5 (total   355) without +   350
Noah & Jacob    1,040     and  50 +   7 (total 1,097) without + 1,090
Adam & Joseph     900     and  30 + 110 (total 1,040) without +   930
   Totals       2,140         230    122        2,492             2,370
                                              [   122 ]
                                              [ 2,614 ]
```

We find with some examination that while the figures come out close, they do not come out exact. So we go back to the text, and find out that another age is given us for Abraham (who seems to be the key to quite a lot of these figures), and that is 99 when he was given the *promise* of Isaac's birth date, and when he was circumcised. So let's rewrite that same chart with 99 instead of 100:

```
Abraham & Isaac   199     and 150 +   5 (total   354) without +   349
Noah & Jacob    1,040     and  50 +   7 (total 1,097) without + 1,090¹⁰⁸⁷
Adam & Joseph     900     and  30 + 110 (total 1,040) without +   930
   Totals       2,139         230    122        2,491             2,369
                                              [   122 ]
                                              [ 2,613 ]
```

Suddenly we're making a lot more sense. The first column's total, **2,139** is precisely 3 x 713, the number of years in Genesis after the flood. The last column's total is precisely the number of years from Adam to Joseph's death at the end of Genesis. Subtracting the two, we get 1,656, the exact number of years from Adam to the flood.[1088]

So what are we to do with the extra 122 years which have not yet been used? (They're in brackets at the bottom of the chart.)

We do the same thing we've done each time so far; we add them again to the total. That brings the lower figure in the fourth column of numbers above to **2,613**[1089].

[1087] 1,090; note that 1,090 of Jacob and Noah x 11, minus the "+ 110" from Adam and Joseph = 11,880 from the original chart again.

[1088] The central figures around which the others pivot are Noah and Jacob. Were we to remove the +7 from there, the fourth column would read 2,484, which doubled is 4,968. 4968 is precisely 3 x 1656, the number of years before the flood.

[1089] 2,613; We might also note that Jacob''s utterance, *For your salvation I hope, Jehovah*, in 49:18 has the gematria value of 1,388 which when added to 2,613 comes to 4,001. This brings us to the date of the Messiah's birth.

The first time we did this, we found that the 20 first patriarchs represent 33 cycles of 360°. The second time we found that the last three patriarchs were perfectly proportional with the first 20, by a multiple of 27, the number of Hebrew letters. So if we are to continue the journey, we will be looking for what **2,613** is proportional to, and what it means.

In each case before, the numbers correlated to **11,880**, the total of the 20 patriarch's ages.

So we simply take the proportion: **11,880** divided by **2,613** is **4.54649827784**. What do we do with a figure like that? We find out how many years it is in 360° cycles. Thus:

- 4.54649827784 x 360° = 1,636.73938   or
- **1,636 years**, 266 days, 4 hours, 14 minutes, and 36 seconds.

And here the great secret unfolds. *From the death of Joseph at the end of Genesis to the birth of the Messiah was . . .* **1,636 years**.

Furthermore, the 266th day of the year is September 23rd, which is known as the closest estimate for the day of year that Jesus was born. And once again we end up with the number 23, which by the way, means *full action in every capacity*.

Hidden in the dates and ages of the patriarchs in Genesis is the date of the birth of the Messiah.

Appendix XIII
Themes Within Themes: the Ephesian Pattern

The book of Genesis is unique even among Biblical narratives. Its scope is vast, yet the accounts with which it is filled resonate with normal human lives of every culture. Attempts to summarize it characteristically fall so short as to be insulting to the text. Thus we turn to the only competent entity available for summary: scripture itself. Specifically, Ephesians 4:4-6.

One body, and one Spirit, even as also you were called in one hope of your calling. One Lord, one faith, one baptism. One God and Father of all, who: over all, and through all, and in you all.

We have here the trinity pattern mentioned in Appendix VII (Time) but somewhat enhanced. To reiterate the trinity pattern: there is the Father who is source of everything, the Son who is manifestation of everything, and the Spirit who is the active power of everything. They share no part of their respective characters with each other except that each of them is fully God.

Here we have their characters multiplied. Each of the three is described in three parts, yet in a way that folds back on itself, as follows:

This is the meta-pattern of all things and how they exist in relationship to one another. The relationships fold like a Klein Bottle in mathematics, because the smallest summary (the last part) is actually a model of the entire structure, and is repeated in each section. This is one of the most compact and complex patterns found in scripture. Some familiarity with the workings of the trinity function, when applied, will demonstrate that these three verses were laid out with a sensitivity and skill that belies the casual manner in which it was introduced in the text.

A look at the order in which it appears...

3A (Power)
       3 (Power of Power)
       2 (Manifestation of Power)
       1 (Source of Power)

2A (Manifestation)
       3 (Power of Manifestation)
       2 (Manifestation of Manifestation)
       1 (Source of Manifestation)

1A (Source)
       1 (Source of Source) summarizing **1A**, and thus 1, 2, and 3 here.
       2 (Source of Manifestation) summarizing **2A**
       3 (Source of Power) summarizing **3A**

...suggests the following parallel to Genesis, where the breaks into different sections are conveniently noted in the text by "These are the generations..." or a similar statement:

Adam
    1:1 to 2:3 (No genealogical introduction)
    2:3 through 4 *These: Generations of the heavens and the earth*
    5 through 6:8 *This: Scroll of genealogies of Adam*
Noah
    6:8 through 9 *These: Genealogies of Noah*
    10:1 through 11:9 *And these: Genealogies of sons of Noah*
    11:10 through 11:26 *These: Genealogies of Shem*
Abraham 11:27 through 25:11 *And these: genealogies of Terah*
    Isaac 25:19 through 35 *And these: genealogies of Isaac, Abraham's son*
    Jacob 37:2 through 49 *These: genealogies of Jacob*
    Joseph 50 (No genealogical introduction)

So we see the same pattern going on here. This list includes every time that an introduction is made regarding genealogies <u>except</u> Ishmael in 25:12-18 and Esau in all of chapter 36. Yet the section of the first pattern says *One God and Father of <u>All</u>*, which would include the two rejected bloodlines. The question then becomes, Are the same dynamic relationships at play? If so, Isaac would somehow correspond to Abraham, Jacob would somehow correspond to Noah, and Joseph would somehow correspond to Adam. Let's look at that:

Abraham establishes the promise of being heir to the Seed by facing off with God.
Isaac establishes the promise of being heir to the Seed by facing off with society.

Noah safely gets his family through the judgments of God.
Jacob safely gets his family through the judgments of society.

Adam is sent from his birthplace to establish his family before God.
Joseph is sent from his birthplace to establish his family in society.

So we see that the pattern has merit. Genesis is an enormous construct with links throughout the Bible, yet here we have one way to grasp the picture in its entirety, somewhat like a roadmap that, while it does not tell us what we're going to see, can direct us in how to get there.

Appendix XIV

Where was the 'Field'?

In the process of pointing out *what the text actually says* rather than *what we assume it must mean*, we find ourselves stumbling over many a mystery that only grows deeper with investigation. Such is the secret of the Inner Earth. That fact that few know about it does not change reality.

This work has the Sacred Text as its focus, so we do not embark here on the studies investigating cosmology, seismology, geology, cartography, gravity, history, or exploratory expeditions; suffice to say that I have satisfied myself in each of these arenas as to the veracity of both character and word of the Text.

Let us begin our account by considering these scriptural ideas as simply as they present themselves:

There is an Abyss upon whose face was darkness distinct from the surface waters covering the earth. *And the earth, she becomes chaos and vacancy, and darkness over the face of Abyss, and Spirit of God ready-hovering over face of the waters.*

It is from this darkness inside the earth that the light itself shone on day One, in contradistinction to the light from the "light bearers" of day four who shone on the earth; "...*and they become for light-bearers in space of the heavens to cause to light on the earth;* and, *II Corinthians 4:6, 'For it is God, who spoke that out of darkness light should shine...*"

This Abyss is the path to the inside of the earth, the 'one place' to where the surface waters of the earth were gathered when the dryness appeared; *Genesis 1:9, "They flow together, the waters, from under the heavens toward one place..."* and, *Isaiah 51:10, "Are you not she? The one draining the sea; waters of the vast Abyss, where she places the depths of the sea..."* and, *II Peter 3:5-6, "For this they willfully forget, that heavens were from of* old, and an earth compacted <u>out</u> of <u>water</u>, and <u>through</u> <u>water</u>, by the word of the God; by which means the then world, overflowed with water, perished." I underlined the words "from under" in Genesis 1:9 because this expression consistently means "away from under" in Hebrew.

It is the waters gushing out of the Abyss which provided the Flood waters; *Genesis 7:11, "In this the day, they were torn, all of the springs of the vast Abyss..."* After this—and not before—the oceans are spoken of as being on the surface of the earth, and rain is mentioned.

This inner ocean fed the four streams which watered the whole earth as described in Genesis 2:10-14; and *Ezekiel 31:4, "Waters, they made him great; Abyss, she made him high; streams of her going round her planting, and trenches of her she sent to all of trees of the Field."* and, *Job 38:15, "Have you come to the seepings of the sea? And have you walked in search of the Abyss?"*

The balance of the ocean-borders so often spoken of are the result of the balance between inner and outer waters of the earth; *Proverbs 8:27-29, "In his causing to establish the heavens, there —I; In his causing to delineate the horizon on face of Abyss, in his causing to make rigid skies from above, in his causing to strengthen springs of Abyss, in causing to place to the sea his decree—that waters pass not bidding of him, to cause to delineate the foundations of the earth..."* and, *Ezekiel 31:15, "Thus he says, my Lord Jehovah: In the day of his descent to the unseen, I cause mourning; I cover on him Abyss; and I withhold her streams; and they are shut up, the vast waters."*

The entrances to the abyss are generally covered over: *Revelation 9:1, "And the fifth angel sounded trumpet; and I saw a star out of the heaven fallen to the earth, and there was given to it the key of the pit of the Abyss..."* and, *Psalm 104:6, "You cover over Abyss as with clothing"* and, *Job 38:30, "As stone, waters hide themselves, and faces of Abyss freeze."* This limited access to the inner earth appears to have happened around the time of the great earthquake that occurred in the days of Uzziah, mentioned in Amos 1:1 and Zechariah 14:5; after this time there was a distinct diminishing of the presence of the 'great ones' that are given as 'iron' in the feet of clay in Daniel 2; and though it is prophesied that these 'great ones' will again make their presence known on earth, in the interim the mortals have gotten weaker, and the demi-gods have gotten stronger, as it says there, *"And whereas you saw the iron mixed with miry clay, they shall mingle themselves with the seed of men; but they shall not cleave one to another, even as iron does not mingle with clay."*

The inner earth is a place that animals who supposedly have become extinct on the surface can survive; *Psalm 36:6, "Your judgments: vast Abyss; man and beast you are saving."* and *Genesis 1:22, "And he is blessing them—God—to cause to say, 'You—fruitful! and you—increase! and you—fill the waters in the seas! and the flier increases in the earth:'"*

The last scripture quoted there from Genesis 1:22 brings up a relevant Hebrew word which literally means in the earth. It occurs in the following instances:

- Genesis **1**:22 **2**:5 **4**:12 **4**:14 **6**:4,5,6,17 **8**:17 **9**:7 **10**:8,32 **19**:31 **45**:7
- Exodus **20**:4
- Deuteronomy **4**:17 **5**:8
- Joshua **7**:21
- Judges **4**:21
- 1 Samuel **26**:7
- 2 Samuel **7**:9,23
- 1 Chronicles **1**;10 **17**:8.21
- Job **1**:7,8 **2**:2,3 **14**:8 **18**:10 **38**:33
- Psalms **17**:11 **46**:8,10 **58**:2,11 **67**:2,4 **72**:16 **73**:9,25 **119**:19,87 **141**:7
- Proverbs **11**:31
- Ecclesiastes **11**:20
- Isaiah **40**:24 **42**:4 **62**:7
- Jeremiah **9**:24 **17**:13 **31**:22 **51**:27

- Lamentations **2**:9
- Ezekiel **1**:15 **26**:20 **31**:16
- Daniel **8**:5
- Zachariah **1**;10,11 **6**:7

Let us simply step through the ones relevant to this subject. We find from Genesis 1:22 that birds are given access to the inner earth, and from 2:5 that the plants spread to there. 4:12 & 14 tell us that the place of exile ('Nod') for Cain is in the earth, and that likewise the Giants gravitated to there (6:4), where God first saw the wickedness of man (6:5), and that Adam had been formed there (6:6) and that the inner earth would have everything in it expire just as the outer surface would (6:17).

We will return to the fact that Adam was formed there, but let us go on with the character of the inner earth that scripture gives us.

Genesis 8:17 tells us that the animals released from the ark would also breed abundantly *in* the earth, and that access was given to Noah and his progeny to people it (9:7), but the return of the mighty ones and mixed-race of giants again took it over, as Nimrod in 10:8 & 32 and First Chronicles 1:10. The daughters of Lot lamented the fact that none of these heroes were any longer suitable for husbands in 19:31, likely because the whole kingdom down there had been tainted, though Joseph promised to his brothers that God would preserve them a place there (45:7).

The condition of the inner earth continued to deteriorate, and God has to tell the Israelites in the second commandment (Exodus 20:4 & Deuteronomy 4:17-18; 5:8) not to make images of those beings in the earth. These were the demi-gods which every culture speaks of from the Epic of Gilgamesh to the Greek legends. When reading ancient texts, it is best to assume that they are telling the truth until clearly demonstrated otherwise... and our current culture is in no way competent to be a sounding-board for those ages of whose character we can only guess. Suffice to say that unless one completely disregards all ancient writings of every culture (which is more or less what is happening today), the realities of those times are undeniable.

These "great ones in the earth" are referred to when God compared David's success to them in Second Samuel 7:9 and

First Chronicles 17:8, and the whole of Israel is compared to one of those great races in the earth in First Samuel 7:23 and First Chronicles 17:21. Alexander the Great is spoken of not being able to be touched by these heroes in Daniel 8:5.

Satan has a vested interest in the inner earth, as he tells God in Job 1:7 and 2:2 that he has been going to and fro there, walking up and down in it. And Zechariah 1:10 and 6:1-8 tells us that God has his own observers walking to and fro there; four horses that are remarkably similar to the four horses of the Apocalypse. Indeed, there is a connection between the workings inside the earth and the constellations, as God tells Job in 38:31-33. That God's judgments include this inner realm is plain from Psalms 46:8, 58:2, 67:2,4, Isaiah 40:24 and Proverbs 11:31; as well as the fire consuming part of it in Amos 7:4.

And there are some strange prophecies regarding what happen there. Jeremiah 31:22 mentions that Jehovah creates a new thing in the earth; a female encompasses a male (*geber*; mighty one), and the wheels of the strange creatures in Ezekiel 1:15 are spoken of as operating there. The ancient idea that the dead are kept there is verified by Ezekiel 26:20 and 31:16, and many other references.

The Book of Enoch spends 10 chapters (25-35) describing in detail the inside of the earth which dwarfs Dante's as an elephant dwarfs a gnat; these include a detailed description of the tree of the knowledge of good and evil, birds, beasts, and the locations of the various openings to the surface world and their respective characters.

In the New Testament, Revelation 5:3 & 13 tell us that there are a great many beings under the earth who are then placed on equal ground with the surface-dwellers when faced with God's Christ, as Philippians 2:10 gives us the three classes of intelligent beings who will bow the knee: in heaven, on earth, and under earth.

What does all this tell us about the 'Field' in which was planted the Garden of Eden?

When the 'dryness' appeared and was recognized as earth, it was as Jeremiah 4:23-26 says, "*I see **the earth**, and behold! Chaos and vacancy. ...And to the heavens; and there is not light of them.*

I see the mountains, and behold! Quaking ones, and all of the hills, they stagger. I see, and behold! The Adam is not, and all of the flyer of the heavens, they wander. I see, and behold! The crop, the wilderness, and all of his cities, they are broken down from face of Jehovah; from face of the heat of his anger."

The subject of a previous creation to Adam's will be avoided here as much as is fitting, suffice to say that there is an enormous amount of evidence *for* it, and no evidence whatsoever *against* it, save bias.

So there was a prepared place, the Field, in which the Garden was planted by God himself. The surface of the earth is essentially dry dirt moistened by "Ad" (2:6) until four streams issue out and spread over the ocean-less surface. The Adam is given the job to take the conditions in which he finds himself—the Garden—and duplicate that over the entire surface of the earth. Abel has the wisdom to see that this will require the help of animals. Cain wishes to keep working in the 'Field' as near to the Garden as possible without getting destroyed by the flaming sword 'turning round on herself'.

Yet let us take a step back. If the initial light of day One emanates from the center of the earth, and the sun and moon are merely called 'light-bearers' (as John says as to the baptizer in his gospel, "*He* was not the light, but that he might witness of the light"), then just as in John the true light "shines in darkness, and the darkness apprehended it not," so this light from within the earth—whatever it may be composed of, some have guessed magnetism—is responsible for the light borne by both the sun and moon. We have no problem envisioning the moon as a reflective surface, but we have been conditioned to believe that all the light of day initiates in the sun—merely because we can *perceive* that particular light... and physical perception is always a *surface* condition. What the scripture inexorably suggests is that the light inside the earth is responsible for the operation of *both* the sun and thus the moon. "*By faith we apprehend that the worlds have been framed by the word of God, so that what is seen should not take its origin from things which appear.*" Hebrews 11:3.

In our limited understanding of the actual processes of God's universe, we could simply say: Scripture suggests that the sun is being constantly ignited by whatever is inside the earth. The process seems to be the result of sympathetic movement through geometric magnetic fields, but here we will limit ourselves to what the scriptures say, in which there is more than enough detail supplied.

God declares 'day' and 'night' to light and darkness three days before the sun is operative. Furthermore, the successive days do not utilize these names of day and night that God gave, but instead utilize 'evening' and 'morning', the which are never introduced as a new element, but stated as if they were assumed to have always been there... just as the waters, the Abyss, the Spirit of God, and God. How then did God separate between the light and darkness? If the case were one side of the earth being night and the other day, the sun would be required.

What we have here is a missing element which we have overlooked.

When we return to Genesis 1's parallel in John 1, we find an innocuous statement which almost begs to be overlooked: "In him was life, and the life was the light of men." And a bit farther down, "The true light was, which coming into the world, lights every man." When John writes his epistle in the same genre, he spends all his time with 'life' and while alluding to light, does not in the first section mention it. Something is definitely afoot here regarding this 'life'.

Let us follow the paths of both the waters and the darkness for the first three days. Initially, the darkness is *in* the earth, and the waters are *on* the earth. Then light shines from "out of darkness" *in* the earth, driving the darkness *out* of the earth. Then the waters are gathered together *in* the earth ...leaving both the darkness and the waters in the exact opposite places from which they started. The missing element is the Spirit of God; it is spoken of *in contrast* to the what was on the face of the Abyss; darkness on its face, the Spirit of God on the face of the waters. The Spirit is associated with light.

But we are told nothing in the account regarding the Spirit of God's operative role throughout the successive days. The next mention is when God visits the now shamed Adam in the *wind* of the day; the same Hebrew word as Spirit. We can observe from God's action throughout scripture that when he wants waters moved, he invariably uses wind, as at the crossing of the Red Sea. We can observe from Job 37:21 and 38:24 that the parting of the light is also associated with wind. We observe from Noah's account that dry land is the result of a wind. All these are necessary elements to the Genesis account, yet not stated overtly, lest we bury the impact of *what happened* under *how it happened*—the which we are often wont to do in an attempt to tell God how he should operate. But would we imagine that the Spirit of God hovering ready for the creative process was merely dismissed for the duration?

Let us proceed to the "wind of the day" of chapter 2. If there were an Abyss leading to inside the earth; (indeed, if we are to consider Enoch, many of them) then that invisible light emanating from the earth would—for a short time—be exposed directly to the returning sun-light rather than being filtered through the surface of the earth itself. A person existing in that place would—for a short time until the earth turned the Abyss away from the sun—be exposed to two lights; one from inside the earth, and one from the sun. Likewise the sunlight streaming into the Abyss would produce extreme heat changes to both the passage to inner earth and the immediate area around it. This would invariably produce the same thing that is produced today where sunlight and shade move around: a wind.

In this case it would be a wind alternatively moving in and out of the earth through the passageway of the Abyss, as if the earth were breathing. Now we know that some major physical change came over the Adam after eating of the fruit... and in the account we find him in a protective tent making protective traveling clothes during this double-light period, the "wind of the day". The changes that came over the Adam are discussed in Appendix II; here let us continue the discussion regarding the 'field'.

The Adam and his wife are driven out of the Garden, and cannot approach it because of the *flame of the sword turning round on herself*. The meaning of this expression—as far as its physical form—is becoming plain. The best estimates—decidedly still a guess—for the thickness of the earth between its hollow interior with an inner 'sun' and its outer surface lit by the celestial sun is about 800 miles. If one were sufficiently within this Abyss, there would be no time to escape before the sun once again shone in and exposed one to the double light as the earth turned *round on herself* and exposed one to *the flame of the sword*. Thus without some form of protection such as a 'token' that God placed upon Cain to prevent his being killed, the Garden would be effectively off limits. Thus we can deduce that the 'field' spoken of in the text was the lush border between the inner and outer earth; and that the Garden itself was located in this in-between arena of "morning and evening" rather than "day and night". So it becomes evident from the account that the 'field' spoken of, in which was the 'Garden', was the lush border between the inner and outer earth. The surface of the earth itself was desolate and required the Adam and his progeny to subdue and fill it. We see also that Cain wanted no such job, and wished to keep working with the *fruit* of the garden rather than the *herb* of the ground.

The word translated "ready-hovering" for the Spirit of God is only in three places in scripture; here is the one from Deuteronomy 32:11; "*As Eagle, he is rousing his nest over his fledglings, he is hovering; he is spreading his wings; he is taking him; he is bearing him on his pinions; so Jehovah alone is guiding him; and there is not with Him a strange god.*" In this way—as an eagle must encourage his fledglings out of the nest—so God was prepared to encourage the Adam out of the nest of the Garden to accomplish His plans for the surface of the earth. But the missing element from the Adam which would have empowered him for this work was not his wife, as he initially supposed; nor the fruit of the tree of knowledge of good and evil, as his wife initially supposed; but the Spirit. As Jesus spoke in Luke 11:12, "*If you therefore, being evil, know how to give good gifts to your children, how much more shall the Father who is from heaven give Holy Spirit to them that ask him?*"

I leave you with this picture:

The Adam and his wife find themselves in a perfect paradise between the worlds. Outside, it is all barren dirt that must be cultivated to match their paradise. The job can seem overwhelming, and plans to make it easier are backfiring at an alarming rate. The last backfire results in the degradation of their bodies and expulsion from the Garden. Hand in hand they walk out on to the the barren sea of dirt that awaits thousands of lifetimes of sweat in an unfinished condition to finish. They are naked beneath their clothing; they know that they are not complete, they have no more access to the nest in which they were perfectly happy as they have access to any immediate hope of ever being complete until the promised Seed comes... yet even that hope had backfired, as the one they hoped to be the Seed murdered his brother and was discovered to be "*of the wicked one*".

The horizon is bare, the ground is hard. Scattered thorns and thistles are the only signs of life. A curse is hanging in the air. Somewhere behind them a murderer is skulking, building an empire of oppression and war. Here, there is only the work to be done. The work and the waiting. For four thousand long years.

Appendix XV
Translator's Comment

Genesis is like no other literature within or out sacred writ. It is simply too big. One line from Genesis changes everything we know, yet the stories are so accessible, so down to earth, that they are irresistible. Thus begins the word of God, and thus it continues. It makes no apology for itself, it makes no appeal for or against salvation, in fact it is not in the slightest bit affected by whether we believe it or not. It exists in and of itself. It *is*.

I began the translation process because i needed to know what it actually says. By the time i was halfway through the first chapter, my mind felt like it had been put through a shredder and come out a different kind of being. Then began the roller coaster of grappling with something so large that i was being thrown around like a rag doll in a lion's mouth. The highs of finding the nuance of a particular passage after days of frustration, the lows of seeing how my understanding is only a spark against the roaring blaze of the passages, these began to change me. And i do not think i can describe how.

I can tell you that a great sleepiness has characterized the process. Yesterday, before waking again to type these words, i had woken up newly invigorated to continue the work. I lasted six hours, and barely made it back to my unheated bedroom where i collapsed into a deep sleep. Normally i last days on end without sleep; this work does not allow that.

How much value a person can get from holy writ depends entirely on how much they believe it. Therein lies the difficulty of so many translations. For in order to effectively study a subject, one needs some modicum of objectivity, as well as the ability to explore others' accomplishments without bias. Yet objectivity by itself is a gangrene which puffs up the mind with pride while eroding the soul. Thus we have in academia a vast collection of works that have an underlying soul screaming in pain, thinly veiled by a proud objective veneer: the eternal sneer. It is not a pretty picture. I do not like it.

I have half a dozen translations of the holy writ on my shelf that i truly appreciate. Every single one was done by an individual. There is not a single translation, a single reference guide, or a single commentary done by a committee that is of consistent use to me. This is the nature of the work; you work alone with God, or you fall prey to demons of lust, pride, and educated ignorance. The temptation to excuse away the holy writ as something merely cultural, mythological, or of limited religious application is too strong; these false excuses come rushing in to comfort our pride when in fact we are dealing with something larger than ourselves and will not allow ourselves to admit it.

This is the Word of God. It is larger than we. We do not understand it. We can begin to apprehend it, but only when we have faced off with its Author and come to the full realization that he is bigger than us. That our efforts to put into order something that has already been ordered beyond our imagination is actually the effort of the blind to explain to the blind what something looks like. I do not know what it looks like; i am a fellow blind captive with you. Thus my efforts here are freely admitted to be just that. I do not know Genesis. It is beyond me.

What i have done here then is arrange the words into braille, that in some small measure we might perceive the words once written down in fire. I have attempted to put as many of the original dots as possible on to the pages, which has necessitated making up new braille letters in many cases... but it is only braille. If you are to see the holy writ for yourself, you must do that alone with God. I cannot help nor hinder you in that endeavor.

There have been many prophets in the history of mankind. One thing they have all had in common is that their own relationship with God outweighed the relationship between the people and God that they were seeking to restore. Thus is everything we touch that has the mark of the divine. There is no objectivity. A sword also will go through your own soul. And it is anyone's guess whether you will survive ...or even want to. Elijah learned that.

So what do i have to say here? Little, except that God has been very kind to us in allowing stories of this magnitude to be put into a form that we can read and follow along with. No, i am not capable of making the fire jump off the pages and sear the living Word into the eyes of your soul. I can, however, put them into English in some measure, and you can read them in English. That is the extent of this work, and for now it will do.

www.ingramcontent.com/pod-product-compliance
Lightning Source LLC
Chambersburg PA
CBHW061434300426
44114CB00014B/1686